Engaging Westminster Calvinism

Engaging Westminster Calvinism

The Composition of Redemption's Song

Mark W. Karlberg

WIPF & STOCK · Eugene, Oregon

ENGAGING WESTMINSTER CALVINISM
The Composition of Redemption's Song

Copyright © 2013 Mark W. Karlberg. All rights reserved. Except for brief quotations in critical publications or reviews, no part of this book may be reproduced in any manner without prior written permission from the publisher. Write: Permissions, Wipf and Stock Publishers, 199 W. 8th Ave., Suite 3, Eugene, OR 97401.

Wipf & Stock
An imprint of Wipf and Stock Publishers
199 W. 8th Ave., Suite 3
Eugene, OR 97401
www.wipfandstock.com

ISBN 13: 978-1-62032-798-2

Permission to reproduce the following works has been granted by their respective rights holders.

ARTICLES

"The Glory of God: Archetypal and Ectypal – Part One: The Theophanic Glory." *The Outlook* 60/3 (May–June 2010) 24–27.

"The Glory of God: Archetypal and Ectypal – Part Two: The Image of God." *The Outlook* (July–August 2010) 9–12.

"How Should Moses be Read?: A Debate in Contemporary Reformed Theology," *The Outlook* 62/3 (May–June 2012) 24–26.

"Judgment According to Works: The Crux of Today's Dispute [Part 2]." *The Outlook* 54/5 (May 2004) 6–8.

"Music in Worship: A Historical Sketch and Theological Appraisal," *The Outlook* 49/9 (October 1999) 3–6.

"Patriotic Music in Worship," *The Outlook* 53 (July/August 2003) 4–5.

"Recovering the Mosaic Covenant as Law and Gospel: J. Mark Beach, John H. Sailhamer, and Jason C. Meyer as Representative Expositors." *Evangelical Quarterly* 83/3 (2011) 233–50.

"Today's Church: Standing or Falling? [Part 1]," *The Outlook* 54/4 (April 2004) 5–8.

BOOK REVIEWS

Bryan D. Estelle, J. V. Fesko, and David VanDrunen, eds., *The Law Is Not of Faith: Essays on Works and Grace in the Mosaic Covenant* (Phillipsburg: P & R, 2009), in *JETS* 53 (2009) 407–11.

Richard C. Gamble, *The Whole Counsel of God*, vol. 1, *God's Mighty Acts in the Old Testament* (Phillipsburg: P & R, 2009), in *TrinJ* 31 (2010) 141–43.

G. L. W. Johnson and G. P. Waters, eds., *By Faith Alone: Answering the Challenges to the Doctrine of Justification* (Wheaton: Crossway, 2006), in *JETS* 50 (2007) 640–43.

John R. Muether, *Cornelius Van Til: Reformed Apologist and Churchman* (Phillipsburg: P & R, 2008), in *TrinJ* 30 (2009) 305–8.

Paul A. Rainbow, *The Way of Salvation: The Role of Christian Obedience in Justification* (Bletchley: Paternoster, 2005); and Richard B. Gaffin, *"By Faith, Not by Sight": Paul and the Order of Salvation* (Bletchley, UK: Paternoster, 2006), in *JETS* 50 (2007) 423–28.

Brian Vickers, *Jesus' Blood* and *Righteousness: Paul's Theology of Imputation* (Wheaton: Crossway, 2006), in the *JETS* 50 (2007) 419–23.

Dedicated to the memory of
Meredith G. Kline
(1922–2007)

Biblical theologian *par excellence*
Mentor and friend
Collaborator
Exemplar of Reformed faith and piety

Soli Deo gloria

Contents

Author's Foreword / xi

Prelude: On a Redemptive Theme / 1

SECTION ONE—THE SONG OF REDEMPTION: JUSTIFICATION BY GRACE THROUGH FAITH / 9

1 *Sola Gratia*: The Signature of the Reformation / 11
    Part 1—Today's Church: Standing or Falling?
    Part 2—Judgment According to Works:
        The Crux of Today's Dispute

2 Conflating Faith and Works in Final Judgment/Justification:
   The Teaching of New School Westminster / 21

  REVIEWS:
    Paul A. Rainbow, *The Way of Salvation: The Role of Christian Obedience in Justification*, and Richard B. Gaffin Jr., *"By Faith, Not by Sight": Paul and the Order of Salvation* / 35
    Brian Vickers, *Jesus' Blood* and *Righteousness: Paul's Theology of Imputation* / 45
    G. L. W. Johnson and G. P. Waters, eds., *By Faith Alone: Answering the Challenges to the Doctrine of Justification* / 52

SECTION TWO—SWEET CANAAN: COVENANT LIFE IN ANTICIPATION OF THE END OF THE AGE / 59

3 Recovering the Mosaic Covenant as Law and Gospel: J. Mark Beach, John H. Sailhamer, and Jason C. Meyer as Representative Expositors / 61

4 How Should Moses Be Read?: A Debate in Contemporary Reformed Theology / 81

Contents

REVIEWS:
    Bryan D. Estelle, J. V. Fesko, and David VanDrunen, eds., *The Law Is Not of Faith: Essays on Works and Grace in the Mosaic Covenant* / 87
    Richard C. Gamble, *The Whole Counsel of God*, vol. 1, *God's Mighty Acts in the Old Testament* / 94

SECTION THREE—THE MUSIC OF HEAVEN: WORSHIP IN SPIRIT AND TRUTH / 97

5 The Glory of God: Archetypal and Ectypal / 99
    Part 1—The Theophanic Glory
    Part 2—The Image of God

6 The Distinctiveness of Reformed Worship / 111

7 Music in Worship: A Historical Sketch and Theological Appraisal / 125

8 Patriotic Music in Worship / 133

9 A Brief Interpretive History of Music in the Service of the Church / 137

10 Theological Reflections on Church Music, Arts, and Architecture / 149
    Excursus: Presbyterian Versus Anglican Practice: Two Views on Church Music

REVIEW:
    John R. Muether, *Cornelius Van Til: Reformed Apologist and Churchman* / 155

Postlude: Theme and Recapitulation / 153

Appendix 1: Summary Statement of the Reformed Faith / 163
Appendix 2: Statement on Baptism (from Chapter 6) / 165
Author Bibliography / 167
General Bibliography / 171
Name Index / 175

Author's Foreword

ENGAGING WESTMINSTER CALVINISM is yet another sequel to my study in Reformed covenant theology, past and present. It follows directly upon the previous trilogy of works published by Wipf and Stock: *Covenant Theology in Reformed Perspective: Collected Essays and Book Reviews in Historical, Biblical, and Systematic Theology* (2000); *Gospel Grace: The Modern-day Controversy* (2003); and *Federalism and the Westminster Tradition: Reformed Orthodoxy at the Crossroads* (2006).

This latest collection of writings contains some published articles and book reviews that are not readily accessible to most readers. Many of them are written for a wider audience of informed lay students of Scripture as well as seminarians. They have been brought together here in a fresh way with other new writings. As a result, this study is somewhat unique, drawing upon the author's career in theology and church music. Over the course of four decades of scholarly research and writing the author has also been engaged in the music ministry of the church, serving as organist and choir director. Chief influences in his study and practice of church music have been Robert Elmore and Gerre Hancock, leading organists, choral masters, and composers of our generation. In the course of their stellar careers Elmore and Hancock have served in different ecclesiastical settings—Moravian, Presbyterian, Southern Baptist, and Anglican. What they both share in common is their exceptional skill in the art of improvisation. Part of their accompaniment was "off the written musical score," resulting in service-playing that was creative and engaging. In the spirit of their artistic expression we offer this collection of writings bearing as its theme the great Song of Redemption, composed by "the singing Christ" (Heb 2:12).

Here is what some have said of the author's writings: regarding Karlberg's analysis of the contemporary dispute over the doctrine of justification in *Covenant Theology in Reformed Perspective* R. C. Sproul (Sr.) says it has "penetrated to the heart of the controversy [at Westminster Seminary]." Regarding its sequel, *Gospel Grace*, Sproul writes: "Just today your book

Author's Foreword

Gospel Grace: The Modern Day Controversy arrived, and I am eager to read it. A book on this subject needed to be written, and I'm elated that you took up the task. Like you, I pray for God's illumination and conviction of His gospel in those who lead the church astray." Likewise, Meredith G. Kline spoke of this writing as "a colossal achievement," adding: "We are all greatly indebted to Karlberg for his years of faithful, courageous fighting the good fight and keeping the light on the subtle mischief of the opposition. This study is a thoroughly documented exposé that cannot be ignored, one that will doubtless provoke strong reaction." After reading *Federalism and the Westminster Tradition* a reader posted these comments on Amazon.com: "Reformed theologian Mark W. Karlberg is a man of strong convictions. . . . I highly commend him for his faithfulness to his scriptural convictions and always find his essays in historical Reformed orthodoxy (American Presbyterianism, OPC variety) extremely engaging and constructive. . . . Dr. Karlberg is a must read to accurately understand the disputes at hand within current Reformed systematics."

In the spirit of honest debate and truth-telling, we further our analysis of Westminster Calvinism, where explicit allegiance is given to the confessional teachings contained in the Westminster Standards.

Easter 2013
This Joyful Eastertide (tune: *Vruchten*)
Joachim Oudaen's *David's Psalmen*, 1685

Prelude

On a Redemptive Theme

DISCORDANT NOTES HAVE BEEN sounded in recent decades within Westminster Calvinism, giving rise to divergent schools of biblical interpretation. This compilation of writings, including some previously published essays and book reviews, addresses several issues in the present-day theological dispute. Before introducing these issues, we need to define the boundaries of our engagement with contemporary biblical-theological exposition as they relate to foundational doctrines in Reformed theology. The label "Westminster Calvinism" refers to that tradition in international Reformed orthodoxy which is the culmination of dogmatic reflection in the great age of the Protestant Reformation in England and Scotland. The creed of the Reformed churches in Britain is enshrined in the Westminster Standards, comprising the Confession of Faith and the Larger and Shorter Catechisms. This same theological tradition had been preserved in America largely through the efforts of (old) Princeton and (old) Westminster seminaries. Valiant attempts to contain the onslaught of modernism within Calvinism were largely aborted by the middle of the twentieth century at Princeton and by the end of the twentieth century at Westminster. The chief factor in the departure from orthodox Reformed federalism is to be attributed to the ever-widening influence of Swiss theologian Karl Barth, and the rise of the movement known as Neo-orthodoxy.

Theological exposition is at times a difficult and precarious enterprise, first and foremost because the official confessions of the Reformed churches are subordinate instruments in the propagation and defense of biblical religion. No creedal statement is inerrant, as good and excellent as some may be from the standpoint of the historical development of ecclesiastical dogma. The truth of any statement of faith uttered by the church—or by any biblical expositor/interpreter—is wholly dependent upon the teaching of Scripture itself. But that teaching admittedly is, in the human context, always a matter of interpretation, even though the formal principle of the Reformation rightly insists that Scripture is self-interpreting. So the critical question arises: Which interpretation is correct? That of the Reformed church or the Lutheran (to name only two of the leading Protestant theological traditions)? And within those traditions, is it his interpretation or hers, as one among many dogmatic formulations? At one time it was widely acknowledged by Reformed Christians that the Holy Spirit works illumination and understanding in the hearts and minds of obedient, faithful hearers of Scripture, leading to dogmatic consensus within the church. Today even that conviction is being challenged as inadequate, especially in view of the increased proliferation of interpretations viewed as merely contingent, historically-bound statements of the faith, statements attempting to set forth what the Bible "intends" to teach. In the school of Neo-orthodoxy and the school of (multi-)perspectivalism, mere lip-service is given to the historic doctrines of the faith. Rather, the individual's personal encounter with God in Scripture and in nature is understood to be an *existential* moment/event. Accent here falls decisively upon the subjectivity of faith, what differs with every individual person. Christian dogma, accordingly, is time bound and culture bound. To be sure, the human perspective on truth is limited by creaturely finitude. From this standpoint, the unfathomable truth of God is beyond human comprehension, or theological systematization *in this sense*. This is what is espoused in the Reformed doctrine of the incomprehensibility of God, its corollary being the mystery of (all) divine revelation. Yet it is false to conclude from these truths that theological interpretation/church dogma is merely tentative in nature (and non-binding), as we hear repeatedly in many current theological circles.

Contrary to this viewpoint, we recognize hermeneutics to be a "science" (and theology being the queen of the sciences); there is a proper and there is an improper method of interpretation. Most significantly, Reformed theology has been distinguished by its doctrine of the covenants, notably, the original Covenant of Works in Eden, the intra-Trinitarian Covenant of Redemption entered into by the three Persons of the Trinity (hence *ab extra* with respect to the aseity of God), and the historical Covenant of Grace spanning the period from the fall to the consummation (in classic/historic Reformed terminology). In recent decades, however, this teaching has also been undermined or jettisoned on many and varied fronts. The novel introduction of Framian perspectivalism has helped fuel division and strife within the Westminster School.¹ An account of the departure of Westminster (East and West) from the teaching of Reformed federalism, consistently and uniformly taught, can be gleaned from my published writings.² We have only to look at the output of scores of students trained at Westminster (some now teachers, others pastors and church leaders) to understand both the scope and the gravity of the issues here in dispute. All of this indicates the extent of the inroads that have been made among Reformed congregations and educational institutions since the dismissal of Norman Shepherd from Westminster (Philadelphia) in 1981. Shepherd's departure served only to solidify the teaching advanced most vigorously by his foremost advocate and former colleague Richard B. Gaffin Jr., co-author, if not father, of the theology of New Westminster.³

---

1. Cornelius Van Til, Old Westminster's leading systematician and apologist of the Reformed faith, understood the system of doctrine to be reformed and always reforming *according to the Word of God* (the Scripture principle), ever more consistently by way of biblical exegesis and theological systematization. Van Til defended as integral elements within the Reformed system such doctrines as divine incomprehensibility, the Creator/creature distinction, the distinction between archetypal and ectypal knowledge (what is the difference between knowledge in the mind of God and knowledge in the mind of the creature), and the doctrine of the Covenant of Works. The introduction of Framian perspectivalism signaled the rejection (or radical revision) of Van Til's methodology in favor of new explorations in theological debate and discourse, a decisive departure from Old Princeton and Old Westminster. On Van Til's legacy, see John R. Muether, *Cornelius Van Til: Reformed Apologist and Churchman* (Phillipsburg: P&R, 2008), and my book review in *TrinJ* 30 (2009), 305–8. Cf. also Karlberg, "On the Theological Correlation," and "John Frame and the Recasting of Van Tilian Apologetics."

For a defense of Frame's work, see his *festschrift*, entitled *Speaking the Truth in Love: The Theology of John Frame* (ed. J. J. Hughes; Phillipsburg: P&R, 2009). Contributors were hand-picked by Frame himself; the essays, therefore, offer only one side of the debate regarding the significance and the relevance of Frame's theological hermeneutic for contemporary Reformed theology and practice. In effect, this *festschrift* serves as Frame's own self-defense.

2. See my trilogy: *Covenant Theology in Reformed Perspective*; *Gospel Grace*; and *Federalism and the Westminster Tradition*.

3. In "The Rev. Dr. Richard B. Gaffin, Jr.: *Sancti Libri Theologicus Magnus Westmonasteriensis*," *WTJ* 74 (2012) 1–31, Peter A. Lillback, current president of Westminster in Philadelphia, misleadingly remarks: "The [Shepherd] controversy lasted in the Westminster context until 1982" (7). In the careful orchestration of faculty and administration, dissident voices on the faculty had been removed (many exiled to Westminster West). By this calculated strategy the current faculty achieved a far greater degree of unity with the express purpose of advancing of the work of Gaffin and the so-called "Union with Christ School," a term newly descriptive of New Westminster. It is this theology that is defended in a subsequent article in the same Spring 2012 issue of *WTJ*. See William R. Edwards, "John Flavel on the Priority of Union with Christ: Further Historical Perspective on the Structure

The subject of *Engaging Westminster Calvinism* is the church, reformed and being reformed by the Word of God. Three sections of the book address the following main topics: (1) justification by faith alone (the Gospel of saving grace); (2) the Mosaic Covenant as, in part, a republication of the Covenant of Works made by God with the First Adam, the federal head of all humanity; and (3) the church as the covenant people set apart from the world to be God's holy, "sanctified culture." The church as a spiritual entity or organism is best portrayed by the biblical image of the (corporate) New Man in Christ. By the demonstration of God's justifying work of redemption in the eschatological fullness of times, the saints under the old economy are joined with the resurrected Christ and all the elect, the New Man. The redemptive-historical transition from the Old Man (notably, Israel as a personification of fallen Adam/humanity) to the New Man is accomplished by the atoning, reconciling work of Jesus Christ. In him there is neither Jew nor Gentile; both are one in Christ. Central to the Song of Redemption is the church's confession of justification by faith through sovereign, electing grace. This is the heart of the preaching of the Gospel (as distinguished from the preaching of the Law). By the free gift of God's saving grace, the elect in Christ have the right to be called the sons of God—all to the praise, glory, and honor of his Name. Astonishingly as it may sound to many, it is this doctrine that has come under intense fire at Westminster Seminary since the mid-1970s. Further consolidation within the Shepherd-Gaffin school is evidenced by the latest writings to come from the pens of its leading exponents. This is the subject of the opening section of this book.

Section 2 looks at the corollary doctrine to justification by faith, what in the teaching of the apostle Paul is the transition from the old Mosaic economy to the (semi-)eschatological age of the Spirit, the period lying between the first and second advents of Christ. Here we consider the Bible's teaching regarding the covenant of law entered into with Israel at Sinai. "In some sense"[4] the Mosaic Covenant was a republication of the original Covenant of Works made with Adam in Eden, representative head of all humanity. In many and various respects, Israel's life in the land of Canaan was anticipatory of the great work of Christ in his future accomplishment of redemption in the fullness of times. Like Adam in the garden during his time of probation, Israel in Canaan was under probation, under a covenant of works *as regards*

---

of Reformed Soteriology," *WTJ* 74 (2012) 33–35 (more on this in chapter 2).

4. This language, now widely employed, was coined by me in my doctoral dissertation, "The Mosaic Covenant and the Concept of Works in Reformed Hermeneutics."

temporal life and prosperity, not eternal life, which is secure and indefectible for all those united to Christ through saving, justifying faith. On the one hand, national ("elect") Israel was constituted a peculiar people by the law mediated through Moses. She was uniquely established as a *theocracy*, the only one of its kind in the entire course of redemptive history. This ancient theocracy came to a decisive end with the inauguration of the new and better covenant established in Christ's blood. On the other hand, God's true elect are constituted the Body of Christ (the New Man) by means of forensic, declarative justification. Here we are obliged to distinguish between *decretive election* (i.e., individual election to salvation) and *national election* (the former is eternal and indefectable, the latter temporal and losable).

In the final section we consider the Song of Redemption, the "new song" Christ has given the saints to sing. The ultimate note to be sounded by the redeemed is one that renders all glory and praise to the triune God, the author of salvation. The covenant people are called out of the world, nurtured and sustained wholly by sovereign will and power—a manifestation of God's distinguishing love, grace, and mercy to undeserving sinners. With the establishment of the new covenant the saints of God before and after Christ's first advent are *constituted* the Body of Christ on the sole ground of Christ's perfect righteousness imputed to all those who believe. (Prior to Christ's death the saints of old received the saving benefits of the atonement proleptically, i.e., in advance of its historical accomplishment.) Forensic, declarative justification is one of several distinct benefits enjoyed by believers, notably in union with the *resurrected* Son of God. Glorification remains the final, consummating act of God's redemption of the world. In principle, such is already a present certainty and reality. The church of Christ is the sanctified culture of the Holy Spirit. The Song of the redeemed is a re-creative offering of homage to God, first uttered by the angels in the presence of God (in the midst of his Spirit-Glory). This doxology of praise is the music of heaven come to earth, now rendered by the saints clothed in Christ's righteousness and uniquely gifted by the Spirit of God (see especially Psalm 8). By the transformative power of the Gospel of Jesus Christ—through the regenerating, illuminating work of the Holy Spirit—the people of God are enlisted in the heavenly choir, numbered among the Master's musicians. *In this connection, the Christian Sabbath is the corporate worship of the saints, an observance peculiar to the saints worshipping God at that time of the week which is set apart as holy to the Lord.*

Revelation necessitates the direct encounter of God with humanity, including both the communication of his Word and the establishment/maintenance of spiritual communion (the bond or covenant of love). Faithful reception of God's Word and participation in the fellowship of the Spirit are reflective of humanity's creation in God's own likeness, after the pattern of the angelic host serving God in the heavenly realm. After the fall, it is a matter of refashioning sinful humanity in the image of the Son of God (more exactly, renewal in the likeness of the resurrected/glorified Christ). God manifests himself always and only by way of theophany; the Glory-Presence of God in the Spirit is the place where the Invisible comes to visibility. The "beatific vision of God" is apprehended only through the spiritual eyes of faith. Christ-come-in-the-flesh is the manifestation of God's incarnational Presence made necessary for the reconciliation of God and fallen humanity (the New Man in Christ). For the redeemed, faith gives way to sight at the close of history; the eschaton ushers in the resurrection/glorification of the saints. The church is the product of God's redemptive-historical work in the world, a work resulting in the present-age demarcation between "cult" (the worshipping people in covenant with God) and secular "culture." As a result of sin's entrance into the world, the City of God is sharply distinguished from, and opposed to, the City of Man. In the cult of the sanctified it is the praise of Christ that distinguishes true worship, where the Word of God is confessed in sermon, sacrament, and song. As a church musician of more than four decades, I offer in the closing section of this book some reflections on the role of music in the Christian congregation.

Covenant theology is the wharf and woof of Reformed theology.[5] But such has come under vigorous attack in recent decades, even in what was once the bastion of Reformed orthodoxy. At this junction in the history of Christian doctrine, the future of Westminster Calvinism looks exceedingly bleak. Sadly, J. Gresham Machen's legacy, his unwavering stand for the doctrine of justification by faith alone—what lies at the heart of covenant theology—has been obscured and overshadowed at New Westminster. The teaching recovered by Martin Luther at the opening of the Protestant Reformation was deeply treasured by Machen. It expressed his only hope in life and death. The first generation of faculty and students stood unequivocally with Machen. By the time of Professor Meredith G. Kline's departure from

---

5. Consult the many and varied essays in my foundational study, *Covenant Theology in Reformed Perspective*, which draws upon the distinct, yet complementary, disciplines of historical, biblical, and systematic theology (including ecclesiastical dogmatics).

Westminster (Philadelphia) in 1965, there was growing tension and division at the seminary, division that would only intensify over the course of the next two decades (and beyond). The first major controversy to surface on campus addressed the heterodox teaching of Norman Shepherd, John Murray's hand-picked successor in the department of systematic theology.[6]

Westminster Seminary California has just published a book promoting itself as one of the lone, if not sole, defenders of federal Reformed orthodoxy, seemingly the last haven for "courageous Calvinists" in our generation.[7] The picture, however, is far more complicated, far more disheartening than the faculty of Westminster West would have her readers believe. At no previous time has doctrinal controversy been so divisive, so bitter within the Westminster community. The reason for this is due, in large part, to fear and/or false veneration of prominent members of the faculty, resulting in the deliberate, calculated misrepresentation of the issues in ongoing dispute. Duplicity, prevarication, dissemination, and deceit have become the hallmarks of the faculty and administration at Westminster. What additional evidence supports this charge? To that we now turn in Section 1.

---

6. We have noted on many occasions that, in spite of his novel reinterpretation of the Reformed doctrine of the covenants, Murray's theology falls within the bounds of orthodoxy. But clearly, the time has now come to articulate a (mature) covenant theology that comports more fully with the teaching of Scripture, notably in regards to the controverted points in Westminster teaching. Unquestionably, Murray's theologizing on the doctrine of the covenants laid the seeds for the deviant views that would come to prevail at New Westminster, notably in the work of Norman Shepherd and Dick Gaffin (and their many advocates). See Karlberg, "Works and Grace," 23.

7. W. Robert Godfrey and D. G. Hart, *Westminster Seminary California: A New Old School* (Escondido, CA: Westminster Seminary California, 2012). In the estimate of Godfrey and Hart, "It is not too much to say that [Robert] Strimple became Murray's truest successor as a Reformed systematician, blending faithfulness, learning, and piety" (41). At Westminster's critical hour Strimple, then dean of the faculty, failed to denounce Shepherd's unorthodox teaching on justification, election, and the covenants. Happily, he did come to change his stance after President Edmund Clowney had studied the issues more closely for himself, thus reversing previous support for Shepherd. This turn of events altered the course of the seminary controversy, leading to Shepherd's ouster from the seminary. Overall, however, both Clowney and Strimple, as leading administrators and faculty members, mishandled the theological controversy. Misrepresentation of the seminary's decision to remove Shepherd (including the "reason and specifications" for his dismissal as announced to the public) and fierce criticism of Shepherd's critics (who were in the right) would come to haunt the institution.

SECTION ONE

The Song of Redemption: Justification by Grace through Faith

It was the Protestant reformers, beginning with Martin Luther, who recovered the biblical doctrine of justification by faith alone (apart from good works). Inwrought righteousness—produced by the sanctifying work of the Spirit of Christ in the elect—plays no role in the justification of sinners. Justification and sanctification are two distinct, inseparable benefits among many in the application of redemption, or more specifically, in the believer's "union with Christ" by grace through faith. And among the many benefits of redemption, justification was rightly viewed by the reformers as providing the judicial (i.e., legal) basis for the sinner's reconciliation with God. By means of the imputation of Christ's perfect righteousness to sinners justified by faith, the guilt and the penalty of sin have been removed once and for all. The "state of justification" is firmly established and unalterable. *In soteric justification, there is no process.* Good works are evidential of justifying grace. There are two aspects to soteric justification: the *constitutive* and the *demonstrative* (or *evidential*). All said, the doctrine of justification relates to the heart of the Gospel of sovereign, electing grace in Christ Jesus. It stands as the church's "Song of Redemption." Justification by grace through faith is the heartbeat, the musical signature and meter, of the Christian life (in union with Christ).

Section 1 defends the biblical, reformational teaching concerning justification by faith alone by critiquing present-day, ongoing assaults upon the doctrine from one of the least expected places, Westminster Theological Seminary, once the bastion of federal Reformed orthodoxy. The three book reviews at the end of this section underscore the extent to which new teaching on Paul and the law of God, including the doctrine of justification by faith and (good) works, has found a home in contemporary "evangelicalism."

1

Sola Gratia: The Signature of the Reformation

Part 1—Today's Church: Standing or Falling?

A staple in international, orthodox Calvinism from the opening days of the Protestant Reformation has been the theological distinction between the "Law" and the "Gospel." What does this distinction mean, and how important is it? Simply put, it contrasts two, divinely ordained ways to the obtainment of life eternal, one by meritorious works (i.e., by the Law) and one by unmerited grace and favor (i.e., by the Gospel). This fundamental antithesis—reiterated time and again throughout the Bible, both Old and New Testaments—lies at the very core of Protestant evangelical theology, Lutheran and Reformed. Contrary to the claim made by some recent historians of doctrine, there is no disagreement or discord between these two leading Protestant traditions concerning this vital, theological distinction. Differences of interpretation within Lutheranism and Calvinism do appear with respect to how these two principles of inheritance, works versus faith (i.e., law versus grace), apply to the various covenants in the Bible, beginning with the unique Covenant of Works established by God with Adam in the Garden of Eden at creation, and followed by the subsequent covenants spanning the history of redemption, all of which are subsumed under the rubric of the Covenant of Grace (exceptions include God's covenantal pledge to uphold and govern all humankind in accordance with his common grace).

It was this basic, theological antithesis between the Law and the Gospel that led Martin Luther to recover the biblical doctrine of justification by faith alone—justification apart from the works of the Law, even the "good works" of believers (see Eph 2:10). In his classic study, *The Bondage of the Will*, Luther described the desperate plight of sinners. By nature (since Adam's transgression), humankind is in bondage to sin and death. Only the mercy and grace of God in Christ can remedy the consequences of the Fall. The salvation of sinners is the manifestation of the predestinating, electing love of God. The sovereign Lord of the covenant secures for the sinner that which he cannot obtain for himself. Salvation is all of grace.

So important was this teaching of the Bible that Luther insisted it was the defining article (i.e., doctrine) of the standing or falling church. Any admixture of faith and works (obedience which is in accordance with the law of God, the "good works" of those regenerated, sanctified, and renewed in the image of Christ) is, according to the great apostle Paul, anathema. Why are the good works of believers—works that evidence the "obedience of faith" (Rom 1:5), works truly pleasing to God—excluded from justification (with respect to its *constitutive* aspect)? Very simply put, the reason is that what is required by the justice and holiness of God for salvation, (re)union and communion with God, is *perfect obedience*. The purpose of Christ's first coming was to make atonement for sin and to secure the promised inheritance, viz., a people redeemed by the blood of the Lamb. The ground or basis of salvation is the righteousness of Christ alone. His perfect obedience is the exclusive, meritorious basis of life and salvation for sinners, those chosen in Christ by the Father in eternity past. The doctrine of Christ's *meritorious* obedience is meaningful only in the context of the system of doctrine taught in the Bible. Here the interpreter of Scripture must come to grips with the Protestant-Reformed teaching concerning the Law and the Gospel.

Before commenting further upon the distinctive formulations of Reformed covenant theology, views different from classic Lutheranism, we must first consider why at present we are facing a radical shift in theological thinking—a shift that has led to a crisis in modern-day Protestant evangelicalism. The single most important factor giving rise to radical reinterpretations of the biblical doctrine of justification, election, and the covenants is the impact that the Neo-orthodox theology of Karl Barth has had upon evangelicalism, both Reformed and non-Reformed varieties. Barth is (mistakenly) considered by many to be the leading Reformed thinker of the twentieth century. Recognizing the fallacy and bankruptcy of nineteenth-century Protestant theology, Barth undertook a remake of traditional Protestant "orthodoxy," what resulted in a theology having superficial resemblance to the theology of Luther and Calvin (most especially the latter). Barth ended up with a new school of theology known as "Neo-orthodoxy." To be sure, Barth is a complex theologian. But one thing is certain upon a close reading of his work: Barth is no friend of orthodox, biblical Christianity. (Of course, there are "evangelicals" who will challenge this evaluation. They do so erroneously.) From the standpoint of the history of doctrine, it was Barth who spearheaded the transformation of contemporary evangelical theology, the form now dominant. He has vigorously maintained that there is no theological antithesis between the Law and the Gospel. On this subject, argues Barth, the orthodox Protestant scholastics were wholly misguided and misinformed. (It is important to recognize here that Barth distinguished sharply between the teachings of Calvin and that of *scholastic* Calvinism.)

Among the philosophico-theological considerations that entered into Barth's thinking was the (unbiblical) notion of divine grace as that which undergirds and sustains all creation—including the recreation of all things in Christ, the Elect Man, the one man for all. Jesus Christ, according to Barth, is the mysterious, yet sublime, revelation of God's electing and reprobating will, the seemingly contrary motion of God at work in the redemption of the world. Stated in terms of the doctrine of justification, election, and covenant, Barth taught that there is but one covenant in Scripture, the Covenant of Grace (hence Barth's doctrine of mono-covenantalism). Implicit in this interpretation is Barth's christomonism, the notion that Christ is the fountain or source of life and death, so that in him lie the final resolution and reconciliation of all things in heaven and in hell—all to the benefit of the world's redemption (hence Barth's implicit universalism). There is no ultimate conflict between the love and the wrath of God. Christ has overcome evil; such is the triumph of divine grace.

According to Barth, Law and Gospel are merely twin sides of God's promissory command—the divine command that humankind be in subjection to his sovereign rule and reign, and the divine promise that he is Lord of all. Law is an expression of God's grace; Grace is an expression of God's law in the world. God's image-bearer is never in a position of "earning" or "meriting" the love and favor of God. All is received by grace through faith. Humankind's "fall" from grace is remedied in the death and resurrection of Christ on behalf of all humanity. Christ is the New Man, the new humanity. The Old Man—humanity in rebellion against God, in rejection of his grace—has been subdued and renovated by the messianic Lord, the Son of Man. In Christ humanity stands righteous before God, free from all condemnation and sin. Jesus Christ has exhausted the wrath of God for every man. Although evangelicalism may certainly not agree with Barth in all respects of his formulations, there is growing consensus that Law and Grace are not antithetical means of inheriting the favor and blessing of God. In particular, the Reformed doctrine of an original Covenant of Works has been widely denounced as speculative and unbiblical.

Historic covenant theology represents Reformed thinking in its most consistent expression. From the beginning of the Calvinistic tradition, the doctrine of the covenants—in conjunction with the traditional Protestant Law/Gospel contrast—played a determinative role in the exposition of Scripture. What gives covenant theology its peculiar character within the broad stream of Christian interpretation is the emphasis placed upon the history of redemptive revelation and the relation of this history to the original goal of creation (biblical protology and eschatology). For purposes of this presentation, we highlight five crucial and essential biblical-theological elements within the system of covenant theology: (1) the doctrine of probation as that pertains to Adam's original assignment in the Garden of Eden, Israel's temporal life and prosperity in the land of Canaan, and the Son of God's messianic fulfillment of all righteousness (under the law of Moses); (2) the doctrine of meritorious reward (i.e., legal obedience) associated with the original Covenant of Works (which covenant was perfectly fulfilled by the Second Adam, Jesus Christ, and by him alone); (3) the term "grace," which, in accordance with the Protestant Law/Gospel distinction, pertains exclusively to the *postlapsarian* situation (the revelation of God's saving grace to undeserving sinners after Adam's transgression in the Garden); (4) the doctrine of the imputation of the First Adam's sin to all humankind and the subsequent imputation of the Second Adam's righteousness to all the elect of God; and (5) the explanation of the continuity/discontinuity between the old and new covenants (including the letter/Spirit contrast).

These five elements—elucidated over the course of five centuries of biblical interpretation—are vital to the system of Reformed doctrine. Regarding the evangelical doctrine of justification by faith specifically, modern-day detractors would have us abandon or radically reinterpret each of these points of doctrine. Current debate within several American-Reformed communions (reflecting developments in contemporary evangelicalism at large) focuses upon the distinctive teachings of Norman Shepherd, former systematics professor and successor to John Murray at Westminster Seminary (see his *The Call of Grace: How the Covenant Illuminates Salvation and Evangelism* [Phillipsburg: Presbyterian and Reformed, 2000]). My exposé, *The Changing of the Guard: Westminster Theological Seminary in Philadelphia*, republished in my *Gospel Grace: The Modern-Day Controversy* (2003), chronicles developments at Westminster. This case study is illustrative of changes within contemporary evangelicalism—changes that are for the worse, not the better. (The debate over Open Theism within the "Evangelical" Theological Society underscores the plight of biblical Christianity at the opening of this third millennium of church history.) To be sure, new questions require a fresh restatement of biblical teaching. Traditional views must always be reevaluated and reformulated in the light of the Scriptures. That task ever remains for the faithful guard, those standing in defense of the biblical, Reformed faith. The responsibility of our generation of exegetes and dogmaticians, and of the generations to follow, is to carry through consistently the insights of our Reformed forefathers concerning the biblical doctrine of the covenants. In Part 2 we turn directly to the question regarding the relationship between the doctrine of justification by faith alone and the doctrine of judgment according to works, what stands as the crux of the contemporary dispute.

Part 2—Judgment According to Works: The Crux of Today's Dispute

Rightly, we individually and corporately confess what Scripture teaches after a careful, exegetical study and elucidation of the text of Scripture, not because it is the view of our Reformed forebears. Having reflected upon the text of Scripture, we may or may not agree with the teachings of historic, confessional Reformed dogmatics. It is the case that I write in defense of traditional covenant theology. Minor differences aside, I remain persuaded that our tradition has rightly interpreted the biblical doctrine of justification, election, and the covenants. Not all within the Reformed camp today assume this same posture. What stands as our chief disagreement? What causes divisions within our camp? Unity in the faith requires conformity to teachings of the Word of God. Let Scripture be our guide, our standard of truth.

The apostle Paul in his second letter to the Corinthians declares that we shall all appear before the judgment seat of Christ, in order that we might be judged according to our works, whether good or bad (5:10). This judgment includes believers. Similarly, in Romans the apostle writes in the same vein: God will render to each "according to his deeds" (2:6). Paul proceeds to demarcate two classes of people: those who obey God and keep covenant with him, and those who disobey and fall under divine condemnation. It is a minor disagreement among biblical commentators whether or not the class of individuals who keep the law is actual or hypothetical in this passage of Romans (2:6-13). I maintain that the apostle Paul instructs his readers here concerning the twofold classification of humankind: covenant-keepers and covenant-breakers. Those keeping covenant with God obey his commandments. They are the "doers of the law" (2:13). Paul is not telling his readers at this point in his argument *how* sinners become "doers of the law." Nor is Paul suggesting that the "doers of the law" are justified by works, i.e., constituted righteous in God's sight on grounds of the "obedience of faith" (1:5). That would flatly contradict what Paul explains later in this letter and elsewhere in his writings. In summary statement we affirm, in light of Scripture's teaching, that judgment is according to works, but not on the basis of works. There is no conflict between the doctrine of judgment according to works and the doctrine of justification by faith (apart from "good works").

Modern-day revisionists contend that the very notion of "meritorious" reward is unscriptural. These expositors, having imbibed to one degree or another the Neo-orthodox interpretation of Karl Barth, insist that the traditional Protestant-Reformed contrast between the Law and the Gospel is entirely speculative. God's covenantal commitment to humankind, so they reason, is all of grace, never a matter of human "works" (i.e., works antithetical to faith). Many of these revisionists conclude that the relationship between the Father and the Son in the eternal covenant (or pact) is purely gracious, not legal. What is accented here is the paternal love and grace of God, not the just requirement of Christ's satisfaction of divine law necessary for bringing closure to the period of probationary testing (what pertains to the First and Second Adams in their representative capacities as federal heads of humanity). The idea of a legal requirement associated with God's covenant is jettisoned altogether. Accordingly, Christ's obedience is not meritorious of the Father's favor and reward. Other revisionists inconsistently (and superficially) hold to the meritorious work of Christ in making satisfaction for the righteous demands of the law of God, while denying the prospect of meritorious reward for the First Adam, had he passed his time of probation. Unlike Barth's speculative theologizing, Reformed interpreters have correctly assessed and weighed in their system of doctrine the explicit parallel drawn by the apostle between the "one act of righteousness" of the Second Adam and the "one act of disobedience" of the First Adam (see Rom 5:12–21). Were the First Adam not in a position to merit the reward of the covenant (viz., the Covenant of Works established at creation), then it is utterly meaningless to speak of the necessity of Christ's substitutionary satisfaction of the legal requirement associated with this covenant at creation and reinstituted under Moses. (The legal covenant made in Eden was reinstituted *in part* with Israel at Sinai for pedagogical, typological purposes.) The principle of inheritance in the Covenant of Works is that of works; the principle of inheritance in the Covenant of Grace is that of faith (i.e., grace, *Gospel*-grace). When all is said and done, the classic Protestant-Reformed antithesis between the Law and the Gospel is absolutely essential to the biblical and evangelical doctrine of justification by faith alone.

To be sure, there is room for further clarification and explanation of the role of faith and works in justification and final judgment (judgment according to works). The current controversy in the church has afforded biblical interpreters yet another opportunity to reassess and reevaluate the teachings of confessional orthodox Protestantism, and Reformed orthodoxy in particular. The centerpiece in recent discussion and debate is the relation between Paul and James on justification. We do not have space to give full account of the arguments advanced on both sides of the theological dispute. What follows is a summary restatement of the biblical doctrine, which restatement reflects the positive contributions that have been made in the church's ongoing polemical defense of the truth of Scripture.

There is only one divine act, not two, with respect to the justification of sinners reclothed in the righteousness of Christ. Soteric justification is twofold in signification, constitutive and demonstrative (so Paul and James). In speaking of justification by works James is not contemplating a different justification from that taught by Paul. (The Protestant reformer Martin Bucer, for example, mistakenly spoke of a "double" justification.) Nor is James introducing good works as the meritorious grounds or instrument in the justification of the ungodly. Rather, James brings into view the demonstrative aspect of God's justifying act in the salvation of the elect.

Good works are demonstrative (i.e., evidential) of God's saving grace in the lives of believers. As such, they are necessary in the Christian life. But they are not the meritorious grounds of salvation. These two aspects of justification, the constitutive and the demonstrative, must never be confused or confounded. They are distinct, though inseparable, in the divine act of justification. Believers are constituted righteous on the grounds of Christ's meritorious obedience imputed through saving faith, faith being the sole instrument receiving the righteousness of Christ. We are justified by faith alone, on the exclusive grounds of Christ's active and passive obedience. Nevertheless, good works are evidential of true, saving faith. "Justification by works" (as taught by James) brings into view the role of good works as evidential of our righteous standing in Christ. Those united to Christ by faith are "the doers of the law."

Similarly, there is only one divine act, not two, with respect to the sanctification of sinners, those remade in the image of Jesus Christ. It was John Murray, longtime professor of systematics at Westminster Seminary, who carefully and convincingly explained the biblical doctrine of sanctification in its twofold aspects, definitive and progressive. Union with Christ at the moment of spiritual regeneration not only places the sinner in right relationship with God (by means of justification on grounds of the imputed righteousness of Christ), but union with Christ also sets the sinner apart unto God as wholly sanctified (see Romans 6 and 8). To be sure, the emphasis in Scripture falls upon the progressive aspect of God's sanctifying power at work in those regenerated and renewed in Christ. But this teaching must not obscure the aspect of the believer's definitive sanctification. Only in terms of this teaching can we understand and heed the biblical admonition to be perfect as our Father in heaven is perfect (Matt 5:48). To be sure, we are not yet what we shall be. But the final glorification of the saints of God has *already* been secured through the redemptive work of Christ (Rom 8:28-30). We are pilgrims on the way to the Eternal City. What the Spirit of God begins in the life of his children he will see to completion. Perseverance in the faith is the outworking of God's grace in the lives of the saints.

Renewed interest and appreciation for the biblical, Reformed doctrine of eschatology in the twentieth century has served to advance Scripture's teaching on the topic of "realized" eschatology, or more specifically, recognition of the biblical distinction between the "already" and the "not yet" of eschatological life in the Spirit. The day of Pentecost marks the birth of the NT church (the church was already present since the days of the establishment of the Covenant of Grace after Adam's fall into sin); it also marks the eschatological age of the Spirit (or more accurately, the *semi*-eschatological age of the Spirit appearing between the two advents of Christ). Christians live in a period of tension between Christ's accomplishment of redemption and the consummation (final glorification of the saints) at the close of history, and between what has already been realized in their own life experience and what is yet to be realized in the eternal kingdom of God. It is the tension between the "already" and the "not yet" of redemption fully achieved by Christ on the cross; it is the mystery of the believer's union with Christ in his death and resurrection and his existential union with Christ by means of the regenerating work of the Spirit of God in anticipation of the consummation (i.e., glorification). Final judgment includes not only the just condemnation of the ungodly, but also the *vindication* of the saints of God, those who have glorified him in true righteousness and holiness. Good works, evidential of justifying faith, will "prove" the efficacy and power of God's saving grace in the lives of the faithful. Final judgment will be according to works, but not on the ground of works. The decisive verdict of guiltlessness has already been declared, settled in heaven for time and eternity, for those trusting in Christ.

There are some modern-day revisionists who maintain that a proper understanding of the biblical doctrine of justification—set in the context of semi-realized eschatology—yields a new, revised (or improved) understanding of what it means to be justified by faith alone. They speak of justification as something "already" declared, and "not yet" declared in consummate finality—a contradiction of grave consequence. Justification, we are told, is maintained only in the exercise of persevering faith and good works (the "obedience of faith"). Since these revisionists have jettisoned the traditional Protestant-Reformed contrast between Law and Gospel—and along with that the allegedly speculative notion of "meritorious" reward with respect to human, creaturely works—they are comfortable (re)asserting the necessity of good works in justification (somewhat after the pattern of Roman Catholic teaching). Thinking they have disposed themselves of the charge of reintroducing "works" in the article of justification, viz., works as meritorious ground of life (in the order of creation) or of salvation (in the order of recreation), they are quite confident affirming the necessity of faith and works in justification. This modern-day heresy, judged in the light of Scripture and Reformation orthodoxy, undermines the Gospel of grace, the only gospel that saves sinners from God's just recompense for disobedience and coming wrath. In the midst of the present, raging controversy it is our fervent prayer that the Lord will enable the evangelical church to reclaim the teaching of our Protestant-Reformed forebears, to the extent it accurately conveys the teaching of Scripture.

2

Conflating Faith and Works in Final Judgment/Justification

The Teaching of the New Westminster School

AT THE HEART OF New Westminster is its teaching concerning justification/final judgment based upon the fruits of a "working, obedient faith." Traditionally, Reformed theology has taught that faith alone is the instrument that appropriates Christ's righteousness in the justification of sinners. This definitive act in the salvation of God's elect is fixed at the moment that the object of God's love and mercy is experientially united to Christ by grace through faith. The outcome for the elect on the Day of Judgment (at the end of the age) is already fully determined.[1] Ensuing good works are evidential of God's justifying work in the life of the believer; they witness to the efficacy of God's transforming grace in salvation, specifically with reference to sanctification, another benefit bestowed upon those united to Christ. "Final justification," or more accurately, final judgment, is not contingent upon good works. *The good works of believers are purely evidential.*[2] Judg-

---

1. This statement stands in radical contrast to New Westminster's teaching on (eschatological) justification as "already"/"not yet."

2. Good works inevitably flow from justification. Once redeemed by grace through faith, the justified are certain of their full salvation (which includes all the benefits of union with Christ). There are two aspects to soteric justification: the *constitutive* (whereby the perfect righteousness of Christ is imputed to the believer as the ground of salvation), and the *demonstrative* (whereby good works, the righteous deeds of the believer, are evidential of God's saving grace operative in union with Christ). The believer

ment on the Last Day is "according to works," but not "based on works." This is not the view of the Shepherd-Gaffin school, which now prevails at Westminster East. The picture is clouded at Westminster West with respect to its renunciation of Norman Shepherd's heterodoxy, on the one hand, and its endorsement of Richard Gaffin's alleged orthodoxy, on the other.

After the dismissal of Shepherd from Westminster in Philadelphia, it was but a matter of time before the focal issue shifted from the doctrine of justification by faith and works to the doctrine of union with Christ, a subject dear to Shepherd himself. Under the direction and coordination of Westminster's senior systematician, Richard B. Gaffin Jr., New Westminster has become more readily identified as the "Union with Christ School."[3] It

---

is already justified (once and for all), though not yet vindicated publicly (this vindication awaits God's final judgment, the approbation of the saints in glory).

3. See Peter A. Lillback's lead article in the Spring 2012 issue of the seminary journal: "The Rev. Dr. Richard B. Gaffin, Jr.: *Sancti Libri Theologicus Magnus Westmonasteriensis*." Gaffin has denied fathering the "Union with Christ School" at Westminster. Belying Gaffin's assertion is the subject of the inaugural lecture by Lane Tipton, Gaffin's successor in the Charles Krahe Chair of Systematic Theology: "Biblical Theology and the Westminster Standards: Union with Chirst and Justification *Sola Fide*" (November 13, 2012). On this occasion Gaffin gave the charge to Tipton. Incredulously, Gaffin denies his responsibility for and ties to Westminster's Union with Christ School. See his "Response to John Fesko's Review" in *The Ordained Servant Online* at http://www.opc.org/os.html.

Since the early days of the Shepherd controversy on Westminster's campus, the stance of the faculty has been characterized by diversion and duplicity. Understandable is the citation made by President Lillback regarding Ian A. Hewitson's partial account of Shepherd's dismissal from the seminary, as advanced in *Trust and Obey: Norman Shepherd and the Justification Controversy at Westminster Theological Seminary*. In the thinking of Lillback, the faculty of Westminster East considers Gaffin to be "a wise theologian in the midst of community-shaking theological controversy" (an opinion that brings into view Gaffin's role in the Peter Enns dispute regarding biblical inerrancy, as well as the Shepherd case regarding justification). Hewitson's retelling of the Shepherd story, one of conflict and division, echoes the position adopted by the faculty and administration of Westminster in Philadelphia. (Actually, Hewitson's book relies exclusively on Shepherd's version of the seminary's handling of his dismissal.) Regarding the Enns controversy, including history and analysis of teaching leading up to those views held by Enns, see Yeo, *Plundering the Egyptians: The Old Testament and Historical Criticism at Westminster Theological Seminary (1928–1998)*. Favoring a new understanding of what inerrancy means to the modern interpreter, see Bovell, *Inerrancy and the Spiritual Formation of Younger Evangelicals*. Bowell was trained at Westminster. In Muether and Olinger, eds., *Confident of Better Things: Essays Commemorating Seventy-Five Years of the Orthodox Presbyterian Church*, no reference is made to the Shepherd controversy or to debates over biblical inerrancy during these years.

For an accurate, authoritative history of the Shepherd dispute, see Robertson, *The Current Justification Controversy*; and these writings by Karlberg: *The Changing of the*

was this Calvinistic doctrine—reworked in subtle ways—that has given shape to the entire seminary curriculum. All roads in the theological encyclopedia lead to union with Christ (from *redemption accomplished* to *redemption applied*). Agreeably, redemptive history—centering upon the work of Jesus Christ in the execution (and securing) of salvation for all those for whom he died—is made personal by the regenerating work of the Spirit of Christ. It is by the Holy Spirit that individual salvation in Christ is made effectual.

The Spring 2012 issue of the *Westminster Theological Journal* contains, as its second lead article, William R. Edwards' "John Flavel on the Priority of Union with Christ: Further Historical Perspective on the Structure of Reformed Soteriology."[4] The aim of this essay is to explain differences of thinking between the faculties of Westminster East and Westminster West, pitting one institution against the other. Regrettably, Edward's reading is misleading and diversionary. Yet it needs to be said that at Westminster disputants on both sides are equally guilty. All have concealed what is at the very heart of the now three-decades-old controversy. Instead, readers are now offered what amounts to mere nibbling at the edges, straining at a gnat—all of which leads to ongoing confusion and misrepresentation. The reason for this deliberate concealment of the real issue(s) at stake is the concerted effort to shield and protect Gaffin, all in hopes of avoiding yet further division and strife within Westminster and among the churches the seminary serves. *Rather than the doctrine of union with Christ, on which there is really little substantive difference among the disputants, it is the doctrine of justification by faith alone that divides the church and seminary.* More exactly, it is the distinction between the *contrasting principles of faith-inheritance and works-inheritance*. At stake in this long-standing

---

Guard: Westminster Theological Seminary in Philadelphia; *Gospel Grace: The Modern-Day Controversy*; and *Federalism and the Westminster Tradition: Reformed Orthodoxy at the Crossroads*. Compare also Engelsma, *Federal Vision: Heresy at the Root*, critiqued below. Engelsma's analysis is based upon a very different interpretation of the doctrine of the covenants, one that is out of step with mainstream Reformed thinking. Englesma enunciates doctrine that is distinctive of the Protestant Reformed church, summed up in the idea of the unconditional covenant. See my review of Engelsma's *The Covenant of God and the Children of Believers: Sovereign Grace in the Covenant*, in *JETS* 49 (2006), republished in my *Federalism and the Westminster Tradition*, 142–49.

4. Compare especially an earlier essay by William B. Evans, "Déjà vu All Over Again?: The Contemporary Reformed Soteriological Controversy in Historical Perspective." See the most recent exchange in Evans, "*Sic et Non*. Views in Review: Westminster Seminary California Distinctives?," which I have not seen.

controversy is the historic Protestant distinction between the Law and the Gospel, a distinction upheld by both evangelical Reformed and Lutheran traditions since the Reformation.

According to Edwards, "the context for the current debate reaches back most immediately to various critiques of the New Perspective on Paul and the Federal Vision."[5] Regarding the doctrine of union with Christ as debated within this wider theological context, the Westminster School(s) offers two divergent readings. Westminster East accentuates the pivotal role of union with Christ in its exposition of Reformed soteriology. Allegedly, Westminster West, after the pattern of Lutheran teaching, emphasizes the centrality of justification by faith to the exclusion of all other saving benefits accruing to the believer by virtue of union with Christ. Edwards stresses: "It should be noted that both positions vigorously maintain that justification is God's forensic, or legal, declaration of a believer's righteous status dependent entirely on the imputed righteousness of Christ and received by faith alone."[6] This analysis of Edwards is simply misleading and inaccurate.

What proponents of the New Perspective on Paul, the Federal Vision, and New Westminster share in common is antipathy for the works (merit) principle, as that relates to the First Adam, federal head of humankind, and to theocratic Israel, the "Servant of the Lord," during the period of the old economy of redemption (from Moses to Christ). The focal biblical text regarding this teaching is Leviticus 18:5. Proper exegesis of this text is crucial to a sound biblical theology of the covenants.[7] Not to be overlooked is the fact that many, if not most, proponents of the New Perspective on Paul and the Federal Vision credit Shepherd and Gaffin for their pioneering work at Westminster. The result of their efforts has been to carry forward Barthian doctrine concerning justification, election, and the covenants that has long prevailed in much of Reformed scholarship over the last half-century or more.[8]

5. Edwards, "John Flavel," 33. A graduate of Westminster in Philadelphia, Edwards currently pastors a Presbyterian Church in America congregation in Forest, Virginia.

6. Ibid., 33–34.

7. In no uncertain or ambiguous terms, the apostle Paul sets the principle of law, enunciated in Lev 18:5, against the principle of faith. And it is this law-principle that characterizes the peculiar nature of the old covenant, the covenant which passed away with the inauguration of the new covenant of Christ established in the fullness of times.

8. Cornelius Van Til, theologian and apologist of Old Westminster, was noted for his vigorous anti-Barthian polemic. Rightly, Karl Barth was deemed to be a modernist, not a (neo-)Calvinist. See notably, Van Til's *Christianity and Barthianism*. "Although Westminster reserved its harshest criticism for liberal Protestantism, Van Til's critique of Barth's neo-orthodox theology was one of the most forceful examples of the school's

Edwards' study of John Flavel (1627–1691) confirms what the author understands to be mainstream Reformed interpretation on union with Christ (hence it is said, Westminster West errs in thinking differently about its own theological tradition). At the same time the dispute, according to Edwards, reflects "deeper structural differences" between the theology of Westminster East and West.[9] All this leads Edwards to conclude: "The point

---

polemics" (Godfrey and Hart, *Westminster Seminary California*, 37). Godfrey and Hart add: "The identity of Westminster as a Reformed seminary was both its greatest assess and its great difficulty. Because of its attention to careful scholarship and its comprehensive curriculum, Westminster had gained a reputation as the West Point of Protestant orthodoxy" (38). The faculty at Westminster West has come to recognize "The Barthian challenge to the Reformation teaching on justification began to have a growing influence on the evangelical theology [to which we hasten to add, New Westminster]. Barth had suggested that the Reformation had overstated the distinction between Law and Gospel and that reproachment with Roman Catholic theology was possible. Evangelicals who had preferred Barth (and ignored Van Til's repeated warnings about his theology) moved again in a dangerous direction" (87). Regrettably, Godfrey and Hart falsely contend: "Reformed scholars such as Richard Gaffin and Guy Waters provided a clear refutation of these errors" (90). In truth, Gaffin has frequently been hailed by the revisionists as one of their most articulate spokesmen and guiding lights. Westminster West's ambivalence and duplicity can best be explained from its beginnings as a theological institution. Godfrey and Hart explain: "Westminster California was born in the heat of the Shepherd controversy and initially left the Shepherd problem to WTS (especially since Frame tended to defend Shepherd while Strimple and Godfrey had sharply criticized him)." They concede: "But even with the dismissal of Shepherd in 1981, the issue of the doctrine of justification did not disappear. Some in the Reformed churches [led by Richard Gaffin] continued to defend Shepherd, others embraced the New Perspective on Paul, and still others adopted the Federal Vision. Clearly justification by faith alone had become a doctrine that needed restatement and defense" (109). This leads Godfrey and Hart to state boldly (and courageously!): "When it came to justification, the material principle of the Reformation, Westminster California would not be silent or equivocate" (112). Compare the similar sentiments regarding their courageous stand for the faith in Clark and Kim, eds., *Always Reformed: Essays in Honor of W. Robert Godfrey*. In the critiques of Karlberg, Engelsma, and many others, this self-assessment on the part of the Escondido faculty is hollow and inaccurate, designed to mislead and misrepresent the ongoing crisis in the seminary and churches.

9. Edwards, "John Flavel," 33. John Fesko, in *Beyond Calvin: Union with Christ and Justification in Early Modern Reformed Theology (1517–1700)*, speaks of the debate over the Reformed doctrine of union with Christ, and soteriology more broadly, as merely a friendly "in-house" dispute (notably, within the Orthodox Presbyterian Church, where unity in all essentials is said to prevail).

For a favorable reading of the Orthodox Presbyterian Church today (one lacking critical self-analysis), see Hart, *Between the Times: The Orthodox Presbyterian Church in Transition, 1945–1990*; Muether and Olinger, eds., *Confident of Better Things: Essays Commemorating Seventy-Five Years of the Orthodox Presbyterian Church*; and Muether, "Who Narrates the Orthodox Presbyterian Church?: The Church and its Historians."

in question is not whether faith is the alone instrument in justification. The issue is whether this is the alone function of faith. The depiction of faith by those emphasizing the priority of justification appears to lead one to this conclusion."[10] Oddly, it turns out that the nature of faith as the unique instrument procuring God's act of justification lies at the heart of the present-day dispute. Westminster West is correct to view Westminster East with suspicion in regards to the doctrine of covenant, justification, and union with Christ. Edwards' analysis of the two Westminster schools does little to further discussion and debate. The true state of affairs in this controversy yet awaits illumination by the Westmisnter disputants.[11] To reiterate, the heart of the matter is the faith-inheritance principle, antithetical to the works-inheritance principle (or in other terms, the Law/Gospel contrast).

For additional critique of New Westminster we turn in the second instance to Gregory K. Beale's *magnum opus*, entitled *A New Testament Biblical Theology*.[12] Beale taps into much of the same potpourri of writings that

---

These authors, speaking on behalf of the OPC as a whole, are eager to portray their denomination as comprising one happy family. And they prefer to write their own history, rather than hear and learn from "outsiders." This mentality has given birth to a culture of pride, complacency, and self-deception.

10. Edwards, "John Flavel," 57. In recent years Gaffin's reference to Christ's "meritorious" obedience (imputed to believers through "faith alone") is meaningless, having jettisoned the doctrine of the Covenant of Works, the covenant informed by the works-merit principle. Following Gaffin's lead, Shepherd now freely employs the notion of the imputation of Christ's righteousness in *The Way of Righteousness: Justification Beginning with James*. This idea, however, is vacuous, foreign to the Gaffin-Shepherd system of doctrine, which has no place for the works-principle in the covenant with the First Adam. Curiously, Shepherd's book offers no interaction with his critics, nor with any of the important works on the subject.

11. Ongoing efforts have been made to quell further debate and dissent, all in the hopes of avoiding yet further damage to the seminary and her constituency. See Robertson, *The Current Justification Controversy*; Karlberg: *The Changing of the Guard: Westminster Theological Seminary in Philadelphia*; idem, *Gospel Grace: The Modern-Day Controversy*; idem, *Federalism and the Westminster Tradition: Reformed Orthodoxy at the Crossroads*; and Engelsma, *Federal Vision: Heresy at the Root*.

12. Overall, Beale's study in biblical theology suffers from several major structural/hermeneutical misappropriations, due largely to his failure to integrate typological interpretation with Reformed teaching on the Mosaic Covenant. His grasp of the theology of the covenants is inconsistent, resulting in an admixture of Reformed and dispensational elements. Oddly, more than once Beale commends the formulation of Scott Hahn in his *Kingship by Covenant: A Canonical Approach to the Fulfillment of God's Saving Promises*. (After studying under Shepherd at Westminster, Hahn joined the Roman Catholic Church and has become an influential theologian for Rome.) Admittedly, Beale's work is one that is in progress of development and maturation. One would hope that he will

Edwards has surveyed. The meaning of justifying faith for New Westminster is more clearly spelled out for us in these pages. Pivotal in Shepherd's reinterpretation of the doctrine of justification by faith and works is his understanding of the second chapter of James. Adopting this same reading, Beale explains: "James 2:14–26 also speaks of the close link between justification and good works (e.g., v. 14: 'a man is justified by works and not by faith alone'). This text is also likely focusing on a final justification at the end of time."[13] Beale proceeds to relate these righteous works of the believer to final (eschatological) justification as the "consummate, manifestive stage of justification." Accordingly, justification takes place in two stages, the "already" and the "not yet." And it is the final stage that *consummates* the believer's righteous standing in union with Christ.

Citing John Piper's *Future of Justification*,[14] Beale describes the two stages of justification in these terms: "Justification and judgment are grounded in the believer's union with Christ, the former coming by faith, and the latter being an evaluation of works that necessarily arise from the

---

yet come to see the irreconcilable differences between the Gaffin school and historic Reformed federalism. But that remains highly unlikely. Michael Horton, among others, gives high commendation for this work of Beale, without requisite objection to controverted points of doctrine (notably, the role of works in justification).

One of the biblical theologians to whom Beale dedicates his book is Meredith G. Kline (the other two named are Gordon P. Hugenberger and David. F. Wells). The body of Beale's treatise, however, shows heavy dependence upon the views of Richard Gaffin, views which are in direct opposition to those of Kline on many critical points in the doctrinal controversy at Westminster. In a footnote Beale remarks: "Gaffin's seminal idea about Christ's resurrection influenced me years ago, and I am trying to expand on it in many ways in this book. Gaffin argues that in Paul's thinking, Christ's resurrection was his 'redemption'—i.e., deliverance from death. Furthermore, he argues that 'justification, adoption, sanctification, and glorification as applied to Christ are not separate, distinct acts; rather, each describes a different facet or aspect of the one act' of having been raised and redeemed from the dead. When believers are identified with and come into union with the resurrected Christ, they are also identified with these same facets" (354 n. 107).

13. Beale, *New Testament Biblical Theology*, 506.

14. Compare Piper's earlier work, *Future Grace: The Purifying Power of the Promises of God*. See my critique of *Future Grace* in *New Horizons* 17/5 (May 1996), and also my *John Piper on the Christian Life: An Examination of His Controversial View of 'Faith Alone' in Future Grace*, republished in *Gospel Grace*, 137–55. Parenthetically, the Evangelical Theological Society has failed in its effort to hold members of the Society to any meaningful vow or commitment to "evangelicalism," in the true sense of the label. Diverse, conflicting views on justification by faith (and works) and biblical inerrancy are only two subjects on which members are sharply divided.

true faith-union with Christ and by means of the Spirit's empowerment."[15] Then, in a footnote Beale further remarks: "This view is compatible with Klyne R. Snodgrass, 'Justification by Grace—to the Doers: An Analysis of the Place of Rom. 2 in the Theology of Paul,' *NTS* 32 (1986), 72–93. Snodgrass holds that justification excludes 'legalistic works' done to earn salvation but includes an evaluation of imperfect works done that are inspired by grace."[16] This is fully consistent with the Shepherd-Gaffin theology, wherein non-meritorious works (the "righteous, good works" of the believer) are understood to be instrumental in the procurement of (final) justification. The way of salvation is the way of faith *and* works. Beale favorably adopts much of Gaffin's teaching on justification by faith and works (described as a "twofold justification"), all the while assiduously avoiding direct interaction with what he calls the "evangelical Presbyterian" controversy regarding law, covenant, and justification.[17] He misleadingly uses terminology drawn directly from Gaffin and his exponents. To be sure, good works are related to justification; they are evidential. However, the obedience of faith (i.e., good works) plays no role *with regard to the constitutive aspect of justification*. The believer is constituted righteous on the sole basis of the imputed righteousness of Christ, appropriated by faith as the alone instrument.[18]

15. Beale, *New Testament Biblical Theology*, 516.

16. Ibid., 516 n. 119. See discussion of "non-meritorious works" as instrument in soteric justification in my *Gospel Grace*. Of course, Roman Catholicism teaches that the righteousness earned in the sinner's justification is imputed and imparted (inwrought). Lane Tipton's "Union with Christ and Justification" attempts to amalgamate opposing formulations. His staunch advocacy of the theology of New Westminster is unaffected by occasional, evasive disclaimers made in this essay. Compare Norman Shepherd's *The Way of Righteousness: Justification Beginning with James*. This work offers no substantive change in formulation, despite the author's return to the doctrine of the imputation of Christ's passive obedience as "ground" of justification. Shepherd's sparse exposition offers no interaction with his many critics, nor interaction with the voluminous literature on the subject.

17. Beale, *New Testament Biblical Theology*, 471. The author seeks to offer some qualification concerning his own understanding of justification as "already"/"not yet," notably at the conclusion of the book. However, these (re)statements of the doctrine do not comport with those favorably drawn by Beale from the Shepherd-Gaffin theology. The two views cannot stand together; they are wholly incompatible.

18. At a later point in his discussion Beale concedes: "Another, I think better, version of the 'not yet' aspect of justification/vindication is that believers in this age are declared both not guilty because of Christ's substitutionary punishment and fully righteous because of the transferral of his perfect righteousness to them; then at the end of the age, the good works of saints (which are imperfect) justify/vindicate that they were truly justified by Christ in the past. Accordingly, this final form of justification is not

Conflating Faith and Works in Final Judgment/Justification

The apostle Paul's exposition of justification by faith is inextricably tied to the peculiar law-principle at work in the Mosaic Covenant, the old economy of the single, ongoing Covenant of Grace spanning the entire history of redemption (recall: in the old economy of redemption the law-principle is restricted to *temporal life* in the land of Canaan).[19] Beale acknowledges this, in part. He agrees that the Mosaic Covenant does entail a republication of the works-inheritance principle, the principle determinative of the first covenant with Adam as federal head prior to the Fall. Yet this leading feature of historic Reformed interpretation of the covenants is left wholly undeveloped throughout the course of Beale's lengthy treatise.[20]

---

on the same level as the justification by faith in Jesus, though it is linked to it. Good works are the badge that vindicates the saints in the sense of declarative proof that they have been truly already justified by Christ" (ibid., 524). What he states on the next page, however, undercuts this formulation: "Therefore, initial justification and consummative justification (or twofold justification) are grounded in believers' union with Christ (both his death and his resurrection), the former coming by faith, and the latter through the threefold demonstration of the bodily resurrection, evaluation of works, and public announcement to the cosmos" (525).

19. Consult Karlberg, *Covenant Theology in Reformed Perspective*. See also chapter 4 in this book. Of special relevance is the collection of articles in Estelle et. al., *The Law Is Not of Faith: Essays on Works and Grace in the Mosaic Covenant*, which I have reviewed in *JETS* 53 (2009) (republished in *Federalism and the Westminster Tradition*). Cf. also the reviews by Mark Jones and Brian Lee of this book in *The Ordained Servant Online* (April 2010) (http://www.opc.org/os.html.)

20. Beale is unclear on the works-principle operative on the symbolico-typological level of life in Canaan, a reenactment of paradise in Eden, entailing a (modified) covenant of works and time of probationary testing. The same can be said of Beale's previous study, *The Temple and the Church's Mission: A Biblical Theology of the Dwelling Place of God*. Admittedly, the Mosaic Covenant remains largely undeveloped in Beale's thinking. He concedes: "At points throughout this book I have discussed the covenant (e.g., chap. 21 under the subheading 'Hebrews'), though I have not addressed it as a major topic. The discussion here is a limited attempt to relate more formally so-called covenant theology to the overall argument of this book" (Beale, *New Testament Biblical Theology*, 916).

Recently, the attempt was made by the Northwest Presbytery of the Orthodox Presbyterian Church to petition the 2012 General Assembly for a denominational study on the church's teaching concerning the Mosaic Covenant. That attempt was derailed, at least for the present time. It is unlikely the issue can be tabled for any length of time, considering just how divisive the subject has become in the OPC and in the wider Reformed community. See the website of Northwest Presbytery OPC (https://sites.google.com/site/mosaiccovenant/home).

How the Mighty Have Fallen

Where does all this leave Reformed dogmatics? This is also the vexing question posed by David Engelsma in his new publication, *Federal Vision: Heresy at the Root*. For many years since the release of Shepherd's book, *The Call of Grace: How the Covenant Illuminates Salvation and Evangelism*,[21] Engelsma has joined those of us who have sounded the alarm. Regrettably, his critique of the current scene in the Reformed church and academy further fragments the community of scholarship that is standing in defense of orthodox Reformed federalism. It is Engelma's conviction that only the theology of his denomination (the Protestant Reformed Church) is in a position to identify the root of the heresy infecting much of present-day Calvinism, and to resolve the controversy.[22] That is simply not the case. Nevertheless, we do well to consider some of the points raised in Engelsma's book.

First, we need to understand that the term "Federal Vision," as used by the author, includes two related movements in contemporary Reformed theology, the New Perspective on Paul and (what for years I have called) "New Westminster." It is the latter that is of special concern to us in the critique offered by Engelsma, one that echoes much of my own evaluation. Engelsma speaks of this pernicious, heretical teaching as "the *chief* threat to the Reformed faith—the Reformation's Gospel of grace—in our time."[23] Corollary to this new teaching is advocacy of the discipline of biblical theology, employed at the expense of traditional systematics (and confessional church dogmatics).[24] It is a back-to-the-Bible movement that frees the in-

---

21. Published by Presbyterian and Reformed, which, from its founding, has been the "unofficial" publishing house of Westminster Seminary, and for years Gaffin has served as one of its advisors/consultants.

22. Principally, the view of the Protestant Reformed Church and Professor Engelsma, one of this church's leading spokesmen, entails a defective theology of the covenants, notably, with respect to the first covenant made by God with Adam in Eden. Engelsma is entirely misguided in thinking that in this widespread controversy the Protestant Reformed Church alone can come to the rescue. Simply not so! According to Engelsma, the root of the heresy lies in its commitment to a "conditional Covenant of Grace." Scripture, notes Engelsma, teaches an "unconditional Covenant of Grace," the only covenant made by God with man (which accounts in part for Engelsma's rejection of the traditional doctrine of the Covenant of Works at creation). "Only this truth [regarding the unconditional covenant] gives assurance of salvation to the baptized children of believers, old and young. Only this truth gives God the glory for covenant salvation" (Engelsma, *Federal Vision*, 12).

23. Ibid.

24. It is Beale's express aim in his treatise to advance the theological discipline that

terpreter/exegete to see truth afresh (after the example of Neo-orthodoxy). "The threat of the federal vision to Reformed and Presbyterian believers and their children," explains Engelsma, "has not diminished in the slightest in the past ten years or so since Shepherd published *The Call of Grace*. On the contrary, the danger to Reformed churches and church members is greater today than ever before."[25]

Engelsma observes: "The publication of Shepherd's book also occasioned the opening of the floodgates of public defense of Shepherd's teachings and aggressive promotion of them within many of the reputedly conservative Reformed and Presbyterian denominations in North America, including the Orthodox Presbyterian Church, the Presbyterian Church in America, and the United Reformed Churches."[26] Failure to eradicate the new teaching within these denominations—plaguing virtually all quarters of the conservative Reformed community—has led increasingly to silence on the disputed issues, the all-too-common practice of looking in another direction. As a consequence, "The danger of the federal vision remains. It is the more dangerous because now, supposedly overcome, it is being ignored."[27] Multi-perspectivalist John Frame has taken it upon himself to publish the opinion of other like-minded proponents of the Shepherd-Gaffin theology: the critics of Shepherd are "stupid, irresponsible, and divisive."[28]

---

is of special significance for Westminster, namely, biblical theology. Employment of the biblical-theological methodology requires far greater discernment than Beale exhibits in his book. The work of Geerhardus Vos, the father of twentieth-century Reformed biblical theology, and Meredith Kline differs significantly from that of Norman Shepherd and Richard Gaffin.

25. Engelsma, *Federal Vision*, 20.

26. Ibid., 18.

27. Ibid., 20. Engelsma speaks of the "earnest, studied, deliberate, deafening, astounding, inexcusable, blameworthy silence" of those who should know better (42). Indeed, where there is greater light, there is greater responsibility and accountability. The silence (including misrepresentation of facts) is truly reprehensible.

28. Ibid., 21. John Frame has recently published an incendiary attack upon Westminster California, aimed at several of the most prominent members of the faculty in *The Escondido Theology: A Reformed Response to Two Kingdom Theology*. The faculty was "surprised and shocked" by their former colleague's vitriolic critique. But the faculty should not have been unsuspecting in the least! Most on the faculty, including President Godfrey, had increasingly moved away from Frame and his odd teachings, to the point where Frame felt alienated and unwelcome, appropriately so in the circumstance. Once again, questions of the honesty and integrity within the faculty here arise. Certainly one can question Godfrey's judgment regarding Frame's advocacy of VanTilianism. Frame is,

Engelsma locates the root of the heresy in the notion of a "conditional Covenant of Grace." Although there is some legitimacy to Engelsma's analysis, it does not sufficiently address the wider, more fundamental issue on which the Shepherd theology rests, namely, the attack on the idea of the Covenant of Works, as opposed to the idea of the Covenant of Grace as taught in historic, confessional Reformed theology. Most significantly and tellingly, Engelsma acknowledges a partial similarity between the view of the Protestant Reformed Church and that of the Federal Vision respecting God's covenant-making with humankind. Both agree that there is no merit, no earning of reward in any circumstance in which man finds himself *coram Deo*. The reward of eternal life, whether proffered at the opening of human history (i.e., before the Fall) or subsequently (over the course of the Covenant of Grace spanning all of redemptive history), is entirely of grace (unearned).[29] Accordingly, it is argued, only Christ by means of his perfect righteousness *merits* the reward of a kingdom, a people saved by grace.

We need not discuss here the legitimacy of the doctrine of the Covenant of Works, amply taught in Scripture and the Reformed tradition. We need only point out the weakness of Engelsma's critique of the new teaching, once he too has jettisoned the historic Reformed doctrine of the Covenant of Works made by God with Adam at the opening of human history. This covenant informs Adam's time of probationary testing (doctrine likewise ignored by Engelsma). Equally abhorrent to Engelsma is mainstream Reformed teaching regarding the Mosaic Covenant as, in part, a republication of the original Covenant of Works. He maintains: "The federal vision doctrine of justification by faith and works is not some fruit of an

---

at best, a modified VanTilian. (Godfrey and Hart offer a disingenuous, explanatory gloss on Frame's resignation in *Westminster Seminary California*, 117–18.)

Engelsma rightly laments: "There are the board and faculty of Westminster Seminary, who defended Shepherd to the end. They have never confessed their sins of approving the doctrine of justification by faith and works and of unleashing the federal vision upon the Reformed and Presbyterian churches in North America by releasing Professor Shepherd with a good testimonial" (22). Westminster repent? The institution sees no reason to do so; the faculty and administration are convinced Shepherd was on the right track. President Lillback himself, in his Westminster doctoral dissertation, subsequently published as *The Binding of God: Calvin's Role in the Development of Covenant Theology*, erroneously attempts to trace the New Westminster teaching back to Calvin. See the defense of Lillback's interpretation in Coxhead, "John Calvin's Subordinate Doctrine of Justification by Works."

29. See further my *Gospel Grace* for discussion of the biblical concept of grace. The term "grace" in Scripture pertains exclusively to God's *redemptive provision* for fallen humanity.

erroneous view of the covenant with Adam, or of a mistaken doctrine of the covenant at Sinai. It is the fruit of a certain doctrine of the new covenant in Christ"—what Engelsma has identified as "a covenant of conditional grace and conditional salvation."[30]

At the same time, unlike the Federal Visionists, Engelsma acknowledges the *meritorious obedience* of Christ imputed to sinners in soteric justification. He writes: "The Protestant Reformed Churches, in contrast, emphatically teach the meritorious nature of the covenant work of Jesus Christ."[31] This means, according to Engelsma, that Christ's meriting was a matter of "divine justice." In other words, "Meriting was necessary, because the justice of God demanded full payment for sin and adequate basis for inheriting eternal life."[32] Engelsma hastens to add: "That Christ merited does not imply that the covenant of God with him and with those who belong to him (Gal. 3:16, 29) is a covenant of works. Covenant of works describes a covenant in which *mere man* earns with God."[33] His final thoughts: "*God was in Christ* establishing the covenant of grace by meriting, satisfying justice, and fulfilling every demand of the law. *Christ was God's willing servant* earning, paying, and submitting to divine justice."[34] This is the gist of Engelsma's teaching on the merit of the Second Adam's obedience, Christ acting in place of the First Adam. Engelsma's view destroys the explicit parallel drawn by the apostle Paul between the First and Second Adams. In so doing, he eviscerates the *vicarious* obedience of Christ as the exclusive ground of the believer's justification. According to Paul, where Adam failed, Christ succeeded. To turn the tables on the argument of Engelsma, disputing whether the Covenant of Grace is conditional or unconditional is meaningless apart from the biblical, Reformed doctrine of the Covenant of Works (including the idea of human merit) established at creation. In the end Engelsma misidentifies the root of the Federal Vision heresy.

The central issue dividing the Reformed church and academy today is one that brings into view critical elements in the (federal) doctrine of the covenants, including the idea of probation for the First and Second Adams, the demand for (*meritorious*) perfect obedience as the ground for divine approbation (justification), the sole instrumentality of saving faith in the

30. Engelsma, *Federal Vision*, 49.
31. Ibid., 140.
32. Ibid., 144.
33. Ibid.
34. Ibid., 145.

appropriation of Christ's righteousness in salvation (faith apart from good works), the contrast between the Law and the Gospel, the unconditional, electing grace of God (which is unlosable), and the redemptive-historic discontinuity between the old covenant under Moses and the new covenant established in Christ's reconciling blood (his substitutionary atonement). *What governs the historical administration of the Covenant of Grace is the household principle, not decretive election (what is, to be sure, the "proper purpose" of redemptive covenant).* Within international Calvinism not all of the elements have at all times been consistently and uniformly exposited; there are differences of expression, which is to be fully expected. What is at stake in the present-day dispute relates to elements of covenant theology that are essential and non-negotiable. The alarm is sounded once more for a return to Scripture and the teachings of federal Reformed orthodoxy on the subject of covenant, election, and justification by faith alone.

Reviews—Section One

Paul A. Rainbow, *The Way of Salvation: The Role of Christian Obedience in Justification*
(Bletchley, UK: Paternoster, 2005)

Richard B. Gaffin, Jr., *"By Faith, Not By Sight": Paul and the Order of Salvation*
(Bletchley, UK: Paternoster, 2006)

Paternoster has published two works by contemporary Protestant expositors that nicely complement one another. Whether they complement the message and cause of the Protestant Reformation will be the critical question left for readers to answer. It would very hard to miss that the argument of both books is the same in thrust and in substance. While Richard Gaffin (Westminster Seminary in Philadelphia) assumes a less confrontational stance toward the Protestant reformers, Paul Rainbow (North American Baptist Seminary) is uninhibited in his criticism of what he sees to be their glaring misreading of the crucial, biblical doctrine of justification by faith alone. The difference in posture, however, is inconsequential, as we shall see. Rainbow writes as a New Testament scholar with solid command of the history of doctrine, Gaffin as a systematician with expertise in Pauline theology (hence his desire to reformulate the system of Reformed doctrine in accordance with biblical theology, which has its own distinct methodology). Together, these two books will undoubtedly serve to advance the contemporary debate among evangelical and Reformed interpreters through their (attempted) restatement of doctrine—one they deem to be evangelical, faithful to the teaching of Scripture.

In this review of two very similar arguments, focal attention will be directed to the work by Rainbow, the stronger of the two. At times I find his writing highly commendable, other times highly exasperating. The author of *The Way of Salvation* attempts to bridge the chasm between two antithetical, theological positions by postulating a *via media*. Unfortunately, the result is a work characterized by thoroughgoing confusion, contradiction, and misstatement. Rainbow aims to supplement historic Protestant teaching on the doctrine of justification by faith. In the course of doing so, frequent citation is made to Gaffin's prior study, *The Centrality of the Resurrection*. Of special mention in this connection is Gaffin's attention to the doctrine of union with Christ and its relevance for the *ordo salutis*.

Rainbow states his major contention in these words: "To isolate justification from sanctification is one way to erect a safeguard against works-righteousness, to be sure. But it goes too far and renders the 'faith alone' doctrine susceptible to an inherent ethical groundlessness. If justification be wholly independent of sanctification, then the requirement of sanctification becomes an add-on, and does not arise form the very nature of God's gift of righteousness. On that hypothesis, the imperative to do good does not arise out of the fact that good behaviour is part and parcel of righteousness itself, but from a different principle and collection of scriptural texts" (xix). Rainbow is concerned that the judgment of God be based on the presence and operation of genuine holiness within the life of the believer—divine judgment based on fact, not fiction. (The implication is that in classical Protestant Reformed teaching the imputation of Christ's righteousness as the exclusive, meritorious ground of the justification of the sinner redeemed and united to Christ, is insufficient, even illusory.) Ethical change, argues Rainbow, must be inherent and transformational. This contention is by no means peculiar to Rainbow's argument, but it is disturbing to hear it from the lips of one professing to be Protestant and evangelical.

Over a spread of twenty chapters, Rainbow discusses all the important aspects of the debate concerning the doctrine of justification, beginning with a brief sketch of the Protestant Reformation. Other topics include the two covenants (Mosaic and new), two kinds of works (meritorious and those of faith, i.e., the "good works" of believers), the imputation of Christ's righteousness, regeneration, and sanctification. The book closes with a theological synthesis, observations on the order of salvation (*ordo salutis*), and an affirmation of the assurance of salvation. Not to appear too novel in his formulation of the doctrine of justification by grace through faith (alone), he ends his study by identifying earlier theologians he views as "forerunners" of his teaching (in part only). These include Luther, Melanchthon, Calvin, Bucer, Hooker, Baxter, Edwards, and Wesley. The "Concluding Postscript" exhorts Protestants and Catholics today to listen anew to each side of the debate through the lens of contemporary theology and exegesis. An appendix commends the Joint Statement drawn up at Regensburg (1541) as a model and starting point for renewed discussion. An extended bibliography is also provided. (In contrast, Gaffin's treatise is much more narrowly focused on the explication of the doctrine of justification in the Pauline *ordo salutis*, in terms of realized eschatology or, more exactly, union with the resurrected Christ—a preoccupation of Gaffin since his doctoral study in the late 1960s. This presentation began as a series of lectures delivered first at Oak Hill Theological College, London, in May 2004 and then reworked for the Seventh Annual Pastors' Conference, which the reader is told was "sponsored by the session of the Auburn Avenue Presbyterian Church, Monroe, Louisiana, in January 2005." The other main speaker at this conference was none other than N. T. Wright. Auburn Avenue is the seat of the "Federal Vision" school, a movement holding similar views to the New Perspective on Paul and the law, and a hotbed for the teachings of Norman Shepherd.)

Did John Calvin and Martin Luther agree in their understanding of the doctrine of justification by faith (apart from works)? Rainbow answers: "In the matter of justification, Calvin was a disciple of Luther almost all the way" (31). (Gaffin avers otherwise.) Rainbow contends: "In the Protestant outlook, imputation is the thing that saves. Good works are required of the regenerate afterwards, but not with a view to any further aspect of salvation. Justifying righteousness and the righteousness of sanctification rest on different causes, operate in separate spheres, and serve disparate ends. They have nothing to do with each other" (35). In his zeal to advance his own nuanced discussion concerning justification and sanctification (contra the view of the Protestant reformers), Rainbow misstates and exaggerates the case against the reformers. The doctrine of the imputation of Christ's righteousness, to be sure, is absolutely critical, but that in no way suggests that everything has been said that needs to be said with regard to exposition of the doctrine of the salvation of sinners justified by grace through faith. Far from it. (Can Rainbow name one respectable work in Protestant dogmatics that begins and ends the locus on the application of redemption with justification and imputation? Rainbow's reading is mere caricature.) As another example of misstatement on the part of Rainbow, he writes: "Having been justified by reason of Christ, believers, moved by the Holy Spirit, start to bear fruit. But their deeds are irrelevant to their righteousness in God's eyes" (35). What respectable Protestant reformer (past or present) would affirm this statement? Rainbow's manner of argument, his reading of the primary sources, can be justly questioned. His command of the history of doctrine, though impressive, is clearly biased.

Moving to the crux of the issue in this modern day dispute, how are we to view the (genuinely) *good* works of the saints, those justified and sanctified in Christ Jesus? How do we reconcile Paul and James on justification (wherein justification is by faith and by works respectively)? And how do we construe future judgment according to works? These questions are not new. What are new are the answers coming from the "evangelical Reformed" camp (hence the intramural side of the theological controversy). Again, in the words of Rainbow: "Many of these problems revolve around the single question whether the fruit of the Spirit counts toward a finalizing of justification. For this reason, the real Protestant dispute with Rome came to be focused squarely on the issue of Christian works in salvation. Against Augustine's opinion that fulfilling the law with the help of the Holy Spirit leads to justification Luther blasted a No" (46).

To his credit, Rainbow, unlike Gaffin, acknowledges more openly the differences he has with traditional Protestant interpretation. He clearly sets his views over against Protestant Reformed orthodoxy (Gaffin equivocates on this score.) The underlying thesis in Rainbow's interpretation is this: "Whenever Paul says that works of the law form no part of the basis on which God accepts sinners, he means that fallen humanity can do nothing to merit God's favor. By no means is he denying that good works will be the ground on which God will approve of believers on the last day. . . . [B]oth our initial acceptance into divine favour and our culminating approbation involve a judgment on God's part in which God attributes righteousness to us, and therefore they together make up that whole justification on which our entrance into God's eternal kingdom depends" (82–84). As for Luther and Calvin, they "did not acknowledge the distinction in Paul's usage between works of the law and good works. They tried to negate it" (84). Not so, I say. For what it's worth, Rainbow chastises those who deny the doctrine of the imputation of Christ's obedience, active and passive. (We are hearing the same from Gaffin and John Piper in *Counted Righteous in Christ*.) The more important question is, however: What is meant by imputation? What place does it occupy in the *system* of doctrine? Prominent in the current debate is the teaching of James. The second chapter of James, observes Rainbow, "ought to have stopped Luther and Calvin in their tracks" (213). He adds: "The Reformers must have realized that James 2:14–26 is fatal to their 'faith alone' doctrine. They did everything they could to dodge its words and clauses" (223).

Three other affirmations and a conclusion drawn by Rainbow help drive home his point: (1) "[E]vangelical obedience, thus defined, will be critical to God's decision finally to justify people" (155); (2) "The plenary imputation of Christ's righteousness to us by faith by no means obviates the fact that Christians must face a final judgment in which God intends to justify us, to the praise of his glory" (172–73); (3) "Inseparable from the futurity of salvation is its conditionality, God's past favour does not, in and of itself apart from certain favours which God promises to bestow, supply everything needed to pass the last hurdle" (173). The conclusion of this thinking: "[This] is not to cast doubt on the outcome. A robust doctrine of grace holds that God himself provides everything he requires of his elect. . . . It is simply to say that our justification occurs in two phases. The righteousness God gave us when we turned to him, he actuates in another dimension before he admits us into the everlasting state" (174).

Contrary to Rainbow's interpretation, justification is not a process, with a (provisional) beginning and a (final) resolution. Having said that, we are obliged to recognize in the biblical data two aspects pertaining to soteric justification, the constitutive and the demonstrative. Rainbow, like Gaffin, identifies two aspects as "present" and "future." Quoting Gaffin, Rainbow agrees that "Our sanctification is strategically more ultimate than our justification" (185 n. 26). How does this teaching comport with the imputation of Christ's righteousness, understood as the sole meritorious grounds of our justification? It simply does not. For Rainbow, the way of salvation, i.e., justification, is by faith (which serves as the alone "instrument" receiving the imputed righteousness of Christ) and by *good* works. Rainbow reasons: "[I]nsofar as justification remains to be concluded at the final judgment, our increase in sanctity precedes that event and supplies one aspect of the basis for a favorable verdict (Rom 8:1–2). What will weigh with the judge in that day is our faith operative in deeds of love wrought through God's Spirit (Gal 5:5–6)" (187). As though this determination has not already been made (i.e., fixed once for all), Rainbow contends: "The primary purpose of the last judgment, then, is to pronounce definitively on people's everlasting fates, to determine whether they will enter the consummated kingdom of God" (189).

What is at stake for believers at the final judgment "is their eternal destiny, not just the secondary issue of rewards; and that the decision will be based on the criterion of their deeds as having demonstrated the reality of their union with Christ by faith" (203). Rainbow endorses the view of Gaffin, seeing "initial justification [as] contingent upon final justification." This construction appears to be "on the right track" (209). Rainbow, like Gaffin, attempts to ameliorate teaching on faith and works as the way of salvation by explaining: "To say that future justification is contingent upon Christian obedience is not to make it uncertain. Inaugural justification places one within the dynamic field of God's grace which ensures a happy outcome. Contingency means that a further condition stands between our present state and the goal; a condition, the fulfilment of which is guaranteed by the same grace which has launched us into trajectory (1 Cor 1:8–9; Phil 1:6)" (211). The problem here is the notion of contingency. This will not stand with the biblical doctrine of justification. The formulation of Rainbow and Gaffin is misleading. It is erroneous.

Briefly, three other important elements of doctrine are to be noted in this discussion. Firstly, Rainbow, unlike Gaffin, affirms the works-inheritance principle, antithetical to the faith-inheritance principle, in the covenant with ancient, theocratic Israel (a reinstatement of the principle operative in the first covenant with Adam). This teaching Rainbow correctly regards as basic and straightforward in Scripture. (By implication, Gaffin is missing the obvious.) In view here is the contrast between Law and Gospel, a vital and constitutive element in Protestant-Reformed teaching. Rainbow explains: "the outstanding feature of the old covenant was its condition that Israel obey the commandments of the Pentateuch in order to enjoy God's blessings" (72). This raises the question: Why does Rainbow proceed to speak of conditionality in the Covenant of Grace—a present justification (by faith) conditioned on future results (i.e., works of faith)? Simply put: "Under law" blessing is contingent upon obedience; "under grace" it is unconditional (not based on human achievement). Christ secures the blessing on behalf of the elect. Rainbow's formulation is flatly contradictory.

Secondly, there is the matter of the (ongoing) warfare between the "flesh" and the "Spirit," Romans 7 being the classic text. Unquestionably, this subject is elusive in most biblical and theological discussion, and one in which Rainbow and Gaffin would have their differences. All can agree, however, that "A correct interpretation of the passage is critical for understanding Paul's theological anthropology and his doctrine of sanctification" (148). More attention needs to be given here to the relationship of this battle between the flesh and the Spirit and the Law/Gospel antithesis as descriptive of the old and new dispensations. On this subject, Gaffin elsewhere mistakenly equates the two, and in so doing undermines the doctrine of the continuity of the Covenant of Grace throughout the history of redemption.

Thirdly, there is the issue of rewards (i.e., gradations in heaven and hell based upon what has been done in the body). The view of Rainbow and Gaffin is part and parcel of their understanding of the role of faith and good works in the life of the believer (and their view of reward for the moral endeavors of the reprobate). Rainbow posits: "God in fairness judges each person individually according to that person's endowments and opportunities. Of those to whom more is give, more will be required (Luke 12:48), and some who appear last in this age will be first then (Matt 19:30). Apparently the degree of glory we attain will be determined by our zeal in responding to God's imperatives. The more diligently we strive, the more sure we can be that we are standing in God's grace now and that he will welcome us into his eternal dwelling in the end. Paul nowhere states this rule as plainly as does Peter (2 Pet 1:5–11). But by his entire life and apostolic ministry he made himself an example of it" (246). No matter how one qualifies this line of argument with respect to rewards, it reintroduces the notion of merit with regard to one's eternal inheritance, in weal or in woe (as an ameliorating influence with respect to the latter).

All said, strands of Rainbow's thinking move in the right direction, but substantive rethinking and reformulation are needed. The same is true of Gaffin's study. With a view to the longstanding controversy at Westminster Seminary over the views of Gaffin and Norman Shepherd, his former colleague, Gaffin's latest book shows no substantive reformulation whatsoever. *"By Faith, Not by Sight"* might suggest a turnabout of sorts. But that would be a misreading based on wishful thinking. It would be a great mistake to read this book out of context—that being the ongoing seminary dispute. If Gaffin has genuinely revised his thinking in the direction of Reformed orthodoxy, there remains no renunciation of former, erroneous teaching, no repudiation of Shepherd's teaching (which is nowhere mentioned in the book). Despite largely superficial changes in this latest installment of his position, Gaffin aims to leave the door open to rethinking of the issues. (Gaffin concedes that he is still thinking his way through basic biblical, Reformed doctrine.) In the final analysis, deep inherent problems remain. Having jettisoned the classic (biblical) Law/Gospel antithesis, Gaffin remains uncertain how to safeguard his theological interpretation. His terminology of a "present justification" and a "future justification," like that employed by Rainbow, is false and misleading. Equally unsatisfactory is the alternative proposal that we speak of two aspects to justification, present and future. (Gaffin admits uncertainty as to how best to explain the present and future components in the doctrine of justification.) Having served on the six-member committee that produced the "Report on Justification Presented to the Seventy-third General Assembly of the Orthodox Presbyterian Church" (June 2006), Gaffin defies what has been billed there as a "consensus report." In his book Gaffin continues to affirm the contingent nature of present justification by grace—a conditional state looking forward to future justification by works. In so doing, his teaching undercuts the clear affirmation that "justification is a once-for-all accomplished, completed, and perfect act" ("Report," 5). Gaffin cannot have it both ways.

"[T]he antithesis between law and gospel," writes Gaffin, "is not an end in itself. It is not a theological ultimate. Rather, that antithesis enters not by virtue of creation but as the consequence of sin, and the gospel functions for its overcoming. The gospel is to the end of removing an absolute law-gospel antithesis in the life of the believer. How so? Briefly, apart from the gospel and outside of Christ the law is my enemy and condemns me" (Gaffin, 103). This explanation will not do. *Law* (and its principle of works inheritance) pertains to the original Covenant of Works; *Gospel* (and its principle of faith inheritance) pertains to the substitutionary work of Christ, including his fulfillment of all righteousness by means of his active and passive obedience "under the law," which righteousness is imputed to those who believe. Gaffin will have none of this thinking. He calls it a false "polarization." (Let it be said, Law and Gospel are polar opposites with respect to the way of inheritance.) Precisely in this connection, the following explanatory comment by Gaffin serves only to obscure the issue in dispute: "Doing God's will is endemic to the divine image as originally created in Adam and restored in Christ" (101). What is glaringly missing in this connection is the biblical, Reformed teaching on probation as that informs the Covenant of Works. According to Gaffin, Law (in contrast to Gospel) merely denotes the vain attempt of the sinner to obtain God's favor on grounds of obedience. Gaffin argues for continuity in all the divine-human covenants, pre- and postlapsarian. Echoing Shepherd's teaching, Gaffin defines covenant in terms of promise and command, faith and obedience. The Pauline category of "the obedience of faith" might equally describe covenant faithfulness all across the historical continuum, from creation to consummation. Accordingly, justification is a matter of faith and (non-meritorious) works.

Agreeably, some Reformed interpreters did speak of a "double justification," or a "second justification." This was an attempt to reckon with the teaching of James, speaking as he does of a justification by works. Difficulty in theological formulation respecting Paul and James on the doctrine of justification marks Protestant theology from the beginning. What is certain, though now widely challenged, is their conclusion that there are two *different* justifications (rather than a *single* justification having two aspects, the constitutive and the demonstrative). Coordinately, judgment according to works is inextricably related to, but sharply different from, justification. The safeguard in the thinking of the reformers was what is identified in Protestant Reformed orthodoxy as the Law/Gospel contrast. Within the (mature) Reformed wing of the Reformation stands the twofold doctrine of the Covenant of Works and the Covenant of Grace, reflecting the antithetical principles of inheritance, one by works and one by faith.

Gaffin reiterates in this book his view that justification, like adoption, unfolds in two stages, present and future: "Paul's statements on adoption, we may conclude, provide a window on how he would have us view the closely related forensic blessing of justification. As adoption is both present [spiritual] and future [bodily], so too is justification" (93). There is no justification for reading Paul in this manner. Adoption and justification cannot be compared so blithely. What Gaffin is unwilling to acknowledge (without equivocation) is the truth that the justification of sinners saved by grace is definitive and unconditional (i.e., not contingent upon good works, the "doing of the law," to which reference is made in Rom 2:6–13). Judgment according to works (or open acquittal) on the Final Day does not complete justification, but rather demonstrates or verifies God's saving grace in the lives of believers in their exercise of good works—works prepared in advance for those who are united to Christ, who are justified and sanctified.

Lastly, by way of critique, the modern day controversy will not permit the federal, scholastic dichotomy between nature and covenant (or Law and prelapsarian "Grace") to stand or go unchallenged. Given the history of the controversy at Westminster Seminary and within the Orthodox

Presbyterian Church, neither the Reformed nor the broader evangelical community can ignore the twofold doctrine of the covenants as expressive of the Law/Gospel antithesis. Included here is the crucial doctrine of probation (whether in the case of the First Adam, Israel under the Mosaic covenant, or the Second Adam). For more detail and discussion on this wide-ranging controversy, see my *Federalism and the Westminster Tradition*. I would be remiss if I did not point out the fact that Gaffin begins his treatment of Paul on the doctrine of justification by commenting on the interplay between two sister disciplines within the theological curriculum: biblical theology and systematics. Gaffin is convinced that the former has much to contribute by way of reshaping and redefining traditional dogmatics. This book is just such an attempt at needed reformulation of the Protestant Reformed doctrine of justification by faith alone, as he sees it. Whether one is reading *The Way of Salvation* or *"By Faith, Not by Sight"*, the message is the same—one that is out of step with Scripture and orthodox Protestant teaching.

Brian Vickers, *Jesus' Blood and Righteousness: Paul's Theology of Imputation*

(Wheaton: Crossway, 2006)

Skillful coursing through difficult and turbulent waters in contemporary theological debate has earned Brian Vickers our highest commendation and thanks. His study of the apostle Paul's vital teaching on the imputation of Christ's (active and passive) obedience is superb in a great number of respects. That said, the work is not without some lingering problems—problems that must be satisfactorily resolved if we are to do full justice to the teaching of Scripture and its "system of doctrine." (Neither the author nor the reviewer is apologetic when acknowledging and defending the *systematic* coherence and consistency of Scripture's teaching.)

Vickers pursued his doctoral studies under one of today's leading evangelical-Reformed interpreters in Pauline theology, Thomas Schreiner. Both currently teach at Southern Baptist Theological Seminary. Like his mentor, Vickers is openly indebted to the work of Geerhardus Vos and Richard Gaffin on the matter of the interplay between biblical theology and systematics. The collaborative effort to assimilate—at least in part—Princetonian theology into the faculty thinking at Southern Baptist is engaging (and convincing!). *Jesus' Blood and Righteousness* is a revision of Vickers' dissertation, a publication adding to the ever burgeoning literature on this and related subjects. At present, all evangelical seminary faculties are wrestling—to one degree or another—with the modern-day dispute over Paul's understanding concerning the Mosaic law, including the doctrines of justification, election, and the covenants. The prospect of unity in essentials in our day is, however, quite bleak. Here is where Vickers comes to the rescue with a clear-headed exposition that should encourage the evangelical community to rethink the dominant view of our day, which in the opinion of author and reviewer undermines of the Gospel of sovereign, saving grace—the Gospel as revealed in the substitutionary atonement of Christ, the Second Adam. "The contention of this book," writes Vickers, "is that the imputation of Christ's righteousness is a legitimate and necessary synthesis of Paul's teaching. While no single text contains or develops all the 'ingredients' of imputation, the doctrine stands as a component of Paul's soteriology" (18). The work proceeds with a brief, but very helpful, survey of the history of the doctrine of justification (and imputation) and moves on to the exegesis of pivotal texts in Romans 4 and 5, then 2 Corinthians 5:21, concluding with a theological synthesis. The following comments and critique highlight some of the most pressing concerns in this fierce, ongoing contemporary dispute.

In understanding the role of presuppositions in exegesis we must first be clear concerning "presuppositions" themselves. They are not pre-theoretical or speculative notions imposed upon the biblical text, but rather crucial biblical convictions drawn from the text of Scripture itself. Theological interpretation—in which *all* students of the Bible engage—is circular, beginning and ending with exegesis of the text of Scripture. Exegesis brings into dialogue the sister disciplines of biblical and systematic theology. Theological presuppositionalism faithful to Scripture is not a linguistic accommodation to one's cultural-historical milieu—what some say supplies the "language" of theology in any given age, i.e., the rules of the "game." For this reason, the doctrine of the covenant(s) is not an alien or speculative presupposition in classic Reformed federalism, a suggestion that is actually quite unpersuasive and inconsistent with Vickers' own exegetico-theological argument. Vickers reasons, "one does not have to characterize the relationship between God and Adam as a 'covenant of works' to maintain a doctrine of imputation within a covenantal framework" (43). But why *exactly* would one reject or oppose the doctrine of the Covenant of Works? With respect to the twofold doctrine of the Covenant of Works and the Covenant of Grace, the traditional covenant theologian insists that "in the Reformed tradition the covenant framework is *the* interpretive presupposition that lies behind the discussion of the relevant Pauline texts" (ibid.). The question is, simply put: Does the doctrine of the two covenants enjoy the support of Scripture? Here there can be no equivocation.

Raising the propriety of the (Reformed) doctrine of the covenants for an evangelical understanding of the imputation of Christ's righteousness in justification takes us a bit ahead of our critique. Vickers rightly maintains that the Protestant doctrine on justification by faith alone—shared by Luther, Melanchthon, Calvin, and a host of other sixteenth- and seventeenth-century reformers—was essentially the same, whether in seed form or full flowering (the latter being the contribution of international Calvinism, i.e., Reformed federalism). Though the following point made by Vickers is hotly contested by some modern-day exponents of Reformed theology, our author is correct to assert that "in the framework of covenant theology, justification rests on the active and passive obedience of Christ. . . . [T]he Westminster divines did indeed hold to the necessity of the imputation of Christ's active obedience" (40 n. 55). Whatever ambiguities are to be uncovered behind closed doors—in the minutes of the Assembly or in others writings of the time—cannot legitimately call into question or place in doubt the clear intentions of the Westminster divines, namely, the importance of Christ's active (and passive) obedience in the procurement of the redemption of God's elect. The clarity of teaching in the Westminster documents should not be missed or ignored. Our author adds a qualifying comment: "It should be noted that in contrast to the Reformed tradition, the doctrine of imputation in the Lutheran tradition is not based on covenant theology. Thus while the majority of covenant theologians hold to the imputation of positive righteousness and while the covenant framework more or less requires it, the doctrine is not restricted to, nor does it necessarily imply, covenant theology" (34 n. 36). True enough, but the question to be asked is this: Which tradition is more faithful to Scripture? Even the eminent Reformed systematician John Murray questioned the very notion of a covenant of works, since the idea of covenant in his mind signified sovereign, saving grace (i.e., redemptive provision). With that definition of covenant, obviously, the original state of Adam at creation could not be viewed covenantally. Regrettably, Murray did not reckon adequately with Scripture or the Reformed tradition with respect to this oddity in his thinking. We must not let Murray (or others following in his train) "off the hook." The system of biblical doctrine requires nothing less than consistency and fidelity to all of Scripture.

It comes as no surprise in saying that the one major caveat I have with Vickers' presentation is the portrayal of covenant theology as mere window dressing (thus reducing theological summation to what fancies the artist-theologian). Rather, the biblical doctrine of the covenants is basic and formative in the progressive unfolding of redemptive revelation. Not only is covenant doctrine essential to *Reformed* theology, it is very decidedly biblical. It is teaching dictated by Scripture itself. The weight and importance of the divine covenants in biblico-systematic theology ought now, at this time in the history of doctrinal development, be incontestable among evangelical-Reformed interpreters (all those adhering to the traditional Protestant Law/Gospel contrast). Astute readers of this book will have to answer for themselves the question, Why covenant theology? And the answer requires greater conviction than Vickers furnishes. The terms "covenant theology" and "federalism" are synonymous, indicating that the crucial element in this doctrine is the representative principle associated with the work of the First and Second Adams. It is here that Vickers is a bit unclear and unsure of himself. Regarding the principle of federal representation, he writes: "This is the perspective held in the Reformed tradition, as is evident in the phrase 'federal theology.' On the other hand, 'covenant' theology is not limited to the Reformed tradition, and other 'covenant' theologies may differ substantially from the Reformed variety. What matters here is that Paul establishes the concept of representation as the most basic component of God's plan of creation and redemption" (150–51). If federal representation is "the most basic component" in the creation and recreation of humankind, then we all need to be federal theologians. Listening again to Vickers: "'Covenant,' broadly speaking, is the biblical structure and the *modus operandi* of the unfolding of the history of redemption. In a real sense the entire Old Testament [and by extension the New Testament] is a covenantal context" (181).

How do other schools of interpretation measure up? Concerning the views of N. T. Wright, Vickers observes: "The connection Wright draws from Adam through Abraham and Israel and through Christ highlights the essential covenantal relationship between God and his people. It must be pointed out, however, that in spite of points of agreement, Wright's covenant theology and Reformed covenant theology are similar only in name at many fundamental points" (151 n.140). Critical to competing views on Paul and the law is one's assessment of the Mosaic economy (and administration), what Reformed theology has rightly categorized as an episode in the ongoing manifestation of the single Covenant of Grace extending from the Fall to the Consummation. In the opinion of E. P. Sanders, as read by Vickers, "The most significant issue is the fact that the Mosaic Covenant, specifically regarding the law, is not inherently lacking anything; indeed, Paul's complaint is not that the old covenant was insufficient, but that it is obsolete now that the Messiah has come" (56). Both Vickers and the contributors to *Covenant, Justification, and Pastoral Ministry: Essays by the Faculty of Westminster Seminary California* underscore the role and significance of the Mosaic Covenant in the present-day dispute over the doctrine of justification by faith. Of paramount importance is one's reading of the works-inheritance principle associated with temporal life in earthly Canaan, the ancient land of promise, type of the believer's eternal reward in the consummate kingdom of God. Strangely, both volumes have studiously avoided engaging this critical aspect of the contemporary debate in any depth. To reiterate: The operation of the works principle in the Mosaic Covenant has a direct bearing upon Paul's interpretation of justification as the distinguishing feature of the new covenant, in contrast to the old (see, e.g., the passage in 2 Cor 3). Hence, it is not something to be glossed over.

Vickers concedes: "A study of the Mosaic law, including a thorough consideration of the Old Testament and the nature of the obedience required in the law, with a specific view of Christ's obedience in regard to imputation, would be another valuable contribution to the larger discussion. Such a study would have to include thorough evidence outside the purview of this book" (226–27 n. 83). It is not as though our author neglects this aspect entirely. After all, Paul's reading of the Mosaic Covenant is crucial in the text of Romans 4–5, which receives focal attention in *Jesus' Blood and Righteousness*. Much insight is provided in the exegesis of these chapters in Romans. However, some of the issues in interpretation which I see Vickers in need of reassessing are these: (1) the biblical idea of probation occupies a much more formative role in unraveling Paul's summary overview of history (including the federal principle of representation); (2) to be "under law," I contend, means to be under probation (and therefore under a covenant-of-works arrangement); (3) to be "under law" in the postlapsum epoch is to be under the dominion of sin (therefore, under the power of sin and death common to all who are in Adam); (4) the "specific command" of which Vickers speaks is much more specific—it is to stand under a covenant of works requiring obedience as the grounds of blessing (or curse in the case of transgression); and (5) according to Rom 5:19, believers are *constituted* (not made) righteousness on the grounds of Christ's obedience (which parallels the reality of all being *constituted*—not made—sinners in Adam). The weight of Paul's argument in Romans leads our author to conclude: "Finally in this regard, the imputation of Christ's righteousness is not simply a by-product of traditional covenant theology. It is a matter of recognizing a similarity between the relationship of Adam to humanity and Christ to humanity. Romans 5:12–21 is the issue, not a presupposition about whether the relationship between Adam and God was a covenant" (228). Again I ask: How can one contend for the importance of federal representation, yet regard the covenantal framework laid out in Reformed theology as optional, as mere window dressing?

Several closing comments: Firstly, Vickers' reading of Peter Lillback's *The Binding of God: Calvin's Role in the Development of Covenant Theology* differs sharply from mine and that of others (e.g., Scott Clark and Cornelis Venema). In this connection, it will be necessary for Vickers to engage the most recent work penned by Gaffin (*"By Faith, Not by Sight": Paul and the Order of Salvation*) and Paul Rainbow (*The Way of Salvation: The Role of Christian Obedience in Justification*). Vickers informs his readers that the latter work arrived too late in his hands to receive adequate attention. (I have reviewed these two books in a previous issue of *JETS*.) Like Norman Shepherd (whom Vickers bypasses in his study), Gaffin and Rainbow teach justification as present *and* future, a benefit of union with Christ appropriated by means of faith *and* works. In their view present justification is thereby contingent on future judgment according to works. Secondly, Reformed interpreters, as exponents of traditional covenant theology, have yet to apply properly the contrasting doctrines of merit under the Covenant of Works and *Gospel*-grace under the Covenant of Grace to the popular, long-held notion regarding a gradation of rewards for believers in accordance with their exercise of good works. Vickers warns here against the danger of a "Christian works-righteousness" (230 n. 94). (Iain Duguid in *Covenant, Justification, and Pastoral Ministry* espouses a similar position.) Needless to say, much more work needs to be done in support of this disputed teaching. Thirdly, alongside a helpful bibliography the addition of other major, more recent works of Meredith G. Kline, including serious interaction, would greatly enrich Vickers' study and exposition. The author's omission of such works is something of a puzzle to me. True ecumenical theology—what all Christians believe to be the teaching of Scripture—transcends idiosyncratic notions and oddities appearing in the history of doctrine (those associated with one theological tradition or another). Such peculiarities ultimately lack biblical support. Not so in the case of traditional Reformed covenant theology as faithfully expounded by representative, modern-day interpreters like Vos and Kline. Lastly, as Vickers so convincingly argues, Christ's imputed righteousness is, in the first place, not ontological, but covenantal; secondly, it is legal, not transformative (what requires the *imparted* righteousness of Christ). The imputation of Christ's obedience, active and passive, is an act of divine justice, not a legal fiction. *Jesus' Blood and Righteousness* captures the essence of the biblical doctrine. What remains is a greater degree of conviction as to the propriety of the federal (covenantal) implications of this teaching in the system of doctrine. Such an excellent disquisition can be made even better—and when it comes to the defense of the faith, it's all hands to the oar! For further analysis of the Shepherd-Gaffin-Lillback school and other, broader aspects of the contemporary evangelical debate, see my *Federalism and the Westminster Tradition: Reformed Orthodoxy at the Crossroads.*

G. L. W. Johnson and G. P. Waters, editors,
By Faith Alone: Answering the Challenges to the Doctrine of Justification
(Wheaton: Crossway, 2006)

Here is one more book to add fire to the flames of controversy. To be accurate, this volume should have been entitled "Answering *Two* Challenges to the Doctrine of Justification," because there is much that is not addressed that needs to be addressed—given the audience for which this collection of essays was specifically written. More importantly, for a book attempting to shed light on this fierce debate today among evangelical and Reformed interpreters of Scripture, it does not cut the mustard (some of the reasons for this judgment are provided below).

What is quite apparent in reading this work, one intended to be a defense of the historic Reformed faith, is that it falls short of its mark. Neither consensus nor cleared-headed understanding of the issues can be found with any degree of consistency. (And that is exceedingly disappointing, given the prospect the editors held out to me personally.) Subtleties and ambiguities in formulation help explain how theological error has penetrated so deeply into evangelical Protestant-Reformed teaching in recent years. It is also, in part, the consequence of an unwillingness to clarify and to modify (scholastic) Reformed teaching where that is demanded. Such is the contention of my thirty-plus years of study on this subject, first begun at Westminster in Philadelphia.

The voices we hear in *By Faith Alone* come largely from the Westminster Seminary community. David Wells of Gordon-Conwell Theological Seminary and Al Mohler of Southern Baptist Theological Seminary provide the Foreword and Afterword, respectively. These help give the book a broader appeal—and that is most welcome. Wells wastes no time to sound the alarm concerning the credibility and vitality of evangelical theology in the years that lie ahead. The situation looks very bleak indeed. And Mohler concurs. In between sage words by these two highly respected theologians and churchmen lie nine essays, preceded by an Introduction by one of the editors of the book, Guy Waters. Principal topics are these: the New Perspective on Paul and the Mosaic law (notably, the work of N. T. Wright), the imputation of Christ's righteousness in justification, the peculiar teachings of the "Auburn Theology School" (what is doubtless unfamiliar to those outside the Westminster community), and the distinctively Reformed doctrine of the Covenant of Works (the covenant established by God in creation and "republished," in part, in the giving of the Law through Moses, what constitutes Israel as the theocratic people of God in ancient, pre-messianic times).

Symptomatic of the ill health of the (evangelical) church is the near total abandonment of, or disregard for, the biblical doctrine of justification by faith alone. From the vantage point of the history of Protestantism and from testimony to the heroic stand of Martin Luther and other stalwarts of the faith, it is utterly shocking that evangelicals today find themselves in the current state of confusion and disbelief. What has gone wrong? Many well-intentioned pastors and church leaders are not seeing enough results among the flock (i.e., good works), hence the attractiveness of the New Perspective and its variants calling for *faith and works* in the procurement of one's salvation. To be sure, there is nothing new here in the history of Christianity—and in the history of the Reformed churches in particular. Assaults on the biblical teaching concerning justification by faith alone are legion. With regard to the present circumstance, Wells comments: "What is different, when compared with our more recent history, is that these aberrant views on matters so central and fundamental are not outside the evangelical church but inside it" (19).

The remainder of this book review turns our attention to the pivotal issues in the present-day dispute regarding justification by faith, apart from the works of the law. What is the significance of the juxtaposition of faith and works in justification? What precisely are "works of the law"? More basically, how are we to construe the reference to Law as opposed to Gospel, and how do Moses and Christ relate as covenant mediators? What is the human instrument(s) receiving the righteousness of Christ in soteric justification? And how does this relate to the sovereign working of God in the salvation of sinners? The answer to these questions requires careful exegetico-theological interpretation of the text of Scripture, especially the writings of the apostle Paul. Unfortunately, we do not have a great deal of this in *By Faith Alone*. Rather, we hear time and again a *confessional* affirmation of what Reformed theology has taught. There is merit in hearing the testimony of the Reformed church—or what remains of it today! At the same time, however, we understand that church tradition stands under the scrutiny of the Word of God. Calvinistic theology, true to its history, is *reformed and reforming according to the light of Scripture.* So, we need to hear from Scripture.

One of the critical texts in the current dispute is found in the second chapter of Romans. Even those who stand opposed to the Shepherd(-Gaffin) version of the New Perspective are not agreed on the exegesis of this important passage of Scripture. Cornelis Venema writes: "Some authors of the New Perspective appeal to Romans 2:13 in support of the idea of a yet-future justification. . . . The reformational reading of this text takes it as a kind of 'hypothesis contrary to fact'" (58, n. 55). This assertion does an injustice to the controversy, specifically, to those who insist that Scripture speaks for itself (i.e., we do not impose our understanding on Scripture). It is here where reformational teaching may well need correction. (For the record, I do not commend the New Perspective interpretation as summarized by Venema, but I do challenge the hypothetical view. Romans 2:13 speaks of two classes of people, viz., the regenerate and the unregenerate. What this text does not tell us is *how* the "doers of the law" are justified. That we learn elsewhere in Romans and other portions of the New Testament.) At the very least we are safe in saying that the notion of a second (or future) justification is wholly contrary to biblical teaching.

T. David Gordon frankly acknowledges that more study has led him to reconsider N. T. Wright's work. He now finds it highly deficient. Gordon is to be commended for his honest acknowledgment. He locates Wright's failure "to relate the Abrahamic story *back* to the Adamic story [thus rendering] his view of Paul incomplete at best and erroneous at worst" (62). One caveat, and an important one given the attention Wright has properly given to typology in Scripture: Gordon claims that through most of Israel's history "she was *not* justified; to the contrary, she was judged to be in violation of God's law and covenant again and again by the prophets, beginning with Moses. Thus, Israel can be and was (at least during the Sinai administration) the *un*justified people of God. This strikes me as virtually irrefutable . . ." (73). In this opinion Gordon is mistaken. A covenantal-typological reading of theocratic Israel tells us otherwise (see, e.g., the imprecatory psalms). The essay by Fowler White and Calvin Beisner attempts to unravel the symbolico-typological message of the Bible. Though sympathetic to their cause, I have a number of reservations and differences with their exposition. The new idea(s) introduced (what the authors call their "fresh" approach) is not helpful, but confusing. Here I have in mind their take on the commandments of Moses (= the Law) versus the commission to Abraham (= the Promise); also their identification of Noah, Abraham, and David as "mediators" of the Covenant of Grace. Simply put, the Law/Gospel antithesis has reference to two contrasting principles of inheritance, works and faith. Additionally, the authors confuse ontological and economic distinctions in their doctrine of the Covenant of Redemption and the Covenant of Grace—as concerns the work of Christ as divine mediator.

The second essay by Gordon is the more significant of the two, especially for the Westminster community of scholars. Gordon (among others writing elsewhere) has the raw courage to question the views of John Murray. Here too he is to be commended for the open stance he has taken. Gordon reminds us that Murray's teaching, like that of all others (with the exception of the biblical writers) is not inerrant! Many at Westminster need to learn this truth. In my view, this is the greatest virtue of *By Faith Alone*, taken as a whole. Gordon has come to see that the source of New Westminster's deviant teaching lies partly in the views of Murray regarding the divine covenants. "Murray's 'recasting' of covenant theology *per se* remains unopened to discussion in Reformed circles; yet, in my judgment, his recasting has generated several other important divergences from the historic Reformed tradition: the views of Shepherd and Bahnsen, paedo-communion, and now Auburn theology. Murray himself embraced none of these errors" (123). At this point I would commend for Gordon's close reading and study my trilogy, climaxing in *Federalism and the Westminster Tradition: Reformed Orthodoxy at the Crossroads*. A critique of Murray's work has been pervasive in my own writings. Beyond the fact that Gordon decries the widespread silence respecting the views of Murray within the Westminster community, the silence respecting the heterodox teaching of Gaffin is equally disturbing and without justification.

Both Richard Phillips and C. FitzSimons Allison address the doctrine of imputation, noting how it is undermined in the thinking of Robert Gundry and N. T. Wright. Neither of these two contributors, however, probe deeply enough into the controverted issues as raised in the current literature. It is not enough to espouse the imputation of Christ's (active and passive) obedience. Both Richard Gaffin and Paul Rainbow, for example, do so, but add good works—the (non-meritorious) works of faith—to the formula of justification by faith alone. (See my review of their two recent books in a previous issue of *JETS*.) This aspect of the discussion introduces us to the single, most critical element in the current dispute, namely, the theological concept of merit in the procurement of justification/(final) approbation. And it is at this very point that needed consensus is lacking in this collection of essays. Coeditor Waters asserts: "[Federal Vision] arguments against the covenant of works often illegitimately equate *works* and *merit*. In other words, objecting to the claim that Adam's obedience in the first covenant was to be 'meritorious,' they therefore dismiss the *works* principle of the first covenant. But such a conclusion does not follow. Many Reformed theologians, firmly committed to the confessional doctrine of the covenant of works, maintain its *works* principle without speaking of the obedience required of Adam in terms of merit" (30). Here, in no uncertain terms, is where Reformed dogmaticians today are obliged to reconsider the teaching of Scripture. In the pages of this book some contributors do offer a glimmer of hope. And for that we are most grateful. See, most recently, the "Doctrinal Testimony Regarding Recent Errors," issued in May 2007 by Mid-America Reformed Seminary (www.midamerica.edu/pubs/errors.pdf.) Although reflecting strands of rationalistic Reformed scholasticism (notably, concerning the doctrine of man's initial creation in a noncovenantal state), the report firmly holds to the Law/Gospel contrast and *meritorious reward*, by way of (gratuitous) covenant condescension. Two responses: the proper word here is "beneficent," not "gratuitous" (since the term "grace," biblico-theologically defined, refers exclusively to redemptive provision); covenant is concomitant with man's creation in the image of God, not a subsequent administration or overlay upon a prior "state of nature."

In conjunction with the aspect of meritorious accomplishment regarding the federal headship of the First and Second Adams is the crucial matter of *probation*, as that informs every covenant-of-works arrangement in the Bible. The idea of probation is another nonnegotiable in mature Reformed covenant theology. Unfortunately, clear teaching on this element of doctrine is lacking in David VanDrunen's essay. More serious and deficient, however, is the essay by John Bolt who adopts the Barthian construct of *law in grace* (or *grace in law*). What this theological perspective entails is the wholesale rejection of the Protestant-Reformed antithesis between the Law and the Gospel. (Bolt falsely appeals to Murray's teaching to buttress his argument. The fact is, deficient though Murray's formulations are, they have been greatly misused and abused by the *radical* revisionists.) Additionally, Bolt's discussion of the Sabbath—as that informing the nature and meaning of the covenant relationship itself—likewise misses the mark. His appeal to the views of Meredith Kline is likewise mistaken.

Some brief, closing remarks: The last essay by Gary Johnson, coeditor of *By Faith Alone*, seems misplaced in this volume, and his note of appreciation for the theology of Karl Barth is thoroughly inappropriate in this context (197 n. 10). Several theologians in this collection of articles are misidentified: Moisés Silva, Richard Gaffin, and John Piper all espouse a new approach to Paul and the law, one that calls for a revision of traditional theological exegesis. To one degree or another, their position(s) undermines the Reformed doctrine of the Covenant of Works—a doctrine Piper explicitly denies. The controversial work of Norman Shepherd barely receives mention. What is to be gained in this strategy? Gordon wonders why the Federal Visionists did not consult Gaffin. The answer is, they did! (For the record, Gaffin and Wright were featured speakers at the 2005 Auburn Conference. Gaffin's lectures were subsequently published in *"By Faith, Not by Sight": Paul and the Order of Salvation*.)

Parenthetically, both the Orthodox Presbyterian Church and the Presbyterian Church in America have issued reports on justification: *Justification: A Report from the Orthodox Presbyterian Church* (The Committee on Christian Education of the Orthodox Presbyterian Church, 2007, and "Report of the Ad Interim Study Committee on Federal Vision, New Perspective and Auburn Avenue Theologies" (issued in 2007 and available online at http://www.pcahistory.org/pca/07-fvreport.pdf). The latter is superior for its conciseness and for its theological consistency. It is personally gratifying to read the position adopted by the authors of this study on justification; obviously, they did their homework. (The report, however, is deficient in supplying bibliographical sources upon which the conclusions of the report rest.) Most recently, the faculty of the theological department of Westminster Seminary in Philadelphia has issued its latest take on the controversy in Oliphint, ed., *Justified in Christ: God's Plan for Us in Justification*. (The biblical department of Westminster West sees matters quite differently.) At best, the doctrine of justification remains elusive in some of these essays, notably that of Richard Gaffin. Lacking is due consideration of the distinctives of Reformed federal theology, specifically, the doctrine of the Covenant of Works (including the traditional Law/Gospel contrast and the doctrine of probation). These crucial aspects of the debate are slighted in this volume.

One can only hope and pray that a book like *By Faith Alone* will stimulate further, deeper study of the controverted issues facing the Reformed churches today. Unless the lingering differences, which continue to divide orthodox expositors of the Word of God, are addressed openly and frankly (including discussion of the role and impact of the writings of John Murray), there is little hope for a strong, uncompromising witness to the Gospel of Christ. God grant us wisdom and discernment for our times. Without it the church of the Reformation will continue its move back to the dark ages, when the light of the Gospel was obscured, if not denied altogether.

SECTION TWO

Sweet Canaan: Covenant Life in Anticipation of the End of the Age

ONE OF THE MOST perplexing exegetico-theological issues within the Reformed tradition since the opening of the Reformation age is the interpretation of the Mosaic Covenant. The heart of this debate was the extent to which the Mosaic Covenant was understood to convey, in part, the features of a covenant of works, thus echoing the first covenant made by God with Adam as federal head of all humanity. The very same issue continues to perplex and divide Reformed interpreters, perhaps no more intensely than today. Once again, we turn to the teaching of Westminster Seminary as shaped by two principle figures, John Murray (Westminster's first systematician) and Norman Shepherd (Murray's hand-selected successor). From the outset of the theological controversy on Westminster's campus (beginning in 1975 and leading up to Shepherd's dismissal from the faculty in 1981), the leading proponent and formulator of the new teaching at Westminster was, and remains, Richard B. Gaffin, Jr., coauthor and architect of teaching deviating from Reformed orthodoxy. What has stood its ground for over five centuries has now been undermined by the New Perspective on Paul, what at Westminster is termed the "Union with Christ" School (fathered by Gaffin).

Pivotal in the current dispute are questions relating to the nature and operation of the works-inheritance principle within the symbolico-typical sphere of covenant life in Canaan, an administrative principle that pertains only to ancient, theocratic Israel within the Mosaic economy of redemption. This principle functioning within the Covenant of Grace comes to a decisive conclusion with the arrival of Israel's Messiah, Jesus the Christ.

Over the course of the unfolding of redemptive history Israel as "Servant of the Lord" typifies—at certain times and in certain situations—the Lord's anointed. This is part of the messianic foreshadowing of Old Testament revelation given through Moses, the lesser prophet. Of special mention here is the attempt of Professor Richard Gamble to construct a systematic theology in terms of the progressive, historical unfolding of redemption from ancient times to the present. It is the attempt to integrate two theological disciplines, namely, biblical theology and systematics.

3

Recovering the Mosaic Covenant as Law and Gospel

J. Mark Beach, John H. Sailhamer, and Jason C. Meyer as Representative Expositors

CONTEMPORARY EVANGELICAL THEOLOGY HAS taken a fresh look at the biblical teaching on the Mosaic Covenant as an administration of Law and Gospel, wherein two *antithetical* principles of inheritance are operative side by side. This is not a new insight, but one that has engaged the attention of expositors for centuries. It was a special preoccupation of Reformed theologians since the beginning of the Protestant Reformation. In more recent times, it has been juxtaposed to the teaching of dispensationalism, only to be reignited by dialogue among the modern-day *progressive* dispensationalists and other challengers (notably, those who advocate the New Perspective on Paul and the law). Explanations of the operation of two opposing principles within the Mosaic economy, works and faith (Law and Grace), have been exceedingly difficult. Because of the complexity of the subject and the lack of clarity in past formulation, biblical interpreters continue to wrestle with numerous perplexing issues crucial to theology in all its related disciplines (exegetical, systematic, biblical-theological, and historical). Basic is the contention that the works principle of inheritance enunciated in Leviticus 18:5 ("this do and live") is the *merit* principle. It is the principle that informs the federal headship of the two Adams. Reward, i.e., divine blessing by way of covenant and probationary testing, is contingent upon obedience to the law of God.

What unites all evangelical interpreters is unreserved agreement (consensus) on the classic Protestant Law/Gospel contrast. The modern-day Barthian reading of Scripture denies this contrast altogether. In its place, Neo-orthodoxy insists on the compatibility of Law and Grace—as two sides of the same coin. They say that man was never in a position to earn or merit God's reward, reward based upon covenantal obedience and fidelity to God's truth and law. This conviction has resulted in the *radical* reformulation of the system of doctrine (most notably with respect to the doctrine of the covenants, justification and atonement, and election). In terms of the history of doctrinal development, Reformed scholasticism in the period of High Orthodoxy exacerbated the dilemma posed by the medieval, speculative dichotomy between nature and grace as applied to the order of creation and the order of redemption. This being the case, we begin our study with the work of Mark Beach on Francis Turretin (1623–1687), one of the leading exponents of scholastic Reformed federalism. In Beach's judgment, Turretin has given expression to the mature ("pinnacle") form of Reformed covenant theology.[1] True though this is, scholastic federalism is not without its problems and weaknesses. The need of the hour is to learn from its mistakes and misformulations, not repeat them. This will take renewed attention to the exegesis of Scripture. For this our attention focuses upon the recent works of John Sailhamer (OT) and Jason Meyer (NT). Resolution of the current Reformed debate over the nature/covenant dichotomy is requisite for proper interpretation of the relationship between the old and new covenants, between Moses and Christ, as understood within evangelical Protestantism. What follows below accents the very curious and fascinating intersection between divergent Protestant evangelical traditions in recent years.

J. Mark Beach on Reformed scholasticism

Christ and the Covenant: Francis Turretin's Federal Theology as a Defense of the Doctrine of Grace began as a dissertation under Richard Muller at Calvin Theological Seminary. In his defense of Reformed orthodoxy, Beach offers a critical reading of Mark Karlberg (among others), who was accused of imposing a false theological construct on Calvinism. (He falsely aligns John Murray and Karlberg with those who have attempted to drive a wedge

---
1. Beach, *Christ and the Covenant*, 16.

between Calvin and the later Calvinists. The differences between Murray and Karlberg on covenant theology aside, nothing could be further from the truth.) The dispute that receives focal attention throughout Beach's study on Turretin comes down to this: Beach, as a modern-day exponent of scholastic Reformed federalism, upholds the nature/covenant dichotomy. This dualism, rooted in medieval theology, notably in the theology of Thomas Aquinas, rends asunder two inseparable aspects of God's creative work, the fashioning of Adam in the image of God and God's *covenantal* engagement with humankind in the prelapsarian epoch. New insights from the discipline of biblical theology that trace the historical unfolding of divine revelation in Scripture (pre-redemptive and redemptive) provide additional evidence against the error of the scholastic construct under review. Agreeably, this theological construct is deeply embedded within Reformed federalism from the period of High Orthodoxy down to the present day.

Repeatedly, Beach argues against the notion of merit with respect to the creature's obtainment of divine blessing and reward. But on this critical issue Beach equivocates time and again throughout his discussion. Theologians on both sides of the contemporary debate agree that the Creator is sovereign and free over all creation. The creature has no inherent rights over the Creator, rights which place the Creator in the creature's debt. Creation is a free act of God, not a necessity. The decrees of God are acts of his own sovereign, free determination. And what God decrees is consistent with his holiness, wisdom, love, and justice (to name only some of the divine attributes). Beach contends that the idea of reward (i.e., earning God's blessing) "introduces a false doctrine of merit into the divine-human relationship. . . . In short, the doctrine of grace is eclipsed by a false notion of a legal relationship imposed upon man in his original, unfallen state—as if Adam had to earn God's favor through obedience and so by his works merit blessing from God."[2] Turretin, the Reformed apologist, upholds merit *ex pacto*, the granting of reward by way of God's *gracious* condescension, having entered into a covenant relationship with man the creature and having promised to bless him with eternal life on grounds of perfect obedience.[3]

---

2. Ibid., 15. Compare the similar position taken by Stephen Casselli in "Anthony Burgess' *Vindiciae Legis*" and Michael D. Williams in "Adam and Merit." Williams' formulation undermines orthodox Reformed doctrine concerning the Covenant of Works and probation. Historian Carl R. Trueman in *John Owen: Reformed Catholic, Renaissance Man* likewise adopts the scholastic federalist dichotomy on nature and grace (nature and covenant), resulting in ambiguity and doctrinal confusion.

3. Beach, *Christ and the Covenant*, 87.

What more precisely does merit *ex pacto* mean? There are several issues to consider here.

In his polemic against the notion of human merit, Beach rejects the medieval distinction between condign merit ("merit" in the strict sense of the word) and congruent merit (whereby God chooses to bestow a reward that exceeds the worth of the meager condition required in the covenant arrangement, the prohibition not to eat of the tree of knowledge). The legal requirement is humanity's natural duty to God. Contrary to Beach's assertion, however, the scholastic doctrine of merit *ex pacto* is identical to the medieval notion of congruent merit. According to this teaching, God is pleased to accept the meager condition for bestowal of reward that excels the payment of duty exacted. None of those holding this view (neither Beach nor the orthodox Reformed federalists) have extricated themselves from the unscriptural, speculative dichotomy between nature and covenant. The distinction is drawn between the creature's duty to render full and perfect obedience to God in the original *state of nature* as a perpetual obligation, and the privileged enjoyment of greater blessing on condition of that same perfect obedience as a manifestation of God's unearned grace. Under the former arrangement, humanity ever remains susceptible of transgressing; under the latter, there is the unmerited reward of confirmation in righteousness. In terms of the original order of creation God is absolutely free to bring his creation to naught, even if Adam remained faithful and obedient. The opportunity of gaining higher blessing on condition of that same perfect obedience comes by way of the *gracious* covenant of works, which is superimposed on the natural order as a supernatural gift of God's grace. *It is application of the term "grace" to the pre-redemptive epoch that lies at the root of the scholastic error. And here it must be insisted: theological vocabulary must conform to biblical teaching—in substance, if not in terminology (compare, e.g., the term "Trinity," which does not appear in the Bible).*

The theological term "grace" (*Gospel*-grace) applies *exclusively* to God's saving work, accomplished by the atoning death of Christ and applied by the Holy Spirit to the elect of God over the course of history, from the Fall to the Consummation. To be sure, God's goodness and beneficence are evident in his creative work. Grace, however, is God's remedy for the transgression of the First Adam, the federal head of humanity. Grace contemplates human *demerit*; it is God's undeserved favor extended to sinners. And it is fallen humanity's demerit that necessitates the vicarious death of the Second Adam, God's only Son, as satisfaction for sin. By means of his active and passive obedience Christ merits the salvation of the elect. Beach concedes that the pivotal text is found in the fifth chapter of Romans, dealing with the imputation of Christ's righteousness. The parallel drawn between the First and Second Adams requires the idea of meritorious reward in the original Covenant of Works. Requisite also is the notion of probation as that pertains to Adam in the Garden of Eden and to Christ in his earthly mission fulfilling the will of his Father. (Typologically speaking, Israel under Moses is likewise placed on probation in the land of Canaan. Obedience to the law of Moses is the meritorious basis for blessing and prosperity in the promised land, even though there is modification of the legal requirement for Israel, representative of fallen humanity.) *Here lies the biblical foundation for the traditional Protestant Law/Gospel antithesis.*

Beach upholds the Augustinian distinction between the original state of humanity susceptible to falling and the eternal state of humanity confirmed in righteousness (in Augustine's terms, the distinction between *posse non peccare* and *non posse peccare*). Confirmation in righteousness is the reward of the covenant. "In this covenant arrangement, according to Turretin, humans are not subjected to an eternal test of obedience or subjugated to a persistent state of fallibility for eternity."[4] *Crucial to our doctrine of creation is the component of proto-eschatology; there is a goal and purpose to God's creative work, specifically, the consummation of his original handiwork (including the glorification of humanity in the image of God).* Creation is not a divine whim, but a divine commitment to fulfill the Creator's eternal purposes as decreed. Creation gives expression to the integrity and faithfulness of God's sovereign good purpose. Beach summarizes Turretin's (*mis*)formulation of the covenantal structure underlying the history of the world. "Scripture sets forth a 'double covenant' (*Foedus geminum*) scheme: 'of nature' and 'of grace.' These are not two covenants, but God's covenant with a twofold character. In short-hand form Turretin describes the double character of the covenant as that of 'works' and 'faith'; the former is 'legal,' the latter is 'evangelical.'"[5] Surely, Beach does not want to espouse the Neo-orthodox doctrine of monocovenantalism, which dissolves the Law/Gospel contrast and undercuts the radical antithesis between the Covenant of Works and the Covenant of Grace with respect to opposing principles of inheritance, works and faith (= saving faith in Christ). Yet, Turretin's statement here obscures this pivotal contrast, and is symptomatic

---

4. Ibid., 75
5. Ibid., 90.

of an underlying misunderstanding and misconception of the meritorious ground of blessing in the first covenant.

As a countercharge against critics of Reformed federalism on this specific point of doctrine, Beach accuses Stephen Spencer for treating "law here in abstraction, not as the specific law given to Adam by God in paradise as part of the probationary arrangement."[6] The point is this: The probationary command encompasses the entire law of God, even while focusing on the single command not to eat of the tree of the knowledge of good and evil. If anyone is guilty of abstraction here, it is the Reformed scholastics. Probation is an integral part of the original Covenant of Works. As image-bearers, our first parents are obliged to render full and perfect obedience to the Creator, after the pattern of the angelic host.[7] Mistaken also are those like Beach who view the Tree of Life in the Garden as representative of Christ and his saving work. Rather, this tree symbolizes the eschatological goal of creation, the consummation of heaven and earth. Of course, after Adam's breaking of the original covenant the goal of creation is attained only by means of the redemptive work of Christ. At the Consummation, humankind beholds God in his heavenly glory, what in scholastic definition is called the "beatific vision of God."[8] Beach rightly notes: "The covenant of grace is thus wholly centered upon Christ and fulfilled in him. This is why it is *of grace*; and it is not to be thought that humans, as one of the parties of this covenant, offer a contribution or fulfill a prescription or meet a condition apart from Christ and all that he does for them, bestowing every benefit and blessing of the gospel covenant."[9]

Our thoughts are directed once again to the crucial Law/Gospel antithesis, which pertains to opposing principles functioning in the Covenant of Works and the Covenant of Grace. It is entirely wrong to suggest that the legal requirement tied to the Covenant of Works could not be fulfilled by the creature in his "natural strength." Nor is the law of God given to Adam in creation "impotent to supply for Adam what was needed to secure his conformity to it."[10] Neither is the covenant of nature (i.e., the law of God) characterized by a "relative weakness," which is the case under the Mosaic

---

6. Ibid., 99.

7. See my essay "The Glory of God: Archetypal and Ectypal. Part Two: The Image of God"; Part One discusses "The Theophanic Glory." (reprinted here as chapter 5).

8. Beach, *Christ and the Covenant*, 134.

9. Ibid., 172.

10. Ibid., 127.

Covenant (given the realities of the fallen human condition). This point of view reintroduces the erroneous medieval scholastic dualism between natural and supernatural ability, wherein it is said that the creature is dependent upon God's *supernatural grace* in order to fulfill the legal requirement of the original covenant. Better is Beach's statement made in these words: "'The first covenant into which God entered with humans was a legal covenant. This covenant of works dealt with man as innocent and unfallen; the promise of eternal life offered therein pending on the perfect fulfillment of the law ('do this and live') and the threat of death prescribed for failure to do so ('cursed is he who continueth not')."[11] In his innocence and creation in perfect righteousness and holiness, Adam was able not to sin (note again the Augustinian teaching, which Beach himself seeks to uphold).[12]

Once we have established the meritorious legal grounds for the obtainment of divine reward, viz., eternal life (symbolized in the tree of life), we are *then* in a position to understand the compatibility of the two antithetical principles of inheritance functioning within the Mosaic Covenant, the contrary principles of Law and Grace. The Reformed theological tradition has been correct in insisting that Scripture teaches only one way of salvation—faith in Jesus Christ. This is true for the saints who lived prior to Christ's death and resurrection. Abraham is called the father of all the faithful. He was justified by faith in Jesus Christ who was yet to come. The benefit of justifying and sanctifying grace is shared by all believers from the time of the Fall to the Consummation (those regenerated by the Spirit of God). So then, the law which was *added* to the promise given to Abraham refers to a unique administration of the Mosaic Covenant regulative of the theocratic life of Israel in the land of Canaan. If the works-inheritance principle is not to undercut the promise (the principle of faith inheritance, i.e.,

---

11. Ibid., 160.

12. Beach (confusingly) concedes: "The language of merit only applies to sinners from divine grace and God's kindly condescension, entering into a gratuitous covenant with human beings, whereby he grants a reward to their works far beyond what those works deserve. In this sense, federal theologians affirmed *ex pacto* merit" (*Christ and the Covenant*, 213). Better is the earlier statement by the author: "whether we are speaking of due reward or the divine gift, we are talking about *ex pacto* blessings of God, for there are no gifts or rewards bestowed to humans that are not rooted in God's goodness or in his salvific grace" (206). The critical question remains: In the Covenant of Works is the reward of God's blessing (viz., confirmation in righteousness) a matter of inheritance by works or inheritance by (unearned) grace? Which is it? There is no middle ground, no place for duplicity or ambiguity. On this point, Beach equivocates. But he would agree, at the same time, that the Protestant Law/Gospel antithesis is a theological nonnegotiable.

justification by grace through faith), then the operation of the former must be restricted in its field of operation. In spite of all the difficulty elucidating this biblical teaching, Reformed interpreters have, by and large, succeeded in recognizing the operation of contrasting principles of inheritance within the Mosaic economy. Some have done so by restricting the legal principle to life in the earthly, typological kingdom. Turretin, as representative of High Orthodoxy, teaches that temporal blessings in the land are based on Israel's own obedience, not the substitutionary obedience of Another. Law inheritance has relevance to life on the typological level of the Mosaic economy.[13] It did not pertain to the antitypical, spiritual level (life in the heavenly, eternal kingdom secured by the merits of Christ alone).

Despite this explanation given by Turretin, he mistakenly identifies the Mosaic law as falling "under the evangelical covenant."[14] Here Turretin and many other Reformed expositors fail to distinguish adequately between law as inheritance principle (Lev 18:5) and law as covenant. The apostle Paul plainly states that '"the law is not of faith." The law *was added* to the Abrahamic promise. In the fullness of time Christ was born under the law to redeem those under the law, held in bondage to sin and death (Galatians 3 and 4). Within the Mosaic administration, regulative of the old economy of redemption as a whole, there is both law and covenant. Specifically, the works-inheritance principle regulates life in the temporal land of Canaan. Faith inheritance pertains to the heavenly session of the saints, who (now, post-Pentecost) live and reign with Christ.[15] The Mosaic economy of redemption, wherein the Mosaic Covenant is an administration of the single Covenant of Grace spanning the history of redemption, anticipates the accomplishment of atonement and reconciliation achieved by Christ and the full outpouring of the Spirit.[16]

Another crucial point to grasp is this: the works obedience required in probationary testing is not "legalism," the quest for *salvation by human*

---

13. Ibid., 253.

14. Ibid., 216 n. 2; cf. also 249 and 252.

15. See Heb 11:40. The "something better" is union with the *resurrected* Christ.

16. "Strictly considered, the Old Testament 'denotes the covenant of works or the moral law given by Moses–the unbearable burden (*abastakto*) of legal ceremonies being added, absolutely and part form the promise of grace'" (Beach, *Christ and the Covenant*, 263, quoting Turretin). The nature/covenant dualism undercuts the biblical teaching on primal eschatology; the Tree of Life points to the life-giving Spirit (before and after the Fall), not immediately to the redemptive work of Christ, who became life-giving Spirit in the work of recreation (1 Cor 15:45–49; cf. 2 Cor 3:17–18).

works. One of the several false assumptions and misreadings of the Reformed literature is Beach's equation of legalism with the doctrine of meritorious reward under the Covenant of Works. The two are not the same. Obedience to the covenant made with Adam as federal head is no more "legalistic" than the obedience required of the Second Adam. The righteousness of Christ is the exclusive meritorious ground of blessing in the Covenant of Redemption (the eternal covenant established between Christ and elect, and them alone). Over the course of redemptive history, the Covenant of Grace includes both elect and non-elect with the "household of faith," the confessing body of saints who acknowledge the true God to be Lord and Savior. It is the elect of God alone who enjoy the eternal, saving benefits of Christ's atonement. Even so, those who are non-elect in the covenant community experience some of the blessings of participation in the life of the (visible) body of Christ. Common grace, extended to the godly and the ungodly (and limited in its effect), is yet another benefit of Christ's atoning work on the cross. Common-grace benefits are only temporary blessings, which in no way convey God's redemptive grace applied by the regenerating, sanctifying work of the Spirit of Christ.

JOHN H. SAILHAMER'S STUDY OF THE OLD TESTAMENT

John Sailhamer has devoted a lifetime of study to the Pentateuch. In his latest work, entitled *The Meaning of the Pentateuch: Revelation, Composition and Interpretation*,[17] the author gives focal attention to the Mosaic law

---

17. The author opens with these words: "This book is a study of the theology of the Pentateuch" (11), adding that "[t]o the extent that theology can rightly grasp God's revelation and accurately translate it into a particular setting, theology can lay claim to some amount of normativity" (61). Although church doctrine is not inspired, yet is authoritative to the degree it faithfully restates the teaching of Scripture. In the words of Sailhamer: "The task of biblical theology is to represent the meaning of the biblical text and to represent it as a word from God" (105). See further Karlberg, "Doctrinal Development in Scripture and Tradition."

Cornelius Van Til understood the system of doctrine to be reformed and always reforming *according to the Word of God* (the Scripture principle), ever more consistently by way of biblical exegesis and theological systematizing. Van Til defended as integral elements within the Reformed system such doctrines as divine incomprehensibility, the Creator/creature distinction, the distinction between archetypal and ectypal knowledge (what is the difference between knowledge in the mind of God and knowledge in the mind of the creature), and the doctrine of the Covenant of Works. The introduction of Framian multiperspectivalism has signaled the rejection of Van Til's methodology and that of the Princeton/(Old) Westminster school in favor of new explorations in

in the covenant God made with Israel at Sinai. The chief message of the Pentateuch, further advanced in the remainder of the OT, is the announcement of the new covenant to come in the messianic age of the Spirit. The essence of the new covenant is the fulfillment of God's promise to Abraham regarding the salvation of sinners—justification by faith through grace, on the basis of Christ's future reconciling death. In what follows, I will provide a theological commentary and analysis of Sailhamer's theology of the Pentateuch. The author is to be commended for grappling with complex issues; his argument and interpretation move us in the right direction. Yet, as will be pointed out below, there is need for rethinking and reformulation on several different, yet related fronts.

Toward the conclusion of his book, Sailhamer remarks: "The nagging problem confronting most evangelical biblical theologies is their lack of success in identifying the central message of the Pentateuch, and the OT as a whole. What remains constant within the historical movement and development of revelation? What is the central theme that draws all the other themes together and links the whole of the OT to the whole of the NT? There has been little agreement on what this center point might be."[18] Here the author has in mind specifically dispensational and covenant theologies. Without taking up the issue of the grand theme of an Old or New Testament biblical theology (or one that encompasses the entire Bible), our interest here is the interpretation of the Mosaic Covenant, specifically, Sailhamer's understanding of the relationship between the old and the new covenants. Another way to view this issue is to consider the eschatological design of God's work beginning at creation and continuing on through the program of redemption. Paramount in the work of creation and re-creation is the realization of the kingdom of God on earth, to be consummated at the close of human history with the arrival of the new heavens and new earth. It is by means of the divine covenants that God's kingdom is administered and regulated. Prior to the Fall, the kingdom of God was a pure theocracy, the direct rule of God over humanity in covenant with God. Humanity, represented in the person of Adam, the federal head (with Eve as his companion), was made perfect in knowledge, holiness, and righteous-

---

theological debate and discourse. On Van Til's legacy, see Muether, *Cornelius Van Til*, and my book review in *TrinJ* 30 (2009) 305–8. Compare also Karlberg, "On the Theological Correlation of Divine and Human Language and "John Frame and the Recasting of Van Tilian Apologetics." For a defense of Frame's work, see his *festschrift*, Hughes, ed., *Speaking the Truth in Love*.

18. Sailhamer, *Meaning of the Pentateuch*, 550.

ness. As image-bearer of God, humanity was holy and righteous. The duty of humankind was to reflect the glory of God. Made a little lower than the angels, humanity would be elevated to a higher status in glory by way of covenant obedience. (Both the human and angelic kingdoms would obtain the initial reward of confirmation in righteousness by means of successful completion of probationary testing. The consummate blessing would await the end of human history.)

"I propose that the big idea of the Pentateuch is 'the importance of living by faith,'" writes Sailhamer.[19] Another way of stating this thesis is to say that the proper purpose of redemptive covenant, to which the Mosaic economy also gives expression, is salvation by grace through faith in Christ. (It is to be recognized that the administration of redemptive covenant is broader than individual election to salvation; that is to say, over the course of its historical outworking redemptive covenant includes some non-elect within its sphere of administration.) What distinguishes redemptive covenant from pre-redemptive covenant, in terms of its *proper purpose*, is the manifestation and realization of God's *gracious* gift of eternal life (the reward first offered to Adam as federal head in the original Covenant of Works), unearned and undeserved. At this critical point, Sailhamer is ambivalent in his understanding. Though wanting to uphold the traditional Protestant Law/Gospel antithesis, he at times undermines this crucial distinction, which is descriptive of the two kinds of covenants unfolding in biblical history. The place of God's covenant at Sinai within the broader scope of redemptive revelation is the exact case in point.

On the one hand, Sailhamer repeatedly (and correctly) asserts, "The Sinai covenant was a broken covenant. The NT contrasted the failure of the Sinai covenant with the new covenant, which succeeded in Christ. . . . In the Pentateuch we are confronted with a call to a new covenant, not to the old."[20] On the other hand, argues Sailhamer, the Sinai covenant *as first established by God* conveyed the faith-principle of inheritance. Accordingly, "Abraham fulfilled the Sinai law [even before it was given] by living a life of faith."[21] One page later we are told: "The Pentateuch lays out two fundamentally dissimilar ways of 'walking with God' (Deut 29:1): one is to be like Moses under the Sinai law, and is called the 'Sinai covenant'; the other, like that of Abraham (Gen 15:6), is by faith and apart from the law, and is

---

19. Ibid., 22.
20. Ibid., 27.
21. Ibid., 13.

called the 'new covenant.'"[22] It is the author's contention that the redemptive (gracious) covenant between God and Moses on Sinai degenerated into a covenant of works when Israel sinned in worshipping the golden calf. From this point onward, the history of the OT narrates the waywardness and the obstinacy of Israel according to the flesh. In the grand view of things, there is life before, under, and after Sinai. "To be situated chronologically 'before Sinai' is, theologically, to be removed from accountability to the law (Gen 15:6; 26:5). To live 'at Sinai' means to be accountable to the law (Lev 18:5). To live 'after Sinai' so to view its covenant in terms of new (spiritual) realities (Deut 10:12–19; 30:1–11)."[23]

The author misapplies the theological concept of grace to the order of creation. (As previously noted, the theological term "grace" pertains only to redemptive provision in the context of human sin and its consequences. Grace is God's remedy for human demerit and transgression.) Sailhamer contends: "From the point of view of the structure of the Pentateuch, the giving of the law, the promises to Abraham, and nature itself are grounded in God's gracious gift of creaturehood. The Pentateuch ultimately is about creation and grace (creation/grace)."[24] He adds: "The future of humanity is tied to God's gracious election to create humankind."[25] Sailhamer's theology of grace and election are in need of rethinking and reformulation. Curiously, Sailhamer expresses his special indebtedness to two Reformed interpreters, John Calvin and Johannus Cocceius, the latter being another of the leading exponents of orthodox federalism, alongside Turretin (federalism is the dominant school in later Calvinism). Sailhamer registers ambivalence on issues that lie at the heart of Reformed biblical theology. He takes Calvin to task for some features and elements of his covenant theology, at places where no substantive issue or dispute exists between Calvin and Cocceius. The objections raised by Louis Berkhof against the views of Cocceius simply reflect the complexity and diversity of thinking within Reformed dogmatics since the period of High Orthodoxy. It is my contention that resolution of these differences, where they are of genuine theological consequence, requires clarification and modification of the Reformed doctrine of the covenants, notably, the Mosaic Covenant. Commendably,

22. Ibid., 14.
23. Ibid., 285.
24. Ibid., 32.
25. Ibid.

Sailhamer is helping Reformed evangelicals move in that direction—with some additional rethinking on his part.[26]

"John Calvin's *Institutes of the Christian Religion*," writes Sailhamer, "is a classic statement of the orthodox view of the OT. Calvin saw little difference between the religion of the OT and the Christian faith. He believed that, like the NT, the faith of the OT was grounded in the notion of covenant. The single covenant (Luke 1:72) through all ages was ultimately sealed by Christ's blood on the cross."[27] To avoid misunderstanding, it must be recognized that Calvin and the theological tradition that followed in his wake taught that this single covenant, termed the "Covenant of Grace," spanned the period of *redemptive* history, from the Fall to the Consummation. (Calvin laid the seeds for the later Reformed doctrine of the Covenant of Works established at creation.) The law given by God through Moses as mediator of the old covenant is contrary to the promise given to Abraham. "Ultimately, I believe, these two themes of law and faith will find their place alongside each other as a juxtaposition of law and gospel. The gospel, that is, justification by faith, is God's means for our fulfilling the law."[28] In distinction from Lutheranism, Calvinism from the outset developed more adequately and more faithfully the teachings of Scripture, including the doctrine of Christian obedience (under the rubric of the "third use of the law"). Setting aside the important subject of the Christian's duty to obey the moral law under the Covenant of Grace (in all ages of redemptive history), our attention focuses upon the foundational Law/Gospel (or Law/Grace) contrast. Christian obedience under the Covenant of Grace is the fruit of the regenerating, sanctifying work of the Spirit of Christ at work in the life of the believer. The inheritance principle of redemptive covenant is grace (grace *in Christ*); the inheritance principle of the original covenant at creation is *works* (the merit principle as that pertains to the First and Second Adams, the federal heads of humanity in creation and recreation). Those who enjoy the saving benefits of Christ's atonement are the elect of

---

26. "The aim of these narratives and their overall structure is to provide an explanation of the purpose and role of the Mosaic law in the Sinai covenant" (Ibid., 366). "Ultimately, the divine guidance that the author has in mind will be resolved through the work of God's Spirit indwelling his people, like wisdom, leading them in the right path. That will come in what the Pentateuch sees a s a different kind of covenant, unlike the one made at Sinai (cf. Deut. 29:1)" (368). While commending typology as a *textual* approach, Sailhamer's view is unclear and undeveloped.

27. Ibid., 136.

28. Ibid., 156.

God. Redemptive covenant and predestination are vital components in Reformed soteriology.

Assessing the relationship of OT to NT, Sailhamer objects to Reformed interpretations that view this relationship in terms of promise and fulfillment. The root of the difficulty, in my estimate, is the author's affinity for elements found in dispensational theology, notably its reading concerning Israel and the church in the history of redemption. Contrary to Reformed teaching on the subject, Sailhamer wants to set the OT on the same playing field as the NT. The OT and the NT, argues Sailhamer, are *of equal weight*.[29] This understanding competes with the pre-Reformation Augustinian view that the NT is concealed in the OT, while the OT is revealed in the NT. Teaching on promise and fulfillment as embodying the essential difference between the two Testaments likewise predates the Protestant Reformation.[30]

Of greater theological weight is Sailhamer's failure to elucidate clearly and unambiguously the essential role of the Spirit of Christ in regenerating and empowering OT believers, those numbered among God's elect. Reference to the Mosaic law as "letter," in distinction from the NT as "Spirit," pertains exclusively to the legal requirement of the old covenant as the meritorious basis of life in the land of Canaan (the reward of temporal, typological blessing). Israel was unable to retain life and prosperity in this holy, theocratic site and thus was punished with exile to foreign lands. In the time of dispersion regenerate OT believers continued to enjoy life and fellowship with God in the anti-typical sphere of heavenly life secured by the Messiah who was yet to come. Cocceius' doctrine of the gradual abrogation

---

29. Although the Bible, Old and New Testaments, comprises the church's Scripture, it is the NT that is the canon for the church (post-Pentecost). It is the NT that is regulative of the new covenant community.

30. Had Walter Kaiser paid closer attention to this interpretive reading of the Bible—and to the concerns of Reformed biblical theology—he might have been prevented from misreading the nature and significance of the law at Sinai, a point on which Kaiser and Sailhamer differ substantially. Sailhamer's own misreading of the promise/fulfillment paradigm likewise prevents him from articulating a genuine *typological* (and *christological*) interpretation of the OT. On the subject of biblical typology Sailhamer equivocates; the author's tribute to Calvin and Cocceius has not fully paid off in his theologizing. In this connection, Sailhamer's distinction between the "biblical Jesus" and the "messianic Christ" is artificial and confusing. The underlying problem is the author's inadequate grasp of typology, based on a failure to understand the relation between OT and NT as promise and fulfillment. Sailhamer also leaves undeveloped the notion of theocracy with respect to Israel's constitution as a chosen people and with respect to her temporal life in the land of Canaan. Compare the assessment by Willem J. van Asselt in *The Federal Theology of Johannes Cocceius*, which I have reviewed in *JETS* 45 (2002), 734–38.

of the Covenant of Works (toward which Sailhamer gravitates) and his doctrine of the forgiveness of sins (partial versus complete remission under the old and new covenants respectively) require rethinking and reformulation. Restricting the works-inheritance principle to the typological level of life in Canaan best explains the operation of conflicting principles of inheritance, Law and Grace, in the covenant made with Israel at Sinai.

Jason C. Meyer's Study of the New Testament

Jason C. Meyer's study in Pauline theology, *The End of the Law: Mosaic Covenant in Pauline Theology*, marks something of a milestone in contemporary evangelicalism, notably among interpreters standing outside the Reformed covenantal tradition. There are, Meyer observes, five approaches to the subject on Paul and the law (utilizing the taxonomy of Walter Kaiser). Situating his own work in terms of this classification, Meyer comments: "I am not a conscious adherent to any theological system within Kaiser's taxonomy." He reasons that "one must not assume that Paul operated with the theological categories that the exegete brings to the text."[31] The success of Meyer's own hermeneutical methodology, described as "thoroughly exegetical," is dubious.

After introducing his subject, Meyer opens with a "transhistorical" overview of the covenant(s) of God in history (ignoring the Reformed doctrine of the original Covenant of Works at creation). The law of Moses is described as a non-soteriological covenant, in that "it did not provide eschatological salvation."[32] The period from Moses to Christ, Meyer implies, serves as a parenthesis in redemptive history; the law was added to the Abrahamic promise in a manner that did not nullify the promise of eschatological blessing to be experienced by the saints in the new heavens and earth. The stage is set for an extended exposition of the antithetical covenants, the old and the new. The principal texts are 2 Corinthians 3–4, Galatians 3–4, and Romans 9–11. Meyer clearly and succinctly addresses many facets of Pauline theology. The question is whether or not his analysis is at all points exegetically grounded and convincing in its theological conclusions.[33]

---

31. Meyer, *End of the Law*, 14.
32. Ibid., 32.
33. Concentrated effort to explain the Mosaic Covenant has its dividends, as this book proves. Meyer's argument conveys many, if not all, of the necessary ingredients to expound meaningfully and accurately the nature and content of the Mosaic Covenant.

Meyer regards the old covenant "as fundamentally non-eschatological," adding "it is not a 'soteriological covenant.'"[34] Summarily stated, "God acted in the old covenant by inscribing on stone tablets. He performs a spiritual work in the new covenant by inscribing on the heart through the Spirit"[35] He further explicates: "The contrasting phrases ['stone tablets'/ 'flesh'-heart tablets—reflective of the letter/Spirit contrast] highlight the *different ways* God acts under both covenants by focusing on the *different objects* of God's inscribing action."[36] Having said this, he yet concedes: "We must remember an important nuance in the language of external versus internal. Interpreters should not read the Sinai covenant as an external covenant in all respects."[37] Equally unclear and contradictory is Meyer's position on membership in the old covenant, which we are told comprises both the remnant of grace and the rest who were hardened.[38] On the preceding page, Meyer asserts: "Membership in the old covenant made one a son of Israel, but not a son of the living God."[39] Which is it? There is the lingering problem for Meyer how to relate covenant to election.

Key to obtaining the promised blessing covenanted to Abraham and his spiritual seed, Meyer admits, is electing grace. Meyer acknowledges repeatedly the operation of saving grace in the Mosaic economy.[40] His position stands as a challenge to dispensational interpretation. But even here, Meyer is not entirely consistent. He distinguishes between two different

---

At the end of the day, Meyer's interpretation comes close to that of *mainstream* Reformed federalism, insisting on the antithesis between Law and (*Gospel-*)grace in the old and new covenants. Indeed, the strength of the book lies in upholding the traditional Protestant Law/Gospel contrast, while viewing the Mosaic law as a covenantal arrangement, not a ("bare") principle abstracted from its context. It is the Mosaic Covenant that gives distinctive character to the Old Testament, wherein the focus of attention is placed upon the Mosaic economy and institution(s), despite the fact that the promise to Abraham is of greater weight and importance in the overall plan of God in redemption. In the course of exposition, Meyer's analysis relies heavily on the exegetico-theological tradition advanced in the works of Thomas Schreiner, his doctoral supervisor, and Douglas Moo (with some modification).

34. Meyer, *End of the Law*, 32.
35. Ibid., 66.
36. Ibid., 70, italics original.
37. Ibid., 70 n. 30.
38. Ibid., 199.
39. Ibid., 198.
40. Ibid., 6 n. 19, 113, 195, and 199 (among numerous other mention throughout the book).

degrees of grace, before and after Pentecost. At the same time he denies the dispensational teaching on ethnic Israel (physical) and the church (true, spiritual Israel), specifically in regards to their placement in the eternal kingdom. Meyer explains: "The old age lacks the dynamic power of the new age because it lacks the distinguishing feature of the new age: the life-giving presence of the Spirit."[41] Better to say that the old covenant bears the trait of the old age (in terms of the legal principle of inheritance by works, which cannot secure eternal life). However, the old covenant is not entirely captive to the old age (in that it accommodates the remnant of saving grace within its field of administration)—just one more indication that the Mosaic legal covenant, in all its peculiarity, is an administration of the single Covenant of Grace spanning the entire history of redemption. (In an excursus Meyer erroneously faults Scott Hafemann for recognizing the regenerating role for the Spirit of God in the old age/economy. It is Meyer himself who cannot have it both ways.)

In acknowledging "the Sinai covenant as one covenant in the historical progression of covenants that carry along God's promise of messianic salvation,"[42] Meyer essentially gives away the distinctive thesis of his book. This statement, along with other similar affirmations scattered throughout the work, places his theology of the Mosaic Covenant in the Reformed federalist camp, a place he does not intend to find himself. Following this school of interpretation, Meyer states: "The two-Adam structure of reality explains why we can come to share in the benefits of Christ's work: He is the representative head of the new creation, just as Adam was the representative head of the old creation."[43] With respect to Paul's explanation of justification by faith apart from the works of the law, Meyer's reading of Leviticus 18:5 is refreshingly clear and sound. Reference here is made to the ground of temporal life in the typological kingdom, viz., on the basis of the works of the law.[44] Here lie the seeds for typology, an essential component in biblical theology. Meyer rightly views Moses as a preacher of the Gospel as well as the Law. Neither Moses' preaching of the Gospel nor Paul's guarantees faith in the hearers. The fruit of true faith and repentance is God's work alone. On this score there is no difference whatsoever in the old and new

---

41. Ibid., 82.

42. Ibid., 29.

43. Ibid., 57. Compare here Brian Vicker's *Jesus' Blood* and *Righteousness*, which I reviewed in *JETS* 50 (2007), 419–23.

44. Meyer, *End of the Law*, 218–19.

economies of redemption. Contrasting the numerical growth of the Christian church with Israel's hardness of heart, Meyer confusingly and mistakenly asserts: "This difference in scope is derived from a difference in grace. God deals with the same sinful people in a remarkably different way in the new covenant, based on the atoning death of Christ and the transforming power of the Holy Spirit."[45] If this were the case, then the grace of the old covenant would indeed be wholly different from the grace of the new. But that runs counter to the witness of Scripture, specifically the teaching that justification by faith in Christ alone is the exclusive way of salvation in all ages of redemptive history.

In drawing this summary critique to a close, we commend Meyer for his work in advancing the debate and in addressing critical issues. Like Sailhamer's, Meyer's argument moves in the right direction, but has a way to go in clarifying further matters that have been disputed among Bible scholars for centuries (since the time of the Protestant Reformation in the sixteenth century, and stretching as far back as the early church). Needless to say, the subject of the meaning and historical unfolding of the divine covenants occupies the attention of the canonical writers themselves, a subject that is unavoidable in the Bible. As the means of bringing resolution to the modern-day debate, the author's attempt at being "thoroughly exegetical"—and only secondarily analytic and synthetic—is flawed and unsuccessful. Clearly, the author's own commitment lies with the Baptist tradition, when, for example, it comes to explaining the new covenant (including the Abrahamic promise) and the covenant signs of circumcision and baptism. From the perspective of Reformed systematics, it bears repeating that Baptist theology mistakenly reduces covenant membership in the church to individual election to salvation. (Church overseers cannot presume regeneration in the administration of the keys of the kingdom. Spiritual regeneration among church members lies hidden from human view, only to be revealed on the Last Day. To be sure, the individual believer can be certain of his/her salvation by the indwelling of the Spirit.) The subject addressed by this book is exceedingly complex and the positions advanced by various interpreters with whom Meyer interacts have shown significant change over time. It is not always easy, therefore, to discern all the various lines of argument and "nuances" that have crept into the discussion and debate. Meyer errs, for example, in his reading of Moisés Silva[46] on

---

45. Ibid., 278.

46. E.g., see Silva's *Explorations in Exegetical Method*. Beach, Silva, and Gaffin, three

the law as a covenant (standing in contrast to the new covenant). A great deal of ambiguity and imprecision remain. Some are convinced that the biblical teaching itself is unclear and imprecise on the subject. Thankfully, Meyer does not agree with this viewpoint.

A couple of other weaknesses mar this otherwise helpful and, in many places, insightful study. Meyer is wrong in arguing that the Mosaic Law-Covenant is "impotent." Rather, we must say that the law effectively advances and enforces the will of God in its execution in the pre-messianic, semi-eschatological economy of redemption. Inheritance by works could not secure temporal blessing in the land of Canaan. Hence, in consigning Israel to sin and exile, the law points to Christ, the end of the law. It is he who fulfills all righteousness, meriting the eternal salvation of God's elect (obtaining life in the eschatological kingdom, which earthly Canaan typified). Perhaps the greatest oversight in this book is its failure to relate the Mosaic Covenant (as a legal arrangement) to the order of creation, what is likewise a covenant arrangement requiring perfect obedience from Adam, our federal head, as the way to confirmation in righteousness and eternal life. Specifically, there is no mention of original probation, what is crucial in explaining the covenantal panorama of biblical history and redemption, most notably the work of Christ as Second Adam. That said, we owe Meyer a great debt for his courage to forge new ground within his interpretative tradition.[47] There is genuine hope that expositors faithful to Scripture may yet come together in setting forth a clear, consistent statement of evangelical Reformed covenant theology.

---

representative modern-day voices, locate themselves within the Murray-Kevan (i.e., Puritan) stream regarding interpretation of the Mosaic Covenant as a pure Covenant of Grace, with no element or principle of works inheritance. In the case of Silva and Gaffin, the traditional Law/Gospel antithesis crucial in Reformed theology has been jettisoned altogether. The leading spokesperson for the (New) Westminster School is Norman Shepherd. See his *The Call of Grace* and *The Way of Righteousness*. For extensive analysis see my trilogy: *Covenant Theology in Reformed Perspective*; *Gospel Grace*; and *Federalism and the Westminster Tradition*.

47. Other important aspects of Paul's covenant theology include the future for ethnic Israel (here Meyer adopts an essentially amillennial understanding of Israel and the church), the role of the sacrificial system of atonement in the old covenant (which begs further elucidation than what is found in Meyer's study), and the nature and content of Christian ethics as laid out in the NT canon.

Conclusion

The recent collection of essays in *The Law Is Not of Faith: Essays on Works and Grace in the Mosaic Covenant* advances the interpretation of the Mosaic Covenant as a republication of the original Covenant of Works at creation (though in modified form after the Fall). It has generated much heated discussion and debate within Reformed circles.[48] Doubtless, this dispute can profit from the work being done in other quarters of the theological world.[49] Reformed covenant theology must fully disentangle itself from seventeenth-century formulations that adopt speculative dichotomizing. There is the urgent need to retrieve teaching that is faithful to Scripture, much of which lies in the pages of Turretin and other stalwart theological expositors, past and present. On the part of Beach there is the need to tap into recent exegetical, biblical-theological studies on the subject. Here I especially commend the work of Meredith G. Kline. Interaction with the teachings of the Federal Vision school, the New Perspective on Paul, and the Shepherd-Gaffin theology would also help bring clarity and relevancy to the ongoing disputes. The doctrine of the Mosaic Covenant remains an element within the system of evangelical Protestant teaching that requires further refinement and rethinking. Genuine headway has been made in recent years, and for that we are most grateful.

---

48. Estelle et al., *Law Is Not of Faith*. My evaluation of this book is found in *JETS* 53 (2009) 407–11. In this connection see also my review of Gamble's *Whole Counsel of God*, vol. 1, in *TrinJ* 31 (2010), 141–43. Criticisms of what has (erroneously) been dubbed the "Escondido hermeneutic" is found in Dennison et al., "Merit or 'Entitlement' in Reformed Covenant Theology"; and in Venema, "The Mosaic Covenant: A 'Republication' of the Covenant of Works?" Neither of these critiques does justice to the teaching of Scripture or to tradition (i.e., the history of Reformed doctrine in all its complexity). The idea that the Mosaic Covenant is "in some sense" a covenant of works first appeared in my doctoral dissertation ("The Mosaic Covenant and the Concept of Works in Reformed Hermeneutics"). An earlier critique of my exposition is found in Schreiner, *Law and Its Fulfillment*, "Appendix: Mark Karlberg's View of the Mosaic Law," 247–51.

49. And here we commend especially the efforts of Sailhamer and Meyer. Scott W. Hahn in *Covenant and Communion* summarizes the views of the current head of the Roman Catholic communion paralleling recent developments in Protestant interpretation, most notably, among advocates of the New Perspective on Paul and the law. The old alignment of Karl Barth and Hans Küng on covenant and justification continues to rear its head.

4

How Should Moses Be Read?

A Debate in Contemporary Reformed Theology

OVER THE LAST HALF-CENTURY or more the dominant view regarding the Mosaic Covenant—though by no means only view—was that it was an administration of the overarching Covenant of Grace *with no antithetical works-inheritance principle*. Recovery of the teaching of early, historic Reformed teaching, namely, the view that the Mosaic Covenant does indeed convey a works-inheritance principle, has generated a good bit of debate over the last few years. Advocates on both sides of the dispute have claimed to be the accurate interpreters of the tradition since the opening days of the Protestant Reformation. Both cannot be true. The present controversy rests partly upon misunderstanding of the issues in dispute, and partly on issues that entail a decidedly different reading of Scripture and tradition. At the heart of the dispute is appropriation or misappropriation of the Protestant Law/Gospel contrast. Simply stated, the Gospel sets forth the principle of justification/salvation by grace through faith, on the merits of Christ's righteousness accruing from his work of substitutionary atonement. The law propounds the principle of inheritance/reward on the basis of the creature's perfect keeping of God's commandments. This principle is formative in the Reformed doctrine of the Covenant of Works, the covenant God made with Adam before his fall into sin. Those who adopt the doctrine of the Covenant of Works, including the idea of meritorious reward with respect to Christ's redeeming work, yet deny the role of merit in the covenant with Adam at creation and in the Mosaic Covenant, have to one degree or another undermined the doctrine of Reformed soteriology, consistently formulated.

The focus of this article is the legal feature of the covenant God made with Moses and all Israel—"legal" here construed as antithetical to "gracious." The doctrine now widely disputed can be stated in these terms: Under Moses there is a *republication* of the works-inheritance principle, the principle operative in the original covenant with Adam prior to his transgression. God's covenant with Moses is *in some sense* a (modified) covenant of works. In current discussion the phrase *in some sense* is drawn from my 1980 doctoral dissertation ("The Mosaic Covenant and the Concept of Works in Reformed Hermeneutics," completed at Westminster Theological Seminary).

There are two aspects of the debate, biblical and historical-theological. Before addressing each of these, a word of clarification is in order: Acknowledgement of the works-inheritance principle in the covenant with Adam (reinstituted with modification in the covenant with Moses) is not optional, the present writer maintains, within the parameters of Reformed evangelical interpretation. To be sure, the theological picture is a bit complicated and clouded. Thanks to genuine progression in theological understanding that comes over the course of the history of doctrine, it is my contention that we are now in a better position to concede that *aspects* of teaching found in Reformed scholastic federalism, i.e., Reformed orthodoxy in the late seventeenth century onwards, are no longer tenable and, therefore, must be rejected. To continue to hold to teachings that are speculative, not biblical, serves only to fuel unnecessary conflict and discord. Given the clarity that has now been attained in theological discourse we are afforded the opportunity to transcend previous conflict. To that end we turn to Scripture, the source of the church's theology.

Scripture Speaks: The Church Listens

Paramount in formulations of the biblical doctrine of justification by faith alone is the Law/Gospel distinction. This distinction is of equal weight to the Creator/creature distinction within the Reformed system of doctrine. Procurement of God's eschatological blessing—what is the consummation of God's purposes in creation—has been granted to creatures (re)made in his own image by means of God's covenant sovereignly administered and maintained over the course of redemptive history. The beneficiaries of this gracious disposition are the elect in Christ. Caution must be exercised against speculative notions of creaturely autonomy, on the one hand, and false dichotomizations between an alleged "order of nature" prior to and distinct from the covenant administration established in creation, on the other. This false dichotomy appears in the writings of several notable Reformed systematicians.

Prominent in the teaching/preaching of the apostle Paul is the role of the Mosaic law in the history of redemptive revelation. The law is Israel's *schoolmaster*, leading her to faith in Jesus Christ as the one who alone redeems sinners from the curse of the law (see especially Galaltians 3–4). In one of his sermons Paul declares: "Therefore let it be known to you, brothers, that through him forgiveness of sins is proclaimed to you, and through him everyone who believes is delivered from all things, from which you could not be delivered through the law of Moses" (Acts 13:38, 39). Space does not permit an exhaustive explanation of the peculiar operation of the works principle within the Mosaic economy, except to say that the legal principle functions on the *typological level of life in the land of Canaan*. Blessing and prosperity in Canaan are contingent upon Israel's compliance with the law of Moses. (Spiritual blessing is contingent upon the merits of Christ's righteousness exclusively.) The works-inheritance principle explains the tutelary, pedagogical use of the law. By frustrating Israel, what results in her exile to the land of Babylon, the law points guilty sinners to Jesus the Messiah for life and salvation. Forgiveness of sins, which comes to all who trust in Christ, is a once-for-all benefit, secure and indefectible. Unlike the temporary forgiveness experienced by corporate Israel under the provisions of the Mosaic law regulative of life in earthly Canaan, this spiritual benefit is of eternal weight and value. (True Israelites enjoyed this benefit by virtue of faith in the Messiah to come.)

Elsewhere the apostle explains: "But now apart from the law the righteousness of God has been manifested, being witnessed by the law and the prophets, even the righteousness of God through faith in Jesus Christ for all those who believe: For there is no distinction; all have sinned and fall short of the glory of God, being justified as a gift by his grace through the redemption which is in Christ Jesus, whom God displayed publicly as a propitiation in his blood through faith. This was to demonstrate his righteousness, because in the patient forbearance of God he passed over the sins previously committed; for the manifestation, I say, of his righteousness at the present time, so that he would be just and the justifier of the one who has faith in Jesus" (Rom 3:21–26). The righteousness of the law, a reference to the works-inheritance principle, is antithetical to the righteousness that comes by faith apart from the works of the law. The tenth chapter of Romans elaborates on these contrasting principles (uniformly referred to as the Law/Gospel contrast in evangelical Protestant theology). Paul makes personal application of this Gospel truth in his autobiography (Phil 3:1–10; cf. Paul's discussion of the role of the regenerating, illuminating Spirit of Christ in 2 Cor 3:13–18).

REFORMED DOGMATICS: THE CHURCH RESPONDS

All of the Reformed confessions adopt the Protestant Law/Gospel antithesis, which antithesis has immediate ramifications for the Reformed doctrine of the covenants, the Covenant of Works (with Adam before the Fall) and the Covenant of Grace (extending from the Fall to the Consummation). This is the *unanimous consensus* of the Reformed churches since the Protestant Reformation, extending into the period of scholastic orthodoxy and well into the twentieth century (at which time the doctrine of the Covenant of Works has come under attack within the "orthodox evangelical" camp). How important is this doctrine? And what are the issues at stake?

Diversity of opinion surrounds the interpretation of the Mosaic Covenant, whether or not there is a works principle functioning at some level within the old economy of redemption. Despite the clarification that has come in recent years, Reformed interpreters (exegetes and dogmaticians) remain polarized. Are we guilty of imposing a false schematization on the biblical text, in either affirming or denying the two-covenant doctrine (the Covenant of Works and the Covenant of Grace)? This is the question today. Space here does not permit a defense of one side or the other. We can only raise the question to those who deny the works principle in the Mosaic Covenant: How can we explain the exile of Israel to Babylon, if the house of Israel had been the beneficiary of God's saving work (by virtue of all the benefits under the Covenant of Grace)? How can we explain Moses' exclusion from entrance into the land of promise (following his disobedience to God)? Is not something else at work within the old Mosaic economy, which comes to a decisive end/abrogation with the coming of Christ and the establishment of the new and better covenant?

Far more serious is repudiation of the doctrine of the Covenant of Works on the part of some. The issue came to a head in the teachings of

Norman Shepherd at Westminster Seminary in Philadelphia back in the mid-1970s (a dispute that extends to the present). If there is no principle of works inheritance in the first covenant at creation, then obviously there is no works principle in any of God's covenants. It was John Murray who first attempted to recast Reformed covenant theology by distinguishing between the original Adamic administration (which he preferred not to call a "covenant") and the Covenant of Grace (which manifested God's gracious, *redemptive* provisions to fallen humankind). Despite the oddities of Murray's formulations, he did not deny the works-*merit* principle in regards to the conditions defining the Adamic administration (specifically, Adam's time of probation). He did entertain the Mosaic Covenant as a purely gracious arrangement (recall that Murray preferred to define covenant as redemptive provision exclusively). All told, Murray vigorously upheld the Protestant doctrine of justification by faith alone. Such was not the case with Murray's successor at Westminster. Shepherd views both faith and the good works of those *united with Christ* as "instruments" in the appropriation of justification, i.e., the "way of salvation." Hence, the believer is justified by faith and good works. Together faith and good works weigh in on the final Day of Judgment (= justification/judgment according to works). Shepherd's theology continues to have its passionate advocates among those who first stood beside him in the seminary controversy and those who espouse a form of "multiperspectivalism" to justify Shepherd's theologizing. (More on this is closely detailed in my trilogy: *Covenant Theology in Reformed Perspective*; *Gospel-Grace: The Modern-Day Controversy*; and *Federalism and the Westminster Tradition*).

Throughout international Calvinism, past and present, the theological tradition under study has indisputably recognized itself to be "reformed and *always* reforming." While sharing high regard for the church's creeds and confessions, the Reformed tradition readily acknowledges that these confessional statements are neither infallible nor inerrant (Scripture alone bears these traits). Not only are there elements of confessional teaching subject to ongoing debate—for example, the Puritan versus Continental understanding of the Christian Sabbath, the meaning and length of the "days of creation" in Genesis 1. There are also more weighty, foundational issues in dispute today, such as the doctrine of justification by faith alone (bringing into view differing assessments of the role of good works, if any, in the procurement of justification/final vindication) and the legal covenant of works with Adam and with Israel at Sinai. These latter two are of great theological consequence.

Expressed in other terms, essential to the doctrine of justification and the covenants is the historic Protestant Law/Gospel antithesis. This subject addresses doctrines intimately related to one another in the biblical text, most notably in the writings of the apostle Paul. When we rightly maintain that perfect obedience is required of the First and Second Adams in their probationary role, and when we say that this perfect obedience is necessary for the attainment of consummate, eschatological blessing (eternal enjoyment and fellowship with God), we are essentially adopting the "merit" principle. It is by the merit of Christ's righteousness (or the merit of Adam's righteousness, had he passed probation in Eden) that all those represented in federal headship are confirmed in righteousness for all eternity. This reward of the covenant is freely granted by God to the creature, the son of God, fashioned in God's own image. (See my previous article, "The Glory of God: Archetypal and Ectypal. Part Two: The Image of God")

For many, lurking behind the modern-day view regarding the Mosaic Covenant as a pure administration of redemptive grace is disdain for the Law/Gospel antithesis, traditionally understood. The Shepherd dispute has served to advance the age-long debate among the churches of the Reformation regarding what is the heart of the Gospel, justification by faith alone apart from works of the law. The spiritual blessings of redemptive covenant are indefectible. Christ in his saving work has secured these benefits to all those united to him by grace through faith. Resolution of the current debate awaits an outcome faithful to Scripture, devoid of speculative notions and false schematizations. May God be pleased to bring unity in the truth in our day.

Reviews—Section Two

Bryan D. Estelle, J. V. Fesko, and David VanDrunen, editors, *The Law Is Not of Faith: Essays on Works and Grace in the Mosaic Covenant* (Phillipsburg: P & R, 2009)

This collection of essays is an exceedingly welcome addition to the literature on Paul and the law, and related topics. It comes on the heels of more than three decades of discussion and dispute originating on the campus of Westminster Seminary in Philadelphia. Debate centered upon the teachings of systematics professor Norman Shepherd (who began as my doctoral advisor in 1977). The topic of the Mosaic Covenant would become the focus of my own academic studies—from the mid-70s to the present. *The Law Is Not of Faith* stands as a compelling answer to many of the questions left unresolved in contemporary evangelical Reformed discussion concerning the Mosaic law, especially as that bears on the doctrine of justification and the covenants of God spanning the history of redemptive revelation. All of the contributors are graduates of the Westminster seminaries, some currently teaching at Westminster West. Each of the three editors is a member of the Orthodox Presbyterian Church, a denomination torn apart by the theological controversy. The dispute is by no means limited to the Westminster/OPC community, however. Reference in the book is made to the Presbyterian Church in America (other denominations might well have been mentioned). More broadly, the subject of this book directly addresses ongoing differences among covenant and dispensational theologians (notably, among the *progressive dispensationalists*).

The editors' Introduction begins with a lengthy fictional account of a seminarian's examination in a court of the church on the subject that for many long years has occupied the minds of presbyters and members of the Orthodox Presbyterian Church. That subject is the doctrine of the republication of the original covenant of works under Moses. Contributors to this collected writing are understood to have reached a consensus in interpretation, *at least in its main outline*. They share "a general sympathy with the republication idea and a general desire to recover serious theological reflection on issues related to it." At the same time they acknowledge a measure of diversity in Reformed exposition, Reformation and modern, and they welcome healthy discussion of "important issues for the doctrine and life of the church" (20). Among the important theological points requisite for the exposition of the doctrine of republication are these: the doctrine of probation in connection with Adam, Israel, and Christ (what is directly related to Estelle's discussion of "entitlement to heaven"); the idea of a national covenant of works (introduced by Charles Hodge, who "raises the issue of the grand narrative of redemptive history, namely, the idea of Israel as God's son who prefigures God's only begotten Son" [13]); and the shift in discussion from matters concerning *ordo salutis* to matters concerning *historia salutis*, anticipating the rise of the distinct discipline of biblical theology, standing alongside systematics (or church dogmatics).

Despite superficial appearances, the editors rightly insist, "The doctrine of republication is not in any way dispensationalism" (14). One of the perplexing questions is why this Reformed doctrine has fallen upon such hard times. "How is it that such a dominant concern with so many Reformed luminaries in the past slipped off the table of discussion and was no longer, generally speaking, a matter that exercised the best minds among theologians, ministers, ruling elders, and educated laypersons?" The editors proceed to ask: "Did such silence, dare we say historical ignorance, lead to a kind of unwitting torpor in the thinking of ministers, exegetes, and theologians in areas of theological inquiry such as the nature of the law, grace, typology, and merit?" (15). Another perplexing question is why John Murray abandoned historic Reformed teaching in his exposition of covenant theology. It is best not to label Murray's aberrant teaching on the biblical covenants "monocovenantal," as the editors confusingly do (16). Murray's preference was to restrict the term covenant to redemptive provision, the post-Fall economy of sovereign, electing grace. Following the lead of Karl Barth, the theology of Norman Shepherd and Richard

Gaffin is indisputably monocovenantal. According to this viewpoint, grace (as opposed to meritorious human works) is viewed as the single way of inheritance/reward in the covenants established by God with humanity, in each and every instance over the course of biblical history. These latter exponents of Neo-orthodox doctrine have jettisoned the merit principle of works altogether, the law principle operative in the creation covenant and republished (in some form) under the Mosaic administration. Radical revisionist teaching at Westminster Seminary has produced no small amount of "agitation in the church" (17). What is principally at stake in this dispute is the Protestant Reformed doctrine of justification by faith alone. Though there are complexities to the doctrine of the republication of the covenant of works in the Mosaic economy of redemption, apprehension of this biblical teaching is "simple enough for a child to understand" (19). We concur fully.

Given the diversity of thought in this collection of essays on the subject at hand, it is best that we begin with the essays of the editors—one historical, one biblical, and one theological. J. V. Fesko ("Calvin and Witius on the Mosaic Covenant") lays out the basic contour of Reformed thinking by comparing two prominent, distinguished Reformed systematicians. He notes that "[T]he differences lay in the emphasis that Witsius places upon the use and role of typology in his explanation of the Mosaic covenant" (27). Fesko concludes: "It is the development of this covenantal framework, a development of nomenclature rather than theological substance, that one finds in Witius's explanation of the Mosaic covenant" (35). But then the picture becomes a bit murky. Fesko indicates that, according to Witsius, the legal arrangement under Moses proffered salvation on grounds of works-righteousness (37). This statement, as it stands, is akin to the teaching of early dispensationalism. Better is the view of Calvin explained by Fesko two pages later.

Bryan Estelle ("Leviticus 18:5 and Deuteronomy 30:1–14 in Biblical Theological Development: Entitlement to Heaven Foreclosed and Proffered") brings the book's discussion to its profoundest level, in so far as it addresses the role and significance of biblical typology. Sound biblical-systematic exegesis ultimately will resolve the dispute in contemporary Reformed theology (building on the work and insights of those who have preceded). Surprisingly, there is no reference here or anywhere in the book to Kline's stupendous work *Glory in our Midst*. This mature work of Kline is essential reading in covenant theology. Problems in theological formulation (noted with regard to Fesko's understanding of the operation of the law principle under Moses) resurface in Estelle's essay. Estelle entertains the notion that the works-inheritance principle enunciated in Leviticus 18:5 posits a hypothetical salvation by works. Better to speak of the "universal implications for the works principle" (115). The difference in formulation is highly important for biblical-theological exegesis and Reformed systematics. A dispensational construction also surfaces in connection with Estelle's understanding of the letter/Spirit contrast in the writings of Jeremiah, whose teachings are anticipated by Moses in Deuteronomy 30. It must be stated emphatically that the same regenerating, empowering Spirit is at work in the salvation of God's elect in the Mosaic economy as in the new. The letter/Spirit contrast must be explained in other terms. Surely it is the case that there is a greater emphasis on the individual (the Spiritual/eschatological) in the new covenant, a decided shift from emphasis on the corporate (the physical/temporal) in the old. Estelle rightly highlights the connection between the typical and antitypical levels of life in the land of Canaan (118, n. 45). This introduces us to some of the richness and complexity of Reformed biblical-theological exposition of the Mosaic institution and economy.

In recent years David VanDrunen ("Natural Law and the Works Principle under Adam and Moses") has become a champion of natural law doctrine. He begins his essay by observing: "No study of the Mosaic law in the Reformed tradition can hope to attain any degree of completeness without attention to the idea of natural law. The ideas of natural law and of the works principle in the Mosaic covenant in fact share an intriguingly similar history. While both concepts were standard features of early Reformed theology—natural law unambiguously and the works principle in the Mosaic covenant with some variation—both have fallen upon hard times in Reformed thought in the last century [especially in the wake of Barthianism]" (282, also 288). Special attention is given to the apostle Paul's teaching in Romans 2:6–15. Here I take exception to VanDrunen's exegesis. In my reading the text indicates that the "doers of the law" are the ones to inherit eternal life. This passage does not tell us *how* this is attained; for an answer to that question we must delve further into Paul's epistle. (The same teaching, as one other example, is stated by the apostle John: "The fine linen is the righteous deeds of the saints" [Rev 19:8].) Pertinent here is the comment of Horton: "Our obedience is not the basis or condition of this justification, but precisely for this reason the law's true purpose can begin even now to be realized in us: perfectly in our representative head, and in us in principle by the new birth as a result of his life, death, and resurrection" (330). Additional clarity needs to be given to the notion of a "strict" versus a "soft" works principle, especially in regards to the issue of Israel's retention of the land of Canaan and her prosperity in the land (cf. 301, n. 30). Better is Meredith Kline's take on the distinction between holy and common institutions—the functioning of natural law in the two respective spheres of administration and governance—and the sharply *antithetical* contrast between the two inheritance principles, Law and Grace. I would suggest that the idea of natural law is more elastic (and knowledge of it more elusive) in the post-Fall epoch than VanDrunen's view seems to allow.

The remaining essayists can be surveyed more briefly. D. G. Hart ("Princeton and the Law: Enlightened and Reformed") offers a defense of the soundness of the Princeton theologians and faults her critics for abandoning—knowingly or unknowingly—the traditional Law/Gospel distinction, as that bears on the Reformed doctrine of the covenants. This entry nicely complements the article by VanDrunen, underscoring the close tie between natural law and the Covenant of Works. Brenton Ferry's essay ("Works in the Mosaic Covenant: A Reformed Taxonomy") closes out Part One ("Historical Studies") by forging a taxonomy covering the array of theological opinion on the subject of the republication of the original covenant of works under Moses. Disappointingly, Ferry's analysis is not entirely helpful, an analysis that results in a partial garbling of issues, however subtle in nuance. Clearer and sharper distinction is required, given the fact that Reformed interpretation of the Mosaic Covenant from the time of the Reformation to the present is replete with vagueness and ambiguity in expression, including some outright contradiction. The Reformed tradition as a whole has been unclear how best to explain the operation of the antithetical principles of Law and Grace within the Mosaic administration of the Covenant of Grace. Ferry's readiness to find continuity and agreement among expositors of federal theology fails to reckon with the untidy side of doctrinal development, prior to theological maturation. Hence, Ferry's readings and conclusions are subject to debate. And with respect to the Westminster controversy in particular, failure to acknowledge change and development in Kline's thinking on the covenants only distorts an accurate reading of the history of Reformed interpretation, past and present.

The bulk of essays appear in Part Two ("Biblical Studies"), and for good reason. Given the long-standing dispute over the doctrine of the republication of the covenant of works in the Mosaic economy and decades of erroneous teaching emanating from the Westminster seminaries, this collection of essays is a vindication of the Scripture principle—that Scripture is its own best interpreter. In the final analysis it is the exegesis of Scripture that brings resolution to all theological controversy. Richard Belcher's essay ("The King, the Law, and Righteousness in the Psalms: A Foundation for Understanding the Work of Christ") deals mostly with the doctrine of the justification of sinners on grounds of the imputed righteousness of Christ. Belcher directly counters the view of Shepherd and the Federal Visionists, here represented in the writings of Peter Leithart. Byron G. Curtis ("Hosea 6:7 and Covenant-Breaking like/at Adam") handles a central OT text, one that has played an important role in the rise and development of covenant theology. In making his case for the covenant made with Adam at creation, some interaction with other texts, notably Isaiah 24:5, would have strengthened his argument.

Indicative of underlying *disagreement* among our essayists is Guy Waters' exposition ("Romans 10:5 and the Covenant of Works"), which is out of sync with this volume of writings intent on upholding the doctrine of the republication of the Covenant of Works under Moses, doctrine Waters explicitly rejects. Explanation of its inclusion may lie in what I see to be the major flaw in this study: inconsistency in theological analysis and failure to hold the line unequivocally. In his taxonomy Ferry makes the attempt to locate Murray's peculiar interpretation within the parameters of Reformed orthodox federalism. Gordon, for one, sees matters quite differently (see below). The position Ferry identifies as the "principle of abstraction" is incompatible with the doctrine of the republication of the original Covenant of Works in the Mosaic economy of redemption. Furthermore, the moral law (and natural law) does not, in and of itself, include the probationary element of eschatological reward for perfect obedience. The former is an expression of natural revelation, the latter of special revelation (these two forms of divine revelation work in tandem.)

The articles by David Gordon ("Abraham and Sinai Contrasted in Galatians 3:6–14") and S. M. Baugh ("Galatians 5:1–6 and Personal Obligation: Reflections on Paul and the Law") conclude Part Two. Gordon aims his critique against Westminster Seminary's most respected systematician, the late John Murray. (Here the author follows in my wake. Meredith Kline, likewise, regarded Murray's deviation from historic Reformed theology as inexcusable.) As one has come to expect, Baugh provides thoughtful insight and careful reflection on issues vigorously disputed within the Westminster community of scholars and pastors. The second of two entries in Part Three ("Theological Studies") is penned by Michael Horton ("Obedience Is Better than Sacrifice"). Horton astutely remarks: "The idea of the imputation of the active obedience of Christ has come under attack by some in contemporary Reformed circles. *At the heart of these misgivings seems to be the notion of merit as a legitimate category in the Creator-creature relationship*" (315, italics added). On the other side of the dispute, it must be noted that the views of Shepherd and Gaffin are substantively identical. Even though Gaffin acknowledges the active obedience of Christ in imputation, he repudiates the notion of merit with respect to the original covenantal arrangement God made with the First Adam. In so doing he destroys the Pauline parallel between the two federal heads and undercuts the need for the active, *substitutionary* obedience of Christ as the *meritorious* ground of the believer's justification. The difference is more than semantics.

In drawing this review to a close, we return once more to Murray's exposition of the covenants. There needs to be a meeting of the minds: On the one hand, Waters remarks that "Some within the Reformed churches are gravitating toward monocovenantalism (often not without grave consequences for their doctrine of justification)" (239). On the other hand, Gordon castigates Murray for his "implicit monocovenantalism" (253). Meanwhile, the book as a whole sets out to counter the worst of these unwelcome developments within the Westminster/OPC community. Interaction with the writings of disputants on the other side, e.g., Sinclair Ferguson and Peter Lillback (as well as interaction with the work of Gaffin), is requisite. Additionally, far greater attention must be given to the doctrine of probation and the crucial role of *meritorious* human obedience in the successful fulfillment of the original Covenant of Works. Also neglected in this volume is discussion of decretive election as that informs covenant theology (what is distinct from Israel's *national, theocratic election*, an essential component in the system of biblical typology). Commendably, the book serves to uphold the teaching of catholic Reformed orthodoxy, as advanced by the federal theologians. I extend a personal word of appreciation for the due diligence of our essayists. It is hoped that this volume will, in turn, commend renewed study and discussion—for the sake of the Gospel of saving grace.

Richard C. Gamble, *The Whole Counsel of God*, vol. 1, *God's Mighty Acts in the Old Testament*

(Phillipsburg: P & R, 2009)[1]

Author Richard Gamble is to be commended for setting as his goal the drawing together of the fruits of biblical, systematic, and historical theology (the last reserved chiefly for the final of the three-volume set). His work has been viewed as groundbreaking. In our reading, however, Gamble's attempt is unsuccessful as a synthesis, ending up as a compilation, a hybrid compendium in theology utilizing distinct hermeneutical methodologies side by side. This assessment is not meant to detract from the usefulness of the study. Gamble, one-time professor at Westminster Seminary in Philadelphia, engages heavily with the writings of this theological faculty. There is no mention of systematicians Michael Horton or David VanDrunen from Westminster California; this may explain, in part, why Gamble avoids hot-button issues that have divided the two campuses. (Redeemer Theological Seminary in Dallas, established in February 2009, marks a third break-off—this in the wake of the turbulent years of the Peter Enns dispute over biblical inerrancy.) With regard to several divisive and disruptive controversies at Westminster, Gamble fails to give the seminary community and the church at large direction and help where it is needed the most. Gamble's compendium relies heavily upon the work of the Dillard-Longman-Enns school for its historical assessment of the OT canonical books.

Gamble expresses genuine reserve concerning John Frame's multiperspectivalism, Harvie Conn's contextualization, and Richard Gaffin's biblical theology as deviations from traditional Reformed interpretation. The last named shifts the emphasis from systematic formulation to redemptive-historical exegesis as the proper and only (?) domain for systematics. For the most part, the material offered in this first volume serves as an introduction to OT theology, which restricts engagement with NT revelation (hence it is different from a true "biblical theology"). Why the author draws on NT revelation in some places of the study and not others is entirely unclear. For example, Gamble's discussion of singing and the use of instruments in corporate worship does not incorporate NT teaching. (The author

---

1. This is a slighty fuller version of the published review in *TrinJ*.

currently teaches at the Covenanter seminary in Pittsburgh, which favors exclusive, unaccompanied Psalm singing.) Several other shortcomings of consequence: the book is slight on exegesis (instead relying on the literature cited, a not-uncommon practice in most systematic theologies); meager attention is given to the theocratic constitution of Israel (what is a unique situation in the postlapsum era), nor is the typological significance of the Solomonic temple sufficiently developed (cf. Gregory Beale's treatment in *The Temple and the Church's Mission*, building on the work of Meredith Kline); there is inadequate analysis of theonomy and no mention of "intrusion ethics" in redemptive history, prior to the Eschaton. Regrettably, Gamble holds simultaneously two antithetical views on the covenant(s); this factor indicates that the author has not thought through carefully issues so fiercely disputed in Reformed circles at the present. Hopefully these problematic features in volume one will be remedied in the remaining two volumes.

With regard to some of the most important issues raised in Gamble's systematics we highlight the following six: (1) the importance of Van Tilian presuppositionalism throughout the theological system ("thinking God's thoughts after him"); (2) the essential role of the covenant idea in revelation, pre- and postlapsum, especially the function of law (the principle of works inheritance) within the Mosaic economy of redemption (see Estelle et al., *The Law Is Not of Faith*, reviewed above); (3) the operation of natural law in the created order (with special attention to the meaning and applicability of Sabbath keeping, a sign of God's covenant with his people); (4) the long-standing question whether the image-of-God concept (explicated in terms of the Spirit-temple of God on both the micro- and macrocosmic levels) is functional and/or ontological; (5) ecclesiology in the OT (contrary to Gamble, theocratic Israel is not synonymous with the church; rather, ancient Israel is distinguished by national, corporate election, not individual election to salvation, what is the *proper purpose* of redemptive covenant); and (6) christological interpretation of the OT requiring, among other aspects, extensive discussion and explication of covenant typology and symbolism in the Bible taken as a whole (what is properly the domain of biblical theology). With respect to the last topic I commend the insightful, path-setting work of Kline, whom Gamble rightly sees as one who "towers over other figures" among conservative American OT scholars of the late twentieth century (130). Kline's work is indispensable for the articulation of a Reformed biblical theology; assimilation would greatly enhance Gamble's systematics. Ancillary issues arising from the theology of the covenants include federal representation and covenant mediation, which are separate and distinct features in the unfolding of biblical history; also, probationary testing in both the angelic and human kingdoms. Gamble's treatment of OT persons tends to move in the direction of moral example, rather than messianic anticipation of the one to come, the true and faithful covenant head, the Second Adam.

In the main, *The Whole Counsel of God* is a beginner's introduction to the teaching of the Bible, yet profitable reading for the advanced student. Many sections have a devotional quality meant to accent the practical side of doctrine, specifically its relevance to the Christian life. Looking ahead, volume 2 will offer a NT theology, volume 3 a discussion of exegetical-dogmatic issues viewed from the perspective of the history of doctrine. Special mention should be made to P & R's 2008 publication of J. van Genderen and W. H. Velema's *Concise Reformed Dogmatics*, frequently cited here, a work that engages primarily the Continental theologians (notably the Dutch Reformed tradition). Clearly, church dogmatics, which for Gamble is equivalent to systematics, has a bright present and future.

SECTION 3

The Music of Heaven: Worship in Spirit and Truth

WE TURN IN THIS final section to the subject of corporate worship in the Reformed covenantal tradition, harmonizing the revelation of God both in terms of his special theophanic manifestation to his covenant people (a manifestation which recurs throughout the entire range of biblical history) and in his inscripturated Word (Christ speaking through the Scriptures). It is the music of heaven, the worship of the saints in Spirit and Truth—in the present, semi-eschatological reality of the New Age that has dawned with the appearance of the incarnate Word, Jesus the Christ. We begin with a look at the Glory of God (the Spirit-theophany) as both archetypal and ectypal—God himself in his self-revelation (the divine Presence) and in residence with his people (the living temple of God in the Spirit, i.e., the church).

The radical transformation of the Old Man (fallen humanity) into the New Man (the Body of Christ) underscores the uniqueness of Christian life, witness, and worship. Bringing together aspects of the author's career in theology and church music, we consider the nature and distinctive character of corporate worship within the Reformed communion, highlighting the role of Christian song and the arts more broadly. Implicit in this discussion is articulation of the Reformed world-and-life view, a subject dear to (Old) Westminster's premier apologist, Cornelius Van Til. We close this section with a review of John Muether's biography of this great stalwart of the faith.

5

The Glory of God: Archetypal and Ectypal

Part 1—The Theophanic Glory

The discipline of Reformed biblical theology—one that accents the progressive, historical unfolding of redemptive revelation—requires us to see Christ in all of Scripture. The famous dictum of Augustine regarding the two testaments is that the New is in the Old concealed, the Old in the New revealed. Reformed teaching on this subject, accordingly, is of ancient pedigree. The apostle John speaks of the crucial tie between the two testaments in terms of shadow and reality, the apostle Paul in terms of promise and fulfillment (after the pattern of OT teaching itself). Of course, it is Christ himself who instructs his disciples in learning to see Christ in the Law, the Prophets, and the Psalms (Luke 24:27, 44–49).

Christology, the doctrine of Christ in the Bible viewed as a whole, is inextricably bound to typology, the study of typical, symbolic precursors of the person and work of Jesus Christ in connection with sundry OT events, persons, and institutions. The single, most important manifestation of God in the midst of his people, however, is the Glory-theophany, what makes its appearance at numerous times throughout biblical history. The theophanic Glory is a complex *eschatological* phenomenon, an anticipation of the Eschaton, the close of history and entrance into the eternal kingdom of righteousness and life. From the outset, the Glory-theophany bears the Immanuel imprint, God with us—supremely so in the incarnate life of God's Son (the incarnation became requisite for the redemption of fallen humankind as decreed by God since the foundation of the worlds).

At times the Glory-cloud manifestation is distinct from the second person of the Trinity; at other times it is an appearance of Christ himself in his supernal existence as the exact radiance of the Father (Heb 1:1–4). It is the coming of God to humanity that is the focus of this essay. (Much of the material developed here builds upon the exegetical and theological analyses of Geerhardus Vos and Meredith G. Kline.)

We begin with the portrayal of the Glory of God given by the psalmist:

> The Lord reigns, let the earth rejoice;
> > let the many islands be glad.
> Clouds and thick darkness surround Him;
> > righteousness and justice are the foundation of His throne.
> Fire goes before Him and burns up His adversaries round about.
> His lightnings lit up the world;
> > the earth saw and trembled.
> The mountains melted like wax at the presence of the Lord.
> At the presence of the Lord of the whole earth.
> > The heavens declare His righteousness,
> > and all the peoples have seen His glory.
>
> The Lord reigns, let the peoples tremble;
> > He is enthroned above the cherubim.
> Let the earth shake!
>
> Exalt the Lord our God
> > and worship at His footstool.
> Holy is He.
> Moses and Aaron were among His priests,
> > and Samuel was among those who called on His name.
> They called upon the Lord and He answered them.
> He spoke to them in the pillar of cloud;
> > they kept His testimonies and the statute that He gave them.
> O Lord our God, You answered them;
> > You were a forgiving God to them,
> > and yet an avenger of their evil deeds.
> Exalt the Lord our God and worship at His holy hill,
> > for holy is the Lord our God.
> (Ps 97:1–6; 99:1–9)

This manifestation of God, his advent, is a heavenly intrusion into the earthly realm—heaven come to earth. It is the very dwelling place of God (in anthropological depiction, since both God and angels are incorporeal). God the Father is seated upon the throne, with Christ at his right hand, surrounded by the seraphim, cherubim, and myriad angels. Taken together, it is the Counsel of God which has called all things earthly and heavenly into being and which sustains all things by his powerful arm (see Gen 1:2). The angels are attending spirits, commissioned at first in God's work of creation and later in redemption. Though created beings, the angels partake in the creative/re-creative work of God as purely ministering spirits, not having divine power unto themselves. God alone is Creator; the angels are subservient creatures. Upon the establishment of the post-diluvian covenant with all creation, what is a modification of the original covenant made at creation, God promises to uphold his handiwork until the close of history, until the extension of his spiritual kingdom throughout all the world has been completed. The retreating storm clouds leave the rainbow in the sky, a sign of God's (common) grace to fallen creation. Never again will God interrupt the course of human history with so catastrophic a judgment as this; the (final) Day of the Lord—the eschatological appearance of God in Glory—will bring his purpose in creation and redemption to its decretive conclusion.

To understand aright the spiritual realm of God's sovereign Presence as a pre-eschatological intrusion into the earthly realm, it is necessary that we make note of its strategic role and appearance over the course of history. Prior to the creation of Adam and Eve, God had fashioned the spiritual world of angels, which at the beginning of time was placed on probation. The angels, as image-bearers of God (hence, "sons of God"), were likewise in covenant relationship with God. Unlike Adam, who would later be placed under similar probation, each angel stood in the integrity of his own act of obedience or disobedience. There was no federal representation here, and no redemption for those angels who transgressed after the instigation of Lucifer. Subsequent to the fulfillment of angelic probation, the heavenly kingdom of light and righteousness broke forth into the earthly realm at the very start of its formation, the earthly kingdom appearing as a replica of the heavenly Glory. This Spirit-theophany hovered over the unformed mass at the beginning of the physical creation; the same Spirit comes in the Garden of Eden in judgment and in prophetic announcement (as regards the promise of salvation to Adam and Eve, the mother of all living, and judgment upon the Serpent). These events mark the opening history of the theophanic Word and revelation—the revelation of God mediated by the Son through the Spirit.

Given all that we have noted thus far, the theophanic Glory is *trinitarian* in essence. The revelation of the (Christian) doctrine of the Trinity is deeply embedded in the biblical record right from the outset. Assuredly, it would be a matter of time before the full, final manifestation of the triune God would appear in the person of Jesus Christ incarnate and in the outpouring of the pentecostal Spirit. Over the course of biblical history the Glory-theophany is identified by the following terms (among others): Spirit, Presence, Face, Hand, Arm, Eyes (cf. "the seven eyes of the Spirit"), Angel (the pre-incarnate bodily manifestation of Christ), Word, and Temple (in anticipation of the consummate arrival of the final heavenly, eternal dwelling of God with his people). A complex, awesome manifestation of the divine for finite humanity to apprehend!

The expression "caught up in the Spirit" has immediate reference to communication of the prophet with the Lord of Glory. Likewise, the expression "walked with God" (after the fashion of Enoch and Elijah) denotes intimate communion with God the Spirit as the eternal Word and source of resurrection life. Comprehensively, OT history and prophecy are written in anticipation of Christ's coming, and are thus preparatory in nature. Encounters with the spiritual world are replete throughout Scripture. The following is but a partial sampling (including instances cited in the above).

In the Law

At the ratification of the covenant with Abraham God manifests himself by theophany, as a smoking oven and flaming torch. This is an aspect of the Glory-representation, one that features both the awe of God's presence and the holiness of his cleansing power in the salvation of sinners (cf. Mal 4:1–3 and John 3:11–12). Having been cleansed and renewed in divine sonship, Abraham converses with God by way of the theophanic Word of revelation, through the mediation of the one who is identified as the Angel of the Lord (Gen 22:15). This is no ordinary angel, nor one having special standing within the angelic kingdom, like Gabriel or the seraphim. The Angel of the Lord is the Lord Christ, also called Michael, the prince of the army of God (cf. the references in Dan 12 and in Rev 12). He is the victor over the enemies of God, the one who conquers sin and death. In John's Gospel (8:56) Jesus declares that Abraham had seen the Lord of Glory (as an instance of the "Day of the Lord," which occurs periodically throughout redemptive history until its consummate realization at the Eschaton). Likewise,

The Glory of God: Archetypal and Ectypal

Stephen recounts that the God of Glory appeared to Abraham when he was yet in Mesopotamia (Acts 7:2).

Similarly, Jacob encounters the angelic revelation of God in pre-incarnate personage; he wrestles with God until he receives the blessing proffered (Gen 30:11). Subsequently in the account, Jacob is again confronted by theophany, when "the angels of God met him" (Gen 32:1). Jacob calls the place God's encampment, his dwelling with humanity. Depicted here is the divine Counsel, the sovereign Lord in the company of his ministering angels. From this encounter, Jacob in turn sends out messengers to prepare the way for his meeting with Esau, an important event in the outworking of Israel's corporate election and the redemption of those who are recipients of God's decretive election in Christ, the true Israel of God. Jacob's (i.e., Israel's) election has both individual and corporate ramifications (see Rom 9).

The pivotal moment in theocratic Israel's formation and subsequent history comes at the revelation of God's law upon Mount Sinai, another instance of the appearance of the Glory-theophany in cloud and fire. (Hebrews 12:18–24 compares the revelational encounter between God and humankind in terms of two contrasting covenants, the Mosaic and the new.) Prior to the giving of the law—what is a covenant of works on the typological level of temporal life in the land of Canaan, wherein prosperity is contingent upon Israel's keeping of the law—Moses meets the Angel of the Lord on the occasion of the blazing fire in the bush, what he describes as a "marvelous sight" (Exod 3:2). Moses stands on Holy Ground, the Rock of salvation. Ascending Mount Sinai, Moses meets God in the presence of his angels, what is an encounter with the divine Counsel (Exod 19:3, 16–20; cf. Gal 3:19). This same Presence (namely, the Angel of the Lord) will go before Israel, bringing her into the land of promise (Exod 23:20). The portable tent was the earthly, symbolico-typological place of meeting with the Lord God, a site overshadowed by the pillar of cloud by day and the pillar of fire by night (Exod 33:7–11). Descending the mountain, Moses' face was aglow with the radiance of God's own Glory (Exod 34:29–35; see 2 Cor 3:6–18, again comparing and contrasting the old and new covenants).

In the Prophets

The experience of prophetic encounter with the God of Glory is resumed in the life of Joshua, who leads Israel into the holy land (Moses had been disqualified entrance into the land because of his transgression of a command of the Lord in the days of wilderness wandering). On that day the provision of manna ceases, and Israel begins to enjoy the fruits of Canaan. At this moment Joshua engages the Captain of the Lord's host, the pre-incarnate, theophanic Angel, who is the Christ of Glory (Josh 5:12–15). Like Moses, Joshua stands on Holy Ground. The prospect of covenant breaking looms large in Joshua's farewell address (Josh 23; see also ch. 24). Life, blessing, and prosperity in the earthly, temporal land of promise is contingent upon the keeping of the law of Moses (eternal life, on the other hand, is secure, based exclusively upon the future, messianic work of God's Son by means of fulfillment of his probationary testing as Second Adam).

The prophetic office arises from humanity's estate of sin and covenant transgression. Originally, as image-bearer and covenantal son of God, Adam was commissioned to rule creation with priestly devotion, hence the twofold offices of priest and king. The role of the prophets is to convey God's word of judgment and sovereign determination; that Word climaxes in bringing God's covenant lawsuit against a disobedient people. The prophet Elijah, whose life and work anticipated that of John the Baptist in the days of Israel's final ultimatum to turn from sin and cleave to Jesus the Messiah in true faith and repentance, encounters the living Presence of God in his awesome theophanic power and judgment. This occasion is clearly reminiscent of Moses' experience on Mount Sinai (1 Kgs 19:11–12). The sound of the Lord on this occasion, like the sound of God's advent in the Garden after the sins of our first parents and like the sound of God's meeting with Moses upon the mountain, was thunderous and terrifying (not the "still small voice, " as commonly translated in the biblical text). It was Isaiah who saw the Lord high and lifted up, seated upon a throne surrounded by the seraphim crying out, "Holy, holy, holy, is the Lord of hosts" (Isa 6:1–7). The cleansing power of God's sanctifying grace is what qualifies and equips the prophet for service in the kingdom. The forgiveness that Isaiah experiences is the fruit of the messianic Lord who is coming to deliver Israel and bring peace to the nations, in fulfillment of God's promise to Abraham.

Eschatological Fulfillment

The Gospels and other books of the New Testament record and interpret the inauguration of the new and everlasting covenant in the blood of Jesus Christ. The Temple of God with humanity is identified as Christ and his Body, the church. The revelatory Word comes as God's abiding Presence in the midst of his people, his dwelling among his sons and daughters, the

The Glory of God: Archetypal and Ectypal

Spirit-Temple of God. The Glory-theophany is thoroughly trinitarian; the kingdom of saints is the beneficiary of God's gracious salvation, accomplished and applied over the course of redemptive history by the Father, the Son, and the Spirit (Col 1:13–20; 2:9–15; Eph 2:19–22; 2 Cor 3:17–18; and 1 Cor 15:47–49). The Book of Revelation, the capstone of inscripturated revelation, details in apocalyptic imagery developments to take place in the latter days, the period extending from the first to the second advents of Christ. The revelation given to John begins with his rapture into heaven, the Glory-Presence of God (Rev 1:10).

Glory-theophany makes several appearances in New Testament times (for example, at the time of the birth of Christ, at his baptism and temptation, at the Transfiguration, at Pentecost, and at Saul's conversion and subsequent "third heaven" experience). The future prospect of every believer is that he or she will likewise see God "face to face," by way of the Glory-Presence. Heaven will come to earth, and the eternal Temple-Kingdom will be consummated in all its reflective Glory, what is the Glory of the Lord God himself. The sons of God, God's image-bearers, will be transformed and glorified, fit for eternity. Oh what a Day that will be!

PART 2—THE IMAGE OF GOD

The idea of the image of God in Reformed theology has never fully jelled. Too often in the minds of interpreters the idea suggests an analogy to be drawn between the Creator and the creature made in God's likeness (the terms "image" and "likeness" are generally understood to be synonymous). The contrast is made between archetype and ectype, between infinite and finite being, and between incommunicable and communicable attributes. It is said that man mirrors God, in some ways more than others. The image is, accordingly, defined in two aspects, the narrower (true knowledge, righteousness and holiness which are lost after Adam's fall into sin) and the broader (including the ability to reason and communicate, to investigate and exercise dominion over creation with moral sensibility, what is a testimony to "natural law").

At best, the concept of man as image of God is elusive in theological exposition. The mistake is that exegetes have missed the immediate context of the revelation concerning man's creation in God's image in the opening chapter of the Bible. God said: "Let us make man in our own image." Is this statement made by the Father to the other two persons in the Godhead (what is implied in the notion of the "plural of Majesty"), or does this assertion bring into view the theophanic Spirit, God's deliberative Counsel, which includes the holy, ministering angels? Above, we gave indication of the prevalence of the Glory-theophany in the history of revelation beginning with the account of creation and extending over the course of redemptive history, old and new economies. Parenthetically, the view that angels lacking physical bodies are thereby denied sonship—and not to be regarded as made in God's image—is in error (see the argument presented in Part 1 above; cf. additionally Job 1:6, Ps 89:6,7; cf. Ps 82:1).

Likeness to God brings into view both priestly and kingly exercise, requiring consecration of and dominion over all creation. (The office of prophet awaits the fallen situation in which humankind finds itself after Adam's transgression in the Garden of Eden.) Essential to the biblical explication of the idea of man as image-bearer of God is the doctrine of probation, pertaining both to the angelic and human realms. The psalmist tells us that the First Adam was created a little lower than the angels (Ps 8); the writer to the Hebrews informs us that the Second Adam, in taking human form with a view to fulfilling all righteousness as covenant head, was also made (i.e., positioned) a little lower than the angels (Heb 2). Here we need to grasp the cosmic scenario laid out in Scripture. Prior to man's creation, the angels were tested as to their allegiance to the Lord of heaven. The obedient angels, who successfully passed probation, were *confirmed* in true knowledge, righteousness, and holiness. This state of glorification ushered the holy angels into the eternal presence of God, thus enjoying everlasting beatitude. Had Adam obeyed God and passed probation, he too would have been confirmed in righteousness (though final glorification would have awaited the fulfillment of the original cultural mandate, including procreation of the human race and dominion over creation as God's vicegerent). The *beatific* vision of God would have come at the close of history, the inauguration of the Eschaton (the arrival of heaven on earth). Though he was without sin, Christ in his incarnation/humiliation as Second Adam was not yet "confirmed" (i.e., justified, exalted) in his work as Redeemer and Lord. Upon completion of his probation (extending from his baptism by John to his death on the cross), Jesus was highly exalted above the heavens as the eternal Son of God, meriting the salvation of God's elect. His reward was the kingdom of kings and priests, those renewed in the image of Christ in true knowledge, righteousness, and holiness (Col 3:10).

It was at the moment of Christ's sacrificial offering up of his own life that Lucifer was barred future contact with the divine Presence in theophanic Glory. The spiritual warfare that now ensues is one that is guaranteed a positive outcome for the saints of God (Eph 6). All things work together for good to those called, justified, and glorified (Rom 8). So certain is the victory of Christ over sin and death, that the redeemed of the Lord are already glorified—at least in principle. As true image-bearers of God, the redeemed have been adopted into God's family as legitimate heirs and sons. Sonship and likeness to God are equivalent concepts in the Bible; sonship means intimate relationship, communion and fellowship with God by way of covenant. The promise of the covenant is that God comes to dwell with his people by way of his eternal Glory-Presence.

The ministering angels labor on behalf of those who are now being saved. At the close of history, sinners saved by grace will be elevated above the angels, so great is the measure of the Father's love displayed in the death and resurrection of his only-begotten Son. The archetypal, deliberative Counsel is designated the "eyes of the Spirit," surveying the events unfolding in the history of humankind (cf. Zech 4:10). Spiritual warfare is cosmic in scope; it is intense and it is unremitting. To the extent that the people of God reflect his glory and truth, (S)piritual maturity and likeness to Christ is attained, though not perfectly prior to the Consummation (Eph 4). We are reminded of the luminescence on the face of Moses when he spoke to God "face to face," a glory that faded with the passage of time (what was a shadow of things to come). The redeemed of the Lord, however, enjoy a true glorification that does not fade or perish (2 Cor 3:18, 1 Cor 15:39–49, and 1 Pet 1:3–9). Our ethical likeness to God and our physical glory/luminescence are aspects of human image-bearing. Just as the heavens declare the glory of God, so do the saints who presently are seated with Christ in the heavenlies, serving as lights in a world of sin and darkness. Our bodies are temples of the Holy Spirit where God indwells (1 Cor 6:19, 20).

There are various degrees of Glory-imaging: there are the lesser and greater lights in the heavenly skies; there is similarly an array of light refraction on the earth below. Differing reflections of God's glory appear in the angelic and human kingdoms. Yet none can compare with the glory to be revealed on the Last Day, when God the Father will be all in all (1 Cor 15:24). The original design of creation was that humankind would be ushered into the consummate kingdom of light and righteousness by way of Adam's successful consecration of his life to the glory of God. Consequent to his transgression, God opened up a new way to secure the proffered kingdom by means of his Son, who became incarnate in human flesh, yet knew no sin. He is the exact image and representation of God (Heb 1:3,4).

In him we take on the divine nature, as finite creatures remade in God's own image (2 Pet 1:3,4). Since the Fall, the cultural mandate is bifurcated—cultic and cultural activities are now distinct. As image-bearers, humanity exercises dominion over creation by means of *common grace*, itself a benefit of Christ's atoning death. Image-bearers renewed in the likeness of Christ are building a spiritual edifice, the Spirit-Temple of God (1 Pet 2:4–10). The latter is exclusively the work of God's *saving grace*. Humanity in its commonality continues to occupy the kingly office appointed to man at creation; redeemed humanity fulfills the priestly office by the cleansing, empowering, and equipping work of the Spirit of Christ. All glory to God who sovereignly rules over his creation with majesty and honor.

Though analogies can be drawn between the natures of God and humanity, the biblical referent to the idea of the image of God is the theophanic Glory manifested at creation and in re-creation. The creature fashioned in God's likeness reflects his glory in terms of the twofold office of priest and king, a calling shared by angels and humankind (before sin entered the world). The image bears both an ethical and a royal component. As heirs of redemption, humanity in Christ experiences the unique electing grace and love of the Father in communion with the Son and the Spirit (1 Pet 1:10–12). Until we experience the consummate (beatific) vision of God in Glory, we are presently "being transformed in the same image from glory to glory, just as from the Lord, the Spirit" (2 Cor 3:18).

Justification for the sanctity and preservation of human life in the present world order—including the institution of civil government associated with the "mark" placed upon Cain and its reinstitution by God with Noah after the flood—is the dignity and royal status of human beings as God's image-bearers (Gen 4 and 9). The apostle Paul speaks of civil magistrates as ministers of God having divine authority (Rom 13). The practice of "holy war" in the time of the Israelite theocracy, the extermination of those living in Canaan (the holy, symbolico-typological site of God's residence among his chosen people), brings into focus the implementation of "intrusion ethics," pointing to the end-time judgment of God upon the ungodly, those who are his enemies. In the modern day, just war theories are not based on "holy war," but upon justice as revealed in natural law. One of the responsibilities of civil governments is to provide safety and protection for the citizens of earthly kingdoms. The goal is that nations might live peaceably. At the same time, however, the operation of God's common wrath against sin and disobedience brings about conflict and destruction upon nations and peoples. Lasting peace is unattainable in this fallen world; both the expansion and the maintenance of the human race and its attending culture in this present evil age are subject to frustration and distortion by the sins of humankind.

The only solution to humanity's plight is the sanctifying, regenerating work of God the Spirit. The prophet Isaiah beheld the Lord of Glory and experienced the cleansing balm of God's mercy and grace. With the removal of Isaiah's iniquity (the benefit of Christ's future atoning death) the prophet became spiritually qualified to minister on God's behalf, declaring the will of God in the covenant lawsuit instituted against disobedient Israel. Exile in Babylon typified the payment requisite for Israel's transgressions; the return to the land of Palestine symbolically announced Israel's satisfaction for sin (see Isa 40:1). Corollary to spiritual cleansing is the idea of investiture, being clothed in the righteousness of Christ by means of God's justifying and sanctifying grace. Under the Mosaic institution, the priestly robes of Aaron were modeled after the tabernacle, which in turn were patterned after the heavenly sanctuary. Ultimately, the resurrection/glorification of the saints is attained in the eschatological replication of the image of Christ in consummate renewal, inner and outer (soul and body), on the Last Day, what is the second advent of the Son of God. The incarnate Glory embodies the exact image/representation of the Father through the Spirit. In his life, death, and resurrection Christ experiences the fullness of the Spirit without measure; upon the completion of his redemptive work Christ is identified as one with the Spirit (2 Cor 3:18 and 1 Cor 15:45). That is to say, in the economy of redemption, Christ and the Spirit are one. Christ has become "life-giving Spirit." As the body of Christ, the Bride is clothed in the likeness of Christ. She is the New Man. In former times, it was only the prophets of the old (Mosaic) covenant who experienced *proleptically* the reality of the consummate, eschatological Spirit in Glory-transformation. The Spirit-rapture of the old covenant prophets was peculiar to their (postlapsarian) office; they uniquely experienced the likeness of the Spirit of the Lord. In the exercise of their prophetic role, they mirrored true likeness in the perfected image of Christ.

Originally, completion of humanity's cultic-cultural labors in the theocratic kingdom that was to encompass the entire world would have ushered humankind into God's eternal Sabbath. Prior to the Eschaton, weekly observance of the seventh-day Sabbath was an anticipation of consummate rest at the close of human history. With the entrance of sin and death into the world, the Sabbath ordinance was modified in a twofold manner. Initially, the seventh-day observance of Sabbath rest (what was a sign of God's covenant established at creation) was withdrawn, only to be reinstituted in the typological, theocratic kingdom made with ancient Israel. Subsequently, Christian observance of God's Sabbath rest is marked by a change in day (from the seventh to the first day of the week) and by the practice of meeting together for corporate worship among the gathered saints, which does not include the requirement of cessation from earthly labors. In fact, the breaking of the original covenant at creation resulted in God placing a curse upon humankind's labors, work that is now characterized by frustration, disappointment, and hard toil. The blessing of seventh-day, physical resting was withdrawn, only to be reinstituted in the theocratic kingdom. The writer to the Hebrews makes clear that our true, eschatological rest awaits those of us who are in Christ, beneficiaries of his redeeming work. Only our cultic activities (the kingdom work of the Christian church in the proclamation of the Gospel and the missionary expansion of God's spiritual kingdom) enjoy the blessing of God signified in the Sabbath ordinance, sign of redemptive covenant. Cultural activities, whether performed by the godly or the ungodly, do not share the Sabbath blessing of God. Presently, the Sabbath is a sign and an ordinance extended to covenant keepers, those who are in covenant with God by way of baptism.

The Sabbath of God for the saints is life in the eternal Presence of the Lord of Glory, communion and fellowship with the triune God. The idea of image-bearing and Sabbath rest (symbolizing entrance into the true sanctuary, the throne room of God) are unintelligible apart from their mutual interplay in the unfolding history of redemptive revelation. Redeemed humanity finds its true identity in its embodiment of the divine Glory, progressively enhanced over the passage of time, notably, over the course of the extension of God's kingdom throughout the world. As God's image-bearers, renewed in the likeness of Jesus Christ, the saints bear witness to God's unmerited love and grace in accordance with the testimony of Scripture, the canons of Old and New Testaments (the authoritative documents of the people of God spanning the old and new economies of the Covenant of Grace). In our corporate worship we come to Mount Zion, the true Spirit-Temple of God indwelling redeemed humanity, an eschatological anticipation of the consummate reality already enjoyed and experienced—to some degree or in one manner of speaking—by the sons of God, both men and angels (see Heb 12:22, 23 and Col 3:1–4). The pre-consummate manifestation of God is by way of Glory-theophany. We now eagerly await the return of the incarnate Son of God in Glory—that we might be transformed "from glory to glory," changed into his glorious likeness.

6

The Distinctiveness of Reformed Worship

ONE OF THE RIPE fruits of Reformed theology is the distinction between special and common grace, between what is holy and what is common. This crucial biblical distinction finds symbolic expression in the Mosaic Covenant in numerous and varied ways. We begin by recognizing that the ancient Israelite theocracy was set apart from all other political-ethnic entities: Israel was God's elect nation. This election, based wholly upon God's sovereign will and good pleasure, is not election to salvation, although the former (national election) does serve the purposes of decretive election (union with Christ) in the overall design of redemptive history, specifically in the unfolding of the Mosaic and New Covenants. The old economy is preparatory and propaedeutic, looking forward to the climax of redemptive covenant accomplished by Jesus Christ in the fullness of times.

Likewise, the distinction between cult and culture is important for the proper interpretation of God's covenantal dealings with humankind, marred though it became by the fall of our first parents in the Garden-paradise (what was holy, theocratic ground). The subsequent rise of the institution of the state, ordained to stand alongside the institution of the church for the governance of the gathered, confessing saints by Word and sacrament, is a manifestation of God's mercy to fallen sinners in a world set against truth and righteousness. The civil state would serve the ultimate purpose of God in the redemption of his elect who would be called out of the world. The ensuing spiritual warfare between the righteous and the unrighteous, what characterizes this world order, was first announced by God in the aftermath of Adam's transgression, as recorded in the third chapter of Genesis. The enmity between God and his (elect) people would be overcome by the sacrificial, vicarious atonement of the Son of God, the true and faithful Seed of the woman. In this One, the many are made (i.e., constituted) righteous; they are justified by grace through faith. Subsequent to the Fall, the provision of garments for Adam and Eve is symbolic of the (imputed) righteousness of Christ which clothes the unrighteous.

Grace: Holy and Common

It is the atonement of Christ that establishes both common and special grace. The blessing and accompanying benefits of temporal life in this fallen world are themselves the fruit of Christ's atonement, alongside the saving benefits of everlasting life received by the elect, and by the elect alone. At the same time, there is the manifestation of God's common wrath, different from his final wrath reserved for the reprobate. The former is temporal, the latter eternal. Believers and unbelievers alike suffer many of the same earthly ravages of sin and death. (Unlike the unbeliever, however, the believer endures these sufferings for the sake of Christ—as witness to his faithfulness and protection in any and all circumstances of life in this present, fallen world.)

Prior to Adam's fall into sin, humanity's habitat in Eden was holy to the Lord; the Edenic garden was the site of God's theophanic revelation to our first parents and the site of Adam's encounter with Satan. It was Adam's task to preserve the holiness of the Garden of God against the encroachments of the Serpent, who challenged both the authority and the wisdom of God, specifically with reference to the probationary command not to eat of the tree of the knowledge of good and evil. To prove what was good, Adam was to obey God's every word with complete fidelity and with full confidence in the justice and the judgment of his Sovereign. It was through transgression that Adam came to know evil with its paralyzing and fatal consequences. Had Adam obeyed, he would have been in a position to fulfill perfectly the original cultural mandate—to propagate the human race and exercise dominion over all creation as the Lord's vicegerent. Had this been accomplished, the site of God's holy presence, at first restricted to the Edenic garden, would have been extended over time to cover the entire earth. All creation would have been holy to the Lord. God's theocratic rule and reign would have included every corner of the globe and would have governed all peoples united in true faith and in the hope of the final consummation of God's purpose in creation, the arrival of the new heavens and earth at the Eschaton (the close of earth's history).

The End from the Beginning

Created in the image of God (or more exactly, in the image of the heavenly, angelic Counsel where the Lord God sits enthroned), human beings serve two historical tasks, the priestly and the kingly. To interpret aright the concept of the image of God, it is necessary to understand the circumstance of the angelic host at the beginning of time. The angels were created good and intelligent beings in need of proving (i.e., confirming) their faithfulness to God by way of probationary testing. Those who followed Lucifer in their rebellion against God were consigned to ultimate death and condemnation. (That final fate would await the conclusion of redemptive history as foreordained by God in his eternal counsel.) The good angels were *confirmed in righteousness,* never again to be tested, never again subject to temptation. According to Psalm 8, Adam was created "a little lower than the angels." That is to say, he was created in a state of perfect righteousness, though not yet confirmed. At the close of history he would have been elevated to the highest state of glorified existence, by means of successful probation and fulfillment of the cultural mandate. Immediately after probation he would have been confirmed in righteousness (likewise, unable to sin). Adam's "one act of righteousness" would have been imputed to all humankind, had Adam obeyed. The exercise of human dominion over all creation would have been accomplished without defeat or frustration. As kings, humankind would have ruled as God's faithful sons/daughters; and as priests, humankind would have consecrated all to the glory and praise of God. (The prophetic office arises as a result of humanity's fall into sin.)

The kingdom of God was from the first regulated by the covenantal pledge and stipulation. Sabbath rest was a (covenantal) sign of the Eschaton, a divine pledge to grant God's vassal people the reward of life eternal upon faithful keeping of the covenant. (Similarly, the tree of life was symbolic of eschatological life, i.e., life everlasting.) The close of probation would have meant the termination of the original Covenant of Works and the inauguration of new phase of covenant life and administration (what might best be termed the "Covenant of Confirmation"), had Adam as federal head exercised his priestly duty in truth and righteousness. The kingdom is administered and regulated by God through the course of human history by means of covenant. And it is redemptive covenant that orders the life of the faith community throughout the course of salvation history. Sabbath pointed to final Rest, what God presently enjoys, having completed the creation of heaven and earth—in anticipation of the future, eschatological glorification of humankind as designed in the original creation. (Here as elsewhere in Scripture and in biblical theology we are speaking in *anthropomorphic* terms concerning God's relationship with creation.)

Postlapsum, the Covenant of Grace is regulative of the kingdom of God in the fallen world. God's spiritual covenant, which orders the ecclesiastical realm of the people of God, does not pertain to the civil realm of earthly kingdoms (the only exception was ancient, theocratic Israel). The church, as the assembly of those called out by God and set apart, is wholly distinct from all geopolitical entities. Hence, the Decalogue, as summary of God's covenant with ancient Israel, is not the moral standard for civic duty among the nations of the world, though the Mosaic law does serve as a *guide* for secular, political jurisprudence (past and present).[1] Originally, it served as the norm for faith and moral conduct in the Israelite theocracy. With the establishment of the new covenant, the Decalogue is *reapplied* within the covenant community—in light of the death, resurrection, and ascension of Jesus Christ into heaven. The kingdom of God is not of this world. It has no ethnic or geopolitical form; rather it transcends the national and political orders of this world. The church of the new covenant is the Body of Christ, the corporate (elect) Man chosen in Christ. The saints who lived before the advent of Christ awaited the day of his appearing and of their inclusion into the Body of Christ.

The distinction between the holy (the church) and the common (the state) pertains to the historical circumstance that sustains after the Fall. As a common grace institution, the state does not bear any ties to the kingdom of Christ. It belongs to the secular order of this world, providentially governed and superintended by God. The sabbath-ordinance, accordingly, belongs to the covenant community alone; it is not something to be observed by all humankind indiscriminately. The kingdom of God is the realm in which God alone rules. The civil ruler, as a temporal servant of God, exercises authority over the political realm of a purely earthly kingdom. And all the kingdoms of this world will one day come to their inglorious end. Their

---

1. See my "Reformation Politics: The Relevance of Old Testament Ethics in Calvinist Political Theory," republished in *Covenant Theology in Reformed Perspective*. See also, my "Westminster and Washington" in *Federalism and the Westminster Tradition*. The state serves no redemptive end; it is a purely common-grace institution lasting until the return of Christ and the establishment of the eternal kingdom that comes to fruition with the wholly supernatural, cataclysmic manifestation of God's Glory and Power. Human efforts do not contribute to this consummating act of God at the close of history. In the meantime, to the extent that the state furthers justice and protection for its citizens, it is an instrument for good, rather than evil.

purpose will have been served. All this to say, *Kingdom* and *Covenant* are holy to the Lord. The end of history is determined by the beginning, the obedience or disobedience of the angelic host and the human race predetermined by God's sovereign, decretive will and good pleasure, for the sake of his own glory.

Humanity's True Calling

Returning to Eden, the first sanctuary of God in the midst of humanity fashioned in the likeness of the heavenly Glory-Counsel, God here revealed himself in Word and in Glory-Presence. The Word was in the beginning, and the Word was God. The incarnation would not have been necessary, had sin not entered the human race. The redemption of fallen sinners required the vicarious sacrifice of the Second Adam to atone for sin and to reconcile sinners to God. Holiness is one of the essential features of life in covenant with the Lord of heaven and earth. God's Presence is a manifestation of his rule and reign; the earthly site of God's reign is constituted a theocracy. (Later, Israel in the land of Canaan was a temporary, provisional symbol of the original theocracy in Eden.)

Confirmation in holiness and righteousness, as a decisive movement closer to the conferment of the eternal kingdom of God at the close of humanity's earthly mission, would only come by way of probationary testing. The fall of Lucifer and his evil minions prepared the way for the temptation of Adam in the Garden; hence, sin lay crouching at the Gate of Heaven, seeking to divert our first parents from the path of life everlasting to converse the path that leads to death and destruction. Part of the creation mandate was to guard the Sanctuary of God from all hostile forces. Success in the War between the Worlds would be the goal of the temptation placed before Adam. His federal (representative) act of obedience would be imputed to all humankind. True worship must be maintained in the holy place of God's dwelling with man. Sabbath was a sign of the eschatological reward proffered to Adam at the close of history, its future realization secured by Adam's "one act of righteousness."[2] It would be the task of the Second Adam to achieve what the First Adam lost.

---

2. Sabbatical observance in the postlapsum world differs significantly from that in the prelapsum world, in that the feature of cessation from earthly labors on the seventh day no longer has relevance or bearing in the common-grace arena. The only exception here is the circumstance that sustained under the Mosaic economy, what was applicable

The Redemptive Mission of the Church in the World

Now in the postlapsum epoch the church of God—already appearing in the earliest days of the historical inauguration of the Covenant of Grace following immediately upon Adam's transgression in the Garden (the consequence of God's mercy and grace extended to sinners)—assumes a prophetic voice in the world. The rise of the school of prophets in ancient times prepared the way for the official theocratic (Israelite) office of prophet. And what preceded this Mosaic institution served to underscore the peculiar redemptive nature of the prophetic office. The message of the prophet contains a word of judgment against the ungodly, a word against covenant breakers. More significantly, the prophet adopts an antithetical posture towards the covenant community with warnings against unfaithfulness. The penultimate climax of this aspect of the Mosaic institution comes in the days of the latter prophets, in the issuing of the covenant lawsuit against a rebellious people. John the Baptist is the messenger of the ultimatum to theocratic Israel.

These days of preparation and patient waiting for the coming of the Messiah finally give way to the establishment of the new covenant in the blood of Christ, the prophet greater than Moses. This hour in redemptive history marks the transition from shadow (the Mosaic economy) to reality (the semi-eschatological, pentecostal church of Christ). The period between the advents of Christ is the time of inaugurated eschatology (hence, the already/not yet character of spiritual life in the new covenant epoch). The Great Commission given by the ascending Christ to his disciples calls for the proclamation of the Gospel and the spiritual discipline of the Word of Christ through the proper governance of the church (exercised by her appointed, ordained leaders). The Great Commission given to the people of God in covenant with him, unlike the original creation mandate, does not call for the establishment of a "Christian" culture to function in the public arena. Covenantal holiness (the outworking of divine sanctification) pertains exclusively to theocracy and to the NT church as the community of faith. Accordingly, in all fields of human science and cultural enterprise

---

to *theocratic Israel*, and her alone. Rest in the land of promise conveyed a symbolic-typological significance. (The Israelite theocracy, as defined by the terms of the Mosaic administration of the Covenant of Grace, lasted in the time from Moses to Christ's first coming; this period was a *parenthesis* in the history of redemption.) Under the new covenant, Sabbath observance pertains exclusively to the corporate worship of the saints.

Christians and non-Christians labor side by side in the development of the arts, the sciences, and humanities. *These activities are common-grace enterprises. And as good and noble as these may be, they serve only a temporal, historical purpose in the maintenance of the human race until Christ comes again.* In brief, this means that (secular) culture is not to be "transformed," but rather given its appropriate place as an expression of the world, as distinct from the church, the saints in witness and worship.

Central to the work of the church is the preaching and teaching of the Word of God, including articulation of a biblical world-and-life view, in which all godly endeavor (in the church and in the world) is subsumed under the lordship of Christ. All activity in the civic arena is religious in orientation; but only Christians are enabled to perform their responsibility to the glory of God from a sincere and contrite heart. To be sure, God is absolutely sovereign in all the affairs of humankind; he rules over the works of the godly and the ungodly. Under his providential superintendence cultural endeavors find their place in the secular workplace, not in the life and witness of the covenant community *as a holy institution set apart by God for a distinct, peculiar mission in the world.* The state, as a secular institution ordained by God, is a non-confessing entity. And in the sovereign outworking of God's all-encompassing will and good pleasure, the actions and deliberations of the nations of the earth are subject to the vicissitudes of human judgment, including the miscarriage of justice, even while all peoples remain the beneficiaries of God's common grace empowered to "do the things of the law" (Rom 2:14,15).

WORSHIP AS THE WITNESS OF THE SAINTS

Whereas (secular) culture is the manifestation of God's common grace in the world (the fruitful labors of the regenerate and the unregenerate working out over the course of earthly history from the Fall to the Consummation), cult pertains to the worship and witness of the saints of God. Those who call upon his name confess and acknowledge God's lordship in all human affairs, temporal and eternal. To the church belong the promises of God, the law (both stipulation and sanction) as expressed in the covenant documents of the Old and New Testaments, the Sabbath institution, the sacraments, and the discipline of the church (cf. Rom 9:4, 5). Neither the church's constitution (the law of God) nor the church's discipline is shared by the ungodly, those who stand apart from the confessing body, the church as the gathered saints. To impose such upon the non-confessing community at large is to make light of the things of God humbly observed by the true sons and daughters of the covenant Lord. "Render to Caesar to things that belong to Caesar, and to God the things that belong to God" (Matt 22:21).[3]

The ministry and mission of the church, accordingly, are wholly spiritual in nature. Teaching and ruling elders rightly ordained to exercise leadership and governance in the church—themselves subject to the Word of God—hold the keys to the kingdom (cf. Heb 13:17). Discipline properly administered in accordance with the teaching of Scripture is one of the marks of the true church. The secular arm of the state serves an entirely different, though complementary, purpose with respect to the wider, more encompassing ordering and governance of human society at large. Whereas the state may make use of the sword for the welfare and the protection of its citizens, such is prohibited in the maintenance and furtherance of the spiritual kingdom of God on earth. Discerning the proper bounds of church and state requires the correct interpretation and application of the inscripturated Word. And that is something that can only be faithfully carried out by the confessing people of God. *The sacred Scriptures belong to the covenant people, not to secular courts of law or civil legislative bodies (though the Scriptures can, secondarily, be viewed as a guide in secular jurisprudence).* In short, the Bible is a covenantal, not a political, document, regulative of the life and witness of the saints. Believers are urged to pray continually for those in civic governance, that such leaders might be responsive to the law of God sovereignly implanted in the human heart, though now corrupted by sin and its effects (in view here is the Reformed doctrine of "natural law"). True interpretation of God's revelation and will requires the regenerating, illuminating work of the Spirit of God granted to the elect, and to them alone.

The nature, shape, and content of corporate worship—what is the cultic practice of the church—are laid out in the canonical documents of the Old and New Testaments, each appropriate to the specific covenantal administration to which the people of God are subject in the course of redemptive history, before and after Christ's first advent. Subsequent to the Fall and the inauguration of the Covenant of Grace, Genesis identifies a

---

3. Americans continue to wrestle with the ramifications of church/state relations in modern-day politics. Evangelicals remain divided over the biblical teaching concerning the institution of the state. Too often, evangelicals work with a (modified) theocratic understanding of the secular state, a view that is at odds with the teaching of Scripture as consistently taught in the Reformed theological tradition.

people, distinct from the ungodly, who by God's grace call upon the name of the Lord (Gen 4:26). The church before Pentecost is the work of the Spirit of Christ (in proleptic manifestation and power). The people of the Word are also the people of the indwelling Spirit, though not yet the Spirit of Pentecost (who inaugurates the semi-eschatological age of the Spirit, the age of the new covenant church). Spiritual regeneration is equally requisite in the time before Christ's atoning work on the cross, as afterwards (cf. Gen 3:15, 21 and Titus 3:5). The same Spirit of saving grace is at work in the individual lives of the redeemed throughout the history of the Covenant of Grace, from the Fall to the Consummation.

As previously noted, one of the signs of the covenant community is the observance of the Sabbath ordinance. There is a question whether the Sabbath was observed in the time prior to the establishment of the theocratic kingdom on earth (i.e., within the household of Israel). However this question is answered (the Scriptures are silent on this point), it is clear that the Sabbath assumes new, heightened significance in the Mosaic economy of redemption. Under the law of Moses, Sabbath keeping bears a twofold signification: (1) cessation from earthly labors with respect to the building of the typological kingdom on earth, in the land of promise; and (2) the weekly gathering of God's people for corporate worship.[4] This is a modification of the circumstance that would have been sustained in the original theocracy that existed in Eden, its goal being the extension of God's kingdom to the ends of the earth. In the original instance, humankind's exercise of world-dominion—apart from the ravages of sin, death, and frustration of all kinds—would have been celebrated by the observance of seventh-day cessation from work. Under the new covenant, only the latter feature, corporate worship, is required of the people of God. *Earthly labors, as part of the common-grace arrangement in non-theocratic societies, do not receive the covenantal sign of God's blessing and promise of consummation.* Only the spiritual fruits associated with Gospel ministry endure for time and eternity (see 1 Cor 3:9–15). The everlasting kingdom of God is not built by human hands, nor is it a product of this world order.

---

4. See the reinterpretation of the Sabbath ordinance in Kline, *God, Heaven, and Har Magedon*. My understanding is incorporated in essays found in my trilogy: *Covenant Theology in Reformed Perspective*; *Gospel Grace*; and *Federalism and the Westminster Tradition*.

Worship in Spirit and Truth

Proper understanding of the relationship between worship in the ancient, typological kingdom on earth—specifically, worship in the Solomonic temple—and worship in the eschatological age of the Spirit requires careful employment of the biblical-covenantal methodology (implicit in Scripture itself).[5] The apostle John characterizes new covenant worship as eschatological (borne by the Spirit of the resurrected Christ), the old as temporal and symbolico-typological. The shadows associated with the old economy of redemption give way to the realities of the eschatological summation of all things in heaven and earth in the fullness of times (what, at present, is *semi*-eschatological). At present, believers even now are seated with Christ in the heavenlies (Col 3:1; cf. Heb 12:18–24).

The Johannine notion of "truth" points to the person and work of Christ, the exact representation or "imprint" of God (cf. Heb 1:3). Christ is not the reflection of God's glory; he is the Glory of God revealed in the incarnation. He is life and truth in human flesh, true Man. Worship of God in the eschatological age of the Spirit is no longer restricted to the Davidic site, no longer prefigured in the symbolico-typological cast associated with the Solomonic temple (John 4:21–24). With the coming of Christ, type gives way to reality. The emphasis in the Old Testament scriptures is upon what is outward and transient, symbolic and typical. The imagery, typology, and symbolism of OT worship, both in terms of its institutions and practices, serve to teach the children of God under age the realities of spiritual, heavenly worship in the true Sanctuary of God. Worship as the realization of the everlasting perfection of God's sanctifying work of grace is reserved for the elect of God in the Eschaton. Presently, worship is experienced in and through the Spirit of Christ in anticipation of that great Day. As the Body of Christ, we are not yet what we shall be. Worship that is pure and unadulterated awaits the Consummation, the glorification of the saints in eschatological fulfillment and perfection.

Worship as Doxological and Dialogical

New covenant worship is characterized by the freedom that has been obtained by way of the Cross (see Hebrews 8–10). This freedom does not give

---

5. See further my "Significance of Israel in Biblical Typology," republished in *Covenant Theology in Reformed Perspective*.

the confessor license to do what he or she pleases in corporate worship. Rather, the gathering of the saints in worship continues to be regulated by the Word of God; specifically, ordained elders are appointed to oversee the life and witness of the congregation. That said, biblical worship is doxological and dialogical, involving clergy and laity hearing and receiving the Word of God as proclaimed in the preaching, the liturgy, and Christian song. New covenant worship, unlike worship under the old, recognizes and emphasizes the priesthood of all believers. Ministers ordained to preach the Word are not priests (contrary to high church theology as taught and practiced in the Roman and Anglo-Catholic communions, for example). Teaching and ruling elders exercise a ministerial authority that comes with ordination to office in the church. Both clergy and laity are subject to the authority of Scripture, the revealed Word of God.

God is worthy of all praise and thanksgiving. All that is done by the creature is to be consecrated to the glory of God and for the advancement of his purpose in creation and recreation, notably, as regards the advancement of the kingdom of Christ through the gathering of the saints in worship and witness. The ordering of corporate worship under old and new covenant administrations is laid out in general terms in the canonical documents. Christians have one Bible, Old and New Testaments, and one canon, the New Testament ordering the life and worship of confessors under the new age of the Spirit of Christ. Whatever the precise form and shape of corporate worship over the span of the history of the Christian church, worship is both doxological and dialogical. Worship begins and ends with the praise of God for his glorious person and work. Included in the assembly of those called out from the world, bearing witness and service to God, is the dialogue between God and his covenant people. In a word, worship is the renewing of the covenant, a reaffirmation of God's lordship in all things common and holy. Worship is a renewal of one's vow to be a faithful covenant-keeper by means of the empowering, persevering work of the Spirit, the Spirit who indwells each believer.

Under the New Covenant, the principle, and essential, elements in corporate worship are these: the reading of Scripture, prayer, song, the presentation of offerings, the preaching and exposition of the Word, and timely observance of the sacraments of the new covenant, baptism and the Lord's Supper. Each of these elements gives expression to the doxological and the dialogical nature of Christian worship. Neither the ordained teaching elder nor other delegated leaders in the house of worship may usurp the voice of the congregation in rendering praise and prayer to God. The principle vehicle for congregational response is the reciting of Scripture, spoken and sung. Here is where Christian freedom, under the supervision and oversight of the elders, is to be recognized. There is no one, uniform "order of service," although many communions have erroneously attempted to impose uniformity in worship and ritual (e.g., the Roman and Anglican communions). The Presbyterian tradition has wisely provided guides to corporate worship. It is left to the discretion and oversight of the elders, informed at all points by Scripture, in deciding the forms used in the weekly order of worship. In this oversight, the minister of the Word exercises the decisive role in subjecting all to the wisdom and counsel of God in Scripture. Christian maturity requires spiritual discernment in all things, including the ordering of the saints in corporate worship.

Illustrative of the freedom granted under the new covenant, the "call to worship" may be spoken by the pastor or sung by choir or congregation. Important here are the words of Scripture, God's summons to enter into his presence as the gathered saints. A choir (with various instruments) may be used to assist the congregation in the singing of psalms, hymns, and spiritual songs. And the choir may prepare in advance anthems of supplication and praise to help the congregation articulate her hopes, fears, and joys in the Christian journey and pilgrimage. Assuredly, the choir, other trained and skilled leaders in worship must shun usurping the voice of the congregation in the worship of God.[6] There is no place for either clericalism or professionalism in Christian worship that limits or impedes the active participation of the congregation. Worship in all of its specific forms or elements is ordered by God; it is not "performance," either in its musical offerings or in its liturgy.[7]

The question of formal versus informal worship (sometimes construed as the difference between morning and evening worship) is itself misleading. All corporate worship that is faithful to Scripture is "formal." Differences arise, first of all, in the location of the gathered saints in worship (e.g., whether in homes, in churches, or in cathedrals). Secondly, there

---

6. One of the great blessings of the Protestant Reformation was the return of music to the people. The various Protestant communions, however, did not agree on the selection of music to be sung or on the use of instruments in worship. For a helpful historical overview, consult Westermeyer, *Te Deum*, and Ogasapian, *Church Music in America, 1620–2000*. More broadly, see Rice and Huffstutler, *Reformed Worship*.

7. Consult Melton, *Presbyterian Worship in America*, which remains one of the best studies on the subject.

are wide variations in liturgy (all worship employs a "liturgy" of some sort). Freedom and diversity find expression in the planning and preparation of the order of worship in terms of the use of creeds and confessions, hymns, and songs (whether traditional, gospel song, or contemporary praise), and in written or spontaneous prayers. Aesthetics plays a role as a "cultural" expression of the local congregation. As Christians who live in a particular historical time and circumstance, we inevitably bring some cultural practices and expectations to our corporate worship in the form of music, liturgy, and architectural design (including accouterments in the place of meeting). Appropriate modifications in worship style are normal—and to be expected and welcomed. (Some practices can be of good benefit to the whole body of believers; others can have negative impact. Here again, wisdom and spiritual discernment are necessary.)

The intellectual, confessional, devotional, evangelistic, and missional dimensions of Christian worship may and do differ among ecclesiastical communions and among individual congregations, both in terms of scope and design. (The most striking differences along these lines can be seen among confessional Calvinists and free Baptists.) Differences also arise with respect to observance of the church year (e.g., Advent, Christmas, Lent, Easter, Pentecost, and other post-biblical observances such as Reformation Day). There are varied, optional ways of remembering God's acts in history, both redemptive-historical (as recorded in Scripture) and in the history of the Christian church (post-Pentecost).

Worship as Word and Sacrament

Central to corporate worship is the (expository) preaching of the Word and the proper administration of the sacraments. The latter need not be a weekly observance, but rather one determined by the wisdom of the elders. The frequency of baptism is, obviously, dependent upon the growth of the church; the frequency of the observance of the Lord's Supper involves both biblical understanding and an assessment of the particular needs of the congregation. The Word preached is essential to the spiritual growth and equipping of the saints for Christian service and mission outreach. And the depth of biblical preaching in any given church is a measure of the spiritual well-being of the congregation. Preaching and the spirituality of the church are intimately bound together, the two maturing over time symbiotically.

Partaking of the elements at the communion table is a visible manifestation of the unity of believers in Christ, the head of the church. Feeding upon Christ's body, represented by the bread and the wine, points worshippers to the spiritual sustenance that Christ alone provides by his Word and Spirit. The (saving) efficacy of the sacrament is received by faith alone. Those who do not partake in faith reap unto themselves the wrath and condemnation of God, should they fail to confess true faith and acknowledgment of their sin and need of Christ's mercy, grace, and love.

Baptism and Christian discipleship are an integral part of the Great Commission. The sacrament of baptism is observed as a directive given by Christ to his church. Baptism by water points to the reality signified in the sacrament, regeneration and rebirth by the Spirit of God. As the outward sign of God's redemptive covenant, baptism identifies the recipient as belonging to Jesus Christ and a member of his Body, the visible church. Baptism is necessary for the governance and the growth of the church as it unfolds over the course of human history. By God's entering into covenant with his people, the spiritual kingdom is formed. The invitation to receive Christ's claim of ownership in baptism is extended to parent and child, even prior to the child's coming of age (the age of personal accountability). The goal of the baptism of infants and adults alike is true, spiritual conversion (which can occur before or after the actual administration of baptism in the name of the triune God). Just as the bread and wine symbolize Christ's body and blood, so also the water of baptism symbolizes one's spiritual cleaning and renewal. In the Presbyterian tradition baptism is administered by the sprinkling of water, rather than immersion.

7

Music in Worship

MUSIC HAS OCCUPIED AN important place in the Christian life down through the centuries. Musical expression itself is part of the common human experience, a natural response of the soul to the sufferings and the joys of life. The use of music in religious worship is likewise universal. In the Bible, the Old and New Testaments, music is everywhere present. In fact, the goal of humanity's redemption is depicted in the Bible as the singing of a "new song." The particular focus of this article is the use of music in corporate worship: what form(s) should music take and how should it be performed? (When all is said and done, music is *performance*. More on this below.) Before turning to these questions, however, we take up a brief historical survey of music in the church, beginning with Old Testament practices.

HISTORICAL SKETCH

Life and worship in the old covenant was closely regulated by the express command of God given to Israel through Moses. A proper assessment of these ancient practices is dependent upon recognition of Israel's status as a nation of priests and kings. Ancient Israel was God's holy nation, a theocracy, chosen and set apart from all the other nations of the world. Once Israel had settled in the land of promise and (in the time of King Solomon) had completed construction of the temple of God on the Mount of Jerusalem, she had, in symbolic terms, entered into God's (sabbatical) rest. God had granted his chosen people physical rest from all the enemies round about her. Israel enjoyed the *typological* realization of the promise previously made to Abraham. (The full *eschatological* fulfillment would await the fullness of times, Christ's coming into the world. The period between the two advents of Christ is that of *semi-eschatological* realization of the ancient promise of salvation by grace.) The performance of music in the Solomonic temple was under the supervision of the Levitical priesthood. Choirs and instrumentalists were part of the symbolism giving expression to the awesome majesty and glory of God's Presence among the people at the site of his holy sanctuary. Solomonic worship was an earthly replica of the heavenly sanctuary, God's true dwelling place in the Spirit. (Quite frequently in the Bible the term "Spirit" refers to the theophanic Glory-Presence of God. Its first appearance is found in Genesis 1:2, the occasion of the Spirit's hovering over the waters at creation in order to fashion the earth, humanity's habitat, as one of several replications of God's cosmic glory.) Prominence is given to Psalms as Israel's hymnbook of praise, confession, and supplication. In divine providence, the Psalms comprises part of the OT canon of Scripture. All of this indicates that worship in the old covenant was tightly regulated. Every facet of worship in the temple was carefully prescribed by God. Such was part and parcel of the burden of the Mosaic law, which served as Israel's tutor or pedagogue until the coming of Christ. The new covenant would open up a new and better way of (S)piritual worship and witness in the world (see John 4:24).

Turning to the pages of the New Testament, we find infrequent reference to music in corporate worship and even less express instruction as to how music is to be employed on such occasions. What we do find is a dramatic contrast between liturgical (cultic) worship under the two covenants. Clearly, the ceremonial (ritual) and sacrificial elements have been abolished by virtue of the death and resurrection of Jesus Christ, the fulfiller of all these things. (Shadows have given way to reality.) At the same time new covenant worship is characterized by a degree of liberty and freedom to the people of God as part of their transition from the status of childhood under the old covenant to that of sonship under the new. But is this new freedom unrestricted? This question has once again become an explosive issue among Reformed churches today. Which songs or hymns are to be sung? What role, if any, do instruments and choirs play? These questions, however, take us ahead of our story. Over the course of the history of the Christian church one finds an impressive array of musical styles and complexities. The story of music in the church is not a simple one:

there is no single line of development, but rather a variety of artistic and philosophico-aesthetic considerations that have influenced the composition and performance of Christian music down through the ages.

Part of the difficulty in summarizing the history of music used in the service of the church lies in the nature of music itself as an expression of the human soul giving praise to God and crying out for help and deliverance. It is the difficulty of distinguishing between worship as life service to God encompassing all Christian endeavor and worship as corporate witness (see Rom 12:1–2 and Eph 5:15–20). Music sung in homes and out in the fields and marketplaces inevitably worked its way into the meetinghouses, the homes of the saints gathered for worship. The prayers and songs of God's people were shared in the context of everyday life and worship. Music was simple and from the heart. The songs of the faith were sung either unaccompanied or accompanied with instruments of various kinds. From the beginning instruments facilitated singing. The Ephesians text to which we have already referred speaks of hymns and psalms and spiritual songs. Biblical commentators are uncertain whether this text refers to three distinct types of musical composition or whether the terms are synonymous (as suggested by the ascriptions given to many of the Psalms). Presently, we lack precise knowledge of the musical terminology employed in ancient times. I suggest that these three terms—hymns, psalms, and spiritual songs—though distinct, nevertheless overlap one another. Hymns are poetic compositions, carefully crafted; psalms are those contained in the Book of Psalms or similar in kind; and spiritual songs characteristically find their origin in spontaneous utterance. Whatever the form, musical song was highly effective in the spread of the biblical faith, an important and exceedingly useful tool in Christian education and catechesis.

It was not until the time of the monastic movement that music began to take on a far more complex idiom, what is called *chant*. Since the early church, many "schools" of chant have developed, for example, Gregorian and Anglican. Common to the tradition of chant singing is the exercise of a distinct priestly office (whether served by monks or priests), including the formation of liturgical choirs functioning in many instances as a type of "priestly" caste. By the close of the sixth century church music was closely tied to the sacraments, especially the Eucharist. In the Roman Church the Mass had become a spectator event for parishioners. Only the ordained priesthood could fully participate in the Lord's Supper. And music served to adorn this "mystery" of the Christian faith and further the great chasm between clergy and laity.

Engaging Westminster Calvinism

By the eve of the Protestant Reformation what began as simple vocal chanting became complex polyphonic singing requiring intense training, skill, and virtuosity. In effect, music was taken away from the people in the pews. Corruption in doctrine and in worship prompted some branches of the Calvinistic tradition to abolish choirs and instruments altogether. In its attempts to reform worship according to the light of Scripture some Reformed churches practiced exclusive Psalm singing (so Calvin in Geneva and the Puritans in England, Scotland, and colonial America). It was one aspect of their application of what has come to be called the "regulative principle of worship" (see below). Both the Lutheran and the Anglican traditions occupied a middle ground between the practices of Catholics and Puritans. In the world of art and music the Renaissance movement climaxed in the age of the Baroque. By this time the Lutheran church had produced its greatest church musician in the person of Johann Sebastian Bach. Bach did for church music what the Westminster Divines did earlier for Reformed theology in their composition of the Westminster Confession of Faith and Catechisms, the epitome of Calvinist teaching during the age of the Protestant Reformation. These were culminating figures and events in this historical epoch. After Bach (1685–1750) and the Westminster Assembly (1648), the church entered the modern era. Protestant scholastic orthodoxy in the seventeenth and eighteenth centuries—both Lutheran and Reformed—served to consolidate the theological gains of the Reformation movement. Comparison has often been made between the intricacies of Protestant scholastic theology and the detailed nuances of Baroque art and music.

It was only a matter of time, however, before many Reformed congregations nurtured in the singing of the Psalms began to write new texts for sacred music through the introduction of scriptural hymns and oratorios based upon biblical narratives. The composers of such music are far too numerous to name, but the best known include Charles Wesley and Isaac Watts, George Frederick Handel and Felix Mendelssohn. Their work has forever transformed Reformed hymnody into the rich collection of biblical texts and musical compositions known the world around. And with the proliferation of hymn writing in particular came the need for trained choirs to assist the congregation in learning new music. Choral anthems became an extension of congregational song, another manifestation of the universal priesthood of believers. Music sung by congregation, choir, or vocal soloists were deemed appropriate in corporate worship (see 1 Cor 14:13–15,

26). The danger, however, is that music can all too readily become an occasion for churchly "entertainment." The cure, however, is not found in the elimination of choral and instrumental music, but rather in its careful use. Although the Protestant reformers may have responded appropriately to the abuses of the Roman church at that juncture in the church's history, the practice of exclusive Psalm singing was not sustainable over time. It had neither the express warrant of the New Testament nor the support of the people of God.

Protestantism has developed a rich array of musical tastes and forms. Among congregations of the Reformed tradition, Welsh Calvinists are noted for their unaccompanied four-part harmony, the English for the development of "cathedral" anthems and hymns (suited to the architecture and the acoustical space of their houses of worship). The employment of new varieties of musical styles was not welcomed in all places at all times. The story of music in the Christian church includes many accounts of conflict and unresolved tensions between congregations and within congregations. That legacy continues down to the present. The Christian Reformed Church and the Orthodox Presbyterian Church exemplify two very different approaches to art and music. Whereas the churchly edifices of Christian Reformed congregations are noted for their architectural design and aesthetics, as well as their appreciation for the pipe organ and the literature composed for it, Orthodox Presbyterians favor plainness in their places of worship and in their liturgy. In most instances, the simpler, the better. And a minority of OPC ministers favor exclusive Psalm singing. The primary factors shaping the distinctive ethos of each of these two Reformed communions are twofold: (1) financial resources, or the lack thereof; and (2) cultural and socio-theological considerations. With respect to the latter, the Genevan and Puritan practice of exclusive Psalm singing (accompanied or unaccompanied) serves to define the ecclesiastical identity of some members within the OPC. Interestingly, it is the Christian Reformed, not the Orthodox Presbyterian, who have shown greater appreciation for music and the fine arts. In contrast to both of these communions, the Presbyterian Church in America adopts a more eclectic approach to architecture, art, and music in the church. That reflects in part the diversity of its Reformed/evangelical heritage.

THEOLOGICAL APPRAISAL

Among the most prominent church musicologists of our day are Donald Hustad (Southern Baptist) and Paul Westermeyer (Lutheran). Though helpful and discerning in many respects, their work fails to articulate a Reformed philosophy of music and the arts. In this second part we offer a theological appraisal of issues important to the contemporary church, especially in the context of present-day social and religious upheaval in America. We begin by asking: What is the nature of corporate worship on the occasion of the weekly gathering of God's people? What did the Westminster Divines intend by adopting the "regulative principle" as that which governs weekly observance of the Christian Sabbath, the Lord's Day? (Here we must carefully distinguish between theological doctrine and the practical application of it in Puritan England, Old and New). Firstly, the saints of God are not at liberty to worship as they see fit. Rather, Christian worship is prescribed by God in the New Testament, just as worship was prescribed by God for Israel under the old covenant. Christian worship includes such elements as prayer, confession of sin, the singing of hymns, the presentation of offerings, the reading of the Scriptures, the exposition of the Word, and the (occasional) observance of the sacraments of baptism and the Lord's Supper. Greater liberty is granted on occasions of "informal" worship of the gathered congregation or small groups meeting in homes or elsewhere for various purposes (for example, Christian weddings and funerals, prayer and Bible studies). Liturgical forms and musical styles may vary at the discretion of the session which has been charged with the oversight of congregational worship and ministry. Prayers may be extemporaneous or prepared, liturgical or musical. The nature of Christian worship is doxological, the praise and service of the living and holy God present in the midst of his people who have gathered in the name of Christ. The observance of worship is distinctively trinitarian: the Father, the Son, and the Spirit are present and they alone are to be worshipped. The people's role is one of response to the Word of God read, sung, and expounded. That response includes the recitation of Scripture and creeds in prayer and in song.

Secondly, Christian worship, unlike worship under the old covenant, is characterized by a greater degree of liberty and spontaneity, though all is to be done decently and in good order (see 1 Cor 14:40). Music belongs to the people of God; they have the right as well as the privilege to render their voices in response to God's Word. And there is genuine room for cultural and artistic diversity in the church worldwide. Church architecture must reflect the prudent use of the congregation's financial resources, what is itself a spiritual exercise of godly stewardship. The use of music and the arts depends in large measure upon the cultural advance of the assembled congregation. Included here is the skillful, professional training of musicians and artisans employed in the service of the church. (This circumstance does not blur or obscure the biblical distinction between "holy" and "common" gifts bestowed by God upon creatures made in his own image and likeness.) Over the centuries biblical Christianity has manifested a variety of traditions which have produced many creeds, hymns, written prayers, and artistic symbols, all giving concrete expression to the living reality known as the people of God, which is the body of Christ. To the extent that a particular congregation or ecclesiastical communion is cut off from this ongoing tradition, whether intentionally or unintentionally, to that extent its worship experience will be impoverished. The Book of Revelation anticipates peoples of every kindred and tribe worshipping together the Lamb who was slain for sinners. Christian worship must presently strive to attain the unity of the faith. What does it mean to worship the Lord in the beauty of holiness? To be sure, there is a marked difference between the old and new economies of redemption. Formerly, outward symbolism and ritual had characterized worship among the OT saints. Now that outward display has given way to the inner realities of (S)piritual communion with Christ. The historical-covenantal transition from old to new covenants, however, does not necessitate the elimination of choirs, instruments, and artistic symbols. At the same time, the worship of God in the beauty of (his) holiness is not dependent upon any outward manifestation; true worship is an exclusively spiritual apprehension of the living God. Nor is there any particular virtue in plainness and austerity. Needless to say, the size, education, and cultural awareness, as well as the affluence of a given congregation will have a direct bearing upon worship practices. In sum, there is liberty within limits. Music and aesthetics are not for the purpose of creating a worshipful "mood," but rather of presenting our best in the worship of God, as in all other things. This requires the prudent and wise use of time, talent, and finances.

Lastly, the history of Christian worship (including music and the arts) has its roots in OT religion: here we must carefully discern both the continuities and discontinuities between the old and new testaments. The slow transition from old covenant to new covenant worship begins with the teaching ministry of Christ and continues on through the NT writings and well into post-canonical times (down to the present). Musical styles and forms will inevitably change within human cultures. Whatever virtue and grandeur are to be found in former days, corporate worship always and necessarily reflects the culture and times in which the people of God live. Maturity in the faith requires that we bear one another's burdens—the prayers and cries from the heart conveyed in musical song (see Gal 6:2).

8

Patriotic Music in Worship

THE REFORMED TRADITION HAS exhibited a range of thinking and practice regarding the use of patriotic music in corporate worship, just as it has given expression to diverse interpretations of the relationship between cult (religious worship) and culture (including freedom of expression in the public marketplace). Does the practice of free speech warrant the state's advocacy of civil religion (whatever the stripe)? And conversely, does this social freedom justify the church's promotion of the state as a quasi-confessional institution (citing the words "In God we trust" found on our currency)? The issue here does not call into question the biblical doctrine of the state as an institution ordained and governed by God through general providence over the course of human history (since the Fall), for good or for ill, but rather the misconception of the state as a confessional organism. It is the contention of this writer that the state, as a minister of divine justice and rule in the world, does not have the duty and responsibility to endorse the Christian religion (or any religion). Its God-ordained task is to protect and provide for its peoples (ensuring their general health and welfare), including the free expression of religious belief and practice by all living within its borders. Christian magistrates, in particular, and members of the body of Christ, in general, have not been given the mandate to establish true religion (i.e., biblical Christianity) as the confession of the state. At the same time, it is inappropriate for the church to confess the name of God (as an act of worship) while extolling the virtues of the nation (as in the lyrics, "My country, 'tis of thee, sweet land of liberty, of thee I sing," a representative patriotic hymn). The confessional church's allegiance is to God and to him alone. Of course, the community of faith in worship prays for governmental leaders and for the general well-being of the nation and nations of the world.

Civil religion, now as in the past, can only foster a distorted and erroneous conception of God, the sovereign Lord of the church, the Creator and Redeemer of humanity. What does true confession of faith mean for the topic addressed here in this essay? We begin by noting what constitutes a patriotic song and, then, proceed to offer reasons for its exclusion from the worship of God.

What Is a Patriotic Song?

It is a lyrical composition written to extol the virtues of the country to which one belongs and for the purpose of expressing one's allegiance to the nation. It is peculiarly focused upon one people and one nation. The text of the song describes the land and the people that inhabit it. It addresses the national consciousness. In contrast, the hymns and songs of the church are directed exclusively to God and they are means of instilling faith, hope, love, confidence in Christ, praise, adoration (and other graces) among the saints of God. Hymns in worship belong exclusively to the people of God wherever they meet. They are not, first and foremost, evangelistic tools aimed at reaching the unconverted (although that is the primary thrust of gospel songs so popular in the last century and a half).

Reasons for Excluding Patriotic Songs from Congregational Worship

The first reason follows from the above. The purpose of singing patriotic music is at variance with, but not in opposition to, witness to the gospel and worship that is exclusively God-centered. This exclusivity is what distinguishes a worshipping congregation from all other gathered peoples. Certainly the Bible calls us to honor those in civil authority and to pray for them. But that is altogether different from using patriotic music in worship.

The second reason may be more difficult to discern and comprehend. As members of the body of Christ, we cannot look to Old Testament practice and make a direct transfer from old to new covenant worship. The very question of the relationship between the two testaments is itself a difficult and complex subject. My comments must be brief. (For further reflection on this subject and other related matters, see my *Covenant Theology in Reformed Perspective*).

In the wilderness of Sinai ancient Israel was constituted by God a special, holy nation—what is properly described as a theocracy. No other nation in the world at that time down to the present was singled out as was Israel of old. This nation was closely identified with the kingdom of God. Since the coming of Christ, no nation, including Israel, now occupies a special place among the nations. In the body of Christ, there is neither Jew nor Greek. We are all one in Christ. No longer is there a comparable holy, geopolitical entity on the face of the earth. (Theocratic Israel *symbolized* the new covenant people of God, a holy nation of spiritual priests and kings.)

As a theocracy, ancient Israel was in a unique position—divinely constituted and divinely ordered. So long as Israel was faithful and obedient, that is, so long as Israel kept the law of Moses, she was promised blessing and prosperity in the land of Canaan. God was painting a portrait in time, in history—in anticipation of the new and better covenant in Christ's blood. The Psalmist declares: "Blessed is the nation whose God is the Lord" (Ps 33:12). That affirmation of faith belongs exclusively to Israel of old. It does not pertain to each and every nation. (This verse, like the teachings of the Old Testament as a whole, must be interpreted in the light of the teachings of the New Testament.)

The nation-states of this world have been instituted by God; nothing occurs in human government that is not under the sovereign rule and control of God. However, the state—with the exception of ancient Israel—has not been granted authority to maintain or enforce religion. The state is not a confessing body; its role is purely civil, not religious. Of course, it is appropriate and dutiful for Christian politicians to testify to their faith and to deliberate all political and social matters in the light of the teachings of the Bible. (The same is true for Christians working in every arena and vocation in life.) The legitimate separation of church and state as distinct institutions ordained by God does not preclude Christian testimony and witness bearing in the marketplace, in the classroom, or elsewhere.

Concluding Remarks

Are Christians free to sing and perform patriotic music? Of course they are. All in its proper place and time. To be sure, Christians have a duty to honor and respect civil leaders and to pray for the welfare of the nation. Are there times when patriotic songs should not be sung? Are there occasions when Christians must voice dissent? Such a time arises when there are blatant offenses committed by a nation against God or humanity. Recall the atrocities committed against the Jews. Should a German Christian extol the virtues of his country in such times? I think not. (See the "Barmen Declaration," as one of the historic confessions of the Reformed church, however one finally assesses its theological "system.")

Can Christians gather together to sing patriotic songs? Yes, but not as the community of faith in worship. In general, singing and playing patriotic music in concert halls, in sports arenas, in shopping malls, in outdoor parks is certainly appropriate and healthy for any nation—without, however, identifying the group as a religious, confessional body. To do so is to confuse the two distinct realms of church and state. Compare the (mistaken) medieval notion of "Christendom," a notion that lingers in many modern-day societies. We honor Christ by singing his praises, and in so doing reserve the singing of patriotic hymns to their own rightful place. "Render to Caesar the things that belong to Caesar, and to God the things that belong to God" (Luke 20:25).

9

A Brief Interpretive History of Music in the Service of the Church

CHRISTIAN HYMN/SONGWRITING COVERS A wide gamut, including various styles of musical and lyrical composition. All music is written in a particular historical and cultural context, hence the differing styles. Church hymnals contain music and lyrics from the earliest centuries of Christianity, even reaching back to the first millennium before Christ, notably, the Psalms of David. One of the oldest styles of music in the church is plainsong (or chant). The well-loved hymn "When I Survey the Wondrous Cross" is based on a Gregorian chant, dating to the seventh century. This hymn text, so appropriate for Lent or the observance of the Lord's Supper, lends itself to the somewhat somber style of chanting. Musical composition creates the context or "mood"—be it meditative or celebratory. Very different from this hymn is the song by James Ward, "On the First Day." Interestingly, it too is written in a (modern) chant style—to be sung in unison, with the addition of instrumental accompaniment. Rhythmically, these two songs are very different. Each is an effective composition, appropriate for the lyrics.

Singing conveys a broad spectrum of human emotion. The salvation Christ has wrought calls forth many responses from those who have been made the beneficiaries of his saving grace—from confession of sin to exaltation of God's mighty power, love, and mercy. As one noted church musicologist has remarked, "Enthusiastic congregational singing, which arises from positive spiritual commitment, may be a dimension far more important than the musical idiom."[1] Worship transcends our own time and our

---

1. Wilson-Dickson, *Story of Christian Music*, 244.

own personal preferences. The Bible, though an ancient text, still speaks. And the music we sing in the church is written for the purpose of impressing upon our hearts and minds God's spoken Word to us. The hymns and songs of the church embody the testimony of the saints, past and present.

It is important to remember that the congregation renders songs old and new as witness to the *oneness of the people of God through time and space*, as a witness to the people of God from ancient times to the return of Christ in glory. Along with creeds, prayers, theological and devotional writings, the songs of the church are part of an exceedingly rich heritage. As members of the Body of Christ we are part of a spiritual community extending around the world, encompassing people of every nation and spanning all historical epochs (see Heb 12:22–24).[2]

> How good and how pleasant it is for brothers and sisters to dwell together in unity. . . . It is like the dew of Hermon coming down upon the mountains of Zion; for there the Lord commanded the blessing, life forever. (Ps 133:1, 3)

The Early Church

The picture is not entirely clear as to the appropriation of music in Christian worship in the earliest decades since Pentecost. We do know that synagogue worship played a significant role in shaping the assembly of Christians in corporate worship in the first century. Many of the basic "elements" of worship—such as the reading (and teaching) of Scripture, prayer, and singing—were already in place. The lyrics of congregational song were drawn from Israel's hymnbook, the Book of Psalms, known from memory. The practice of Psalm singing, consequently, was a staple in religious worship from the very earliest of times. The use of instruments, however, is less clear.

To be sure, choir and instrumental accompaniment were explicitly commanded for worship in the Solomonic temple, what was a type of spiritual worship in the true Sanctuary of God in heaven. The availability of

---

2. Substituting gospel songs or contemporary praise music for the "traditional" hymns of the church (as means of "evangelistic" outreach) is not a genuine option among the worshipping community. One must exercise discernment in the selection of these songs. Especially in the case of contemporary praise songs, the lyrics, more often than not, are trite and focused on the individual (rather than upon superlative work of God in Christ set forth in the biblical text). This note stands as a reminder that the hymns and songs of the church must be thoroughly grounded in the teaching of Scripture.

instruments in the ancient world was limited, though the use of instruments to accompany singing in both the secular and religious culture of the day was by no means uncommon. However, associations of music with sensual, religiously perverse practices and beliefs gave rise to suspicion regarding instrumental accompaniment in worship (the same suspicion would again appear, to some degree, in the time of the Protestant Reformation).

Despite this circumstance, the composition of new hymns and songs appeared at the very outset of Christianity, some of them recorded or alluded to in the writings of the New Testament. Singing the praises of Christ was a spontaneous response of the saints. More importantly, the singing of the Psalms was deemed insufficient for the new covenant people of God. Indeed, the use of the Psalms in the church, whether sung or spoken, are in need of paraphrasing for the sake of the proclamation of the Gospel as revealed by the risen Christ (see, e.g., Luke 24:27). The Psalms were written in a specific historico-covenantal context, one that has changed dramatically with the coming of Christ and the establishment of the new covenant. Our singing of the Psalms must reflect this new reality, viz., the eschatological nature of true worship. Here we must take into consideration the transition from shadow (type) to reality (John 4:24).

By the close of the seventh century the dominant style of Christian singing was plainsong. Variations on chant singing are found within the diverse Christian communities. This would continue to be the case as the church moved through the period of the Middle Ages and into modern times. (Christian chant includes, for example, Ambrosian, Gregorian, Byzantine, Russian, and Anglican). From the earliest times, instrumental accompaniment was frequently seen as competing with unison singing—corporate singing "with one voice"—hence the reticence concerning their use in worship.

Church Artifice in the Medieval Period

Since the time of Constantine, an unholy alliance between church and state had begun to emerge. This alliance would continue to grow in strength and opposition to one another well into the twentieth century, when it would be seriously challenged in the experience of the New World, as elsewhere in the modern age. The union of church and state in the religious, socio-political culture of the medieval world culminated in what is know as

"Christendom." It is this that serves as the historical setting for the Protestant Reformation in the sixteenth century.

Which was the higher power, the ecclesiastical or the civil? Both realms, vying for preeminence, sought to establish its dominance in society and politics. Christian communities devoted great time and money building impressive, towering cathedrals to embody the religious symbolism of a former age—after the pattern of the Solomonic temple, including many of the worship practices of the ancient Israelite theocracy. With the introduction of the stone cathedrals came the rise of scholasticism, a monument of another sort. Complex, sophisticated, even esoteric musical composition was closely associated with worship in the medieval cathedral. All of these developments were earthly attempts to capture the beauty, grandeur, and mystery of God as revealed to humankind. The result was worship that was more symbolic than substantive (i.e., the eschatological realization of the saints worshipping in "Spirit and truth").

It was in this period that the organ, as we now know it, was conceived and employed in the service of the church. The earliest "organs" were handheld instruments; they would become the "king of instruments," in terms of size, splendor, and versatility. No other musical instrument would match the organ in its ability to support congregational or choral singing. The design of organ sound produced by the movement of air through pipes of various sizes, shapes, and material (each producing a distinct sound complementing the entire ensemble) could best blend with the human voice. Hence, the sound of the organ is, first and foremost, associated with "cathedral" or church music. (For some in the contemporary praise movement, the organ is a relic of a past era. This opinion, however, is based upon prejudice, not informed musical understanding.)

The intricacies of musical composition in the medieval church, both vocally and instrumentally, made it impossible for the average worshipper to participate in the singing of the liturgy of the emerging cathedral-tradition, complicated by the fact that services were conducted in ecclesiastical Latin. Only the clergy and (priestly) choir could enact the mysteries of the Christian faith, climaxing in the observance of the Mass. Rome taught the doctrine of the transubstantiation of ordinary bread and wine into the literal body and blood of Jesus Christ. The Protestant reformers rightly viewed this interpretation of the sacrament as blasphemous and ludicrous. Additionally, the laity could not partake of the communion elements, for fear of desecration of the body of Christ. The common people could not be trusted to handle worthily the ultimate (tangible) substance of the faith! Perverse was much of the theology and ecclesiastical accouterments in medieval Catholicism. In this context, the popularity of carols sung outside the church stood in sharp contrast to ecclesiastical choral music.

The Impact of the Renaissance and Reformation

The reformation of the church, begun in earnest in the sixteenth century, set about to reform Christian doctrine along two vital fronts: (1) what came to be called the "material principle" of Scripture, the doctrine of justification by faith alone; and (2) the "formal principle," the doctrine of Scripture as the unique, infallible, and authoritative Word of God. Based on these two principles of interpretation the entire corpus of biblical teaching was reformulated, including the reformation of corporate worship. By the close of the Reformation age in the mid-seventeenth century the final product of this monumental labor was known as *orthodox Protestant scholasticism*. It is here, however, that the two major branches of Protestantism, the Lutheran and the Reformed (at least a major part of the Reformed wing), parted ways. Major differing views included the doctrine of the Lord's Supper, worship liturgy, and evaluations of many aspects of Roman Catholic practice known as adiaphora ("things indifferent"). Parenthetically, the Roman Catholic Church in the time of the Counter-Reformation called for new level of seriousness with regard to church music; at the same time, however, it failed to give music back to the congregation. It remained an exercise of the professionals.

Part of the broader context of the Protestant Reformation was the movement known as Christian humanism (notably, the rediscovery of ancient art, language and literature—Christian, pre-Christian, and non-Christian). This movement, in turn, was part of the renaissance in education and artistic expression, notably in painting, sculpture, architecture, and music. The love of knowledge and learning served as the catalyst for a new rigorous and demanding scholarship that would be unprecedented in intellectual history. No longer would the dogmas of the Roman Catholic Church be sufficient for the establishment of Christian doctrine and practice. Freedom from the dictates of the established church provided inquirers the occasion and incentive to search out the Scriptures without fear of punishment. The acquisition of liberty, however, came only at a great price and only after an extended period of time.

The opulence of the cathedral churches at the time of the Reformation was largely the product of the Renaissance movement (included here is the revival of gothic architecture). The outward splendor and glory of the houses of worship were seen in their buildings, religious paintings and sculpture, and in their complex, ornate musical compositions. Together, all of these creations helped create a sense of overwhelming mystery and awe. Some of the Protestant reformers (over)reacted by destroying much, if not all, of the artistic works in these places of worship. Where possible, the interior and exterior of church buildings were stripped of their accouterments, much of it dismissed as popish and idolatrous. Service music was reduced to unaccompanied Psalm singing, notably, among the Zwinglians and Calvinists. Stained glass windows were destroyed, organs dismantled. Here lay the seeds of austerity in worship associated with many sectors of the Reformed and Presbyterian ecclesiastical tradition. Arguably, abuses in practice did not warrant this extreme response, decadent and idolatrous though much of Roman Catholic worship had become. Corrupt practices do not invalidate the legitimate use of choral and instrumental accompaniment. And it is certainly mistaken to argue that "the Reformed position" on music and arts in the church is that held by Calvin, the English Puritans, and the Dutch Precisionists. They represent only one Reformed point of view—a position, I maintain, lacking scriptural support. (Here is not the place to articulate a biblical theology of music and the arts.)

The practice of exclusive, unaccompanied Psalm singing was, perhaps, the way of least resistance. With respect to the critical concerns facing the church, the Reformers rightly focused attention on the weightier doctrinal and moral issues of the day. Return to the writings of the early church fathers provided reasons and justification for implementing the singing of the Psalms. The need for new renderings of the psalms and new metrical paraphrases led to the adoption of contemporary tunes, carols, and melodies. Of particular distinction was the Protestant hymn-chorale. This is new genre of congregational song would serve as the catalyst for the composition of other musical forms and song-lyrics based on the biblical text. Above all, this development in musical composition was viewed as means of instructing and catechizing the faithful.

A Brief Interpretive History of Music in the Service of the Church

Developments in the Revolutionary Age

The great upheavals that occurred in the aftermath of the Protestant Reformation led to massive shifts in social, political, religious, and intellectual thinking. During this period of time the gilded age of the Baroque was a time of consolidation in cultural, artistic, and intellectual pursuits (especially in the refinements found within Protestant scholasticism). Both in the Enlightenment and in deism man became the measure of all things. Rising nationalism would lead to a new imperialism and expansionism, especially in the New World. The democratic spirit of the American and French revolutions ultimately would have a significant impact on many nations and peoples well into the twentieth and twenty-first centuries. Of special note in this historical epoch was the variety of governance and worship in Christian communities. Differing views regarding the adiaphora and liturgical forms used in corporate worship impacted the observance of rites and customs among the Protestant churches. The new spirit of democracy was to become most evident within the independent Baptist tradition. Lutheranism and Anglicanism granted less freedom to local congregations.

The explosion in artistic creativity, employed in the service of the church, was something altogether new in the history of Christianity; it manifested itself in terms of variety and complexity. This was the age that produced (arguably) the greatest composer of all time, Johann Sebastian Bach.[3] It was the age of George Frederick Handel and numerous other creative luminaries in the field of music. Regrettably, in much of Anglican worship there was the loss of simplicity in Christian worship and, more importantly, loss of congregational participation. Those who "performed" worship were the clergy and the highly trained professionals. Both in theology and in music the preferred language in many quarters had long been ecclesiastical Latin. Happily, by the close of the Reformation age in England and in Germany much more the singing was done in the native tongue, English or German. Musical settings included the Mass, requiems, cantatas and passions (notably those of Bach utilizing Lutheran chorales), oratorios (inspired by the Italian operatic style), and the composition of motets and anthems based on psalms, hymns, and various other biblical and sacred texts. While English cathedral anthems, or high art, flourished throughout the realm, such was not the case in the country churches. The popularity of

---

3. Bach's *Mass* (of which there are many) functions as a prayer of confession, as a creedal statement, and as song of praise; sections of the mass may include the *kyrie*, *gloria*, Nicene Creed, *sanctus* and benediction, and the *agnus dei*.

the English anthem is to be explained in terms of its less complex nature, in contrast to the Latin motet.

Anglicans, and to a lesser extent Lutherans, gave special place to the composition of musical settings for the Mass and for the observance of Evensong, which included settings of the *Magnificat* and the *Nunc dimittis*.[4] (Many of these compositions, as well as the popular English cathedral anthems, concluded with the singing of the words of the Doxology.) The subsequent rise of Anglo-Catholicism reintroduced medieval, Latin church music, notably, plainsong. (In the Anglo-Catholic tradition the choir serves a distinctly priestly function.) Dutch Calvinists were something of a peculiarity in this period of the church's reformation in worship. Their fascination with the sound and the versatility of the pipe organ made them leaders in the field of organ building. Their zeal was only matched by their love for metrical Psalms. Out of this came an impressive organ repertoire based on the Psalms. By the time of the nineteenth century, the evangelical/fundamentalist branches of the Presbyterian, Wesleyan, and Baptist traditions had become rather well entrenched in their provincial musical tastes and understandings, unlike congregations in the Lutheran and Anglican communions. For the former, spirituality and authenticity in worship were more often than not expressed in songs and prayers that were spontaneous and simple, from the heart.

Modernism and Its Plurality of Voices

The advent of the modern period has given birth to a great array of cultural movements yielding yet other artistic styles and forms. Music, at once harmonious and dissident, reflected the modern social habits, tastes and sensibilities—as well as serving as a vehicle for conflicting religious-philosophical viewpoints. Unbridled Romanticism gave birth to certain forms of Impressionism, and ultimately Abstractionism. The cacophony of

---

4. The *Magnificat* and *Nunc dimittis* celebrate the birth narratives, emphasizing the incarnation, rather than the Easter narratives (Christ's resurrection/glorification). What was typological under the old covenant has been sacramentalized in the Anglo-Catholic tradition (with its use of incense and liturgical-priestly vestments and actions). And in the Anglican tradition the homily substitutes for expository preaching of Scripture—the eclipse of Word by sacrament (and music). The text of *Locus Iste* (settings by Anton Bruckner and Richard DeLong, among others) reads: "This place is made by God, an inestimable sacrament without reproach. Amen." (This is the Gradual at Mass for the dedication of a church.)

A Brief Interpretive History of Music in the Service of the Church

voices in the church is reflected in her music and arts. No one style would come to dominate. Alongside the classical tradition stood the ethnic, folk, and popular music of the day, including the spirituals. All of this would be incorporated into the musical tastes of Christian worship. Whereas the tradition of Anglican choral music continued to flourish in episcopal churches across America, many Presbyterian churches adopted the use of semi-professional adult choirs and chamber singers for the singing of more complex and difficult works and for leading the congregation in song.[5] One of the catalysts for renewed interest in America for church choral music was the establishment of such institutions as the Westminster Choir College (Presbyterian) and the music department at St. Olaf College (Lutheran). Before long, Protestant evangelical seminaries began to offer courses in church music and education. Such was the case particularly among the Southern Baptists.[6]

The origin of the gospel song lies in the revival movements of the nineteenth century, made popular in the latter part of the twentieth century by the Billy Graham crusades. More significantly for our day, it was the countercultural movements of the 1960s that would produce a new style of Christian music, known as Contemporary Praise Music. Rejecting traditional forms and liturgies of the established churches, this movement set out to design its own style of worship, giving free reign to spontaneity and self-expression (accompanied by the discrediting of the creedal and

---

5. Anglican liturgy offers a predictable structure and unity to corporate worship in its communion. Presbyterians encourage free style, determined by the discretion of the local church. Presbyterianism is a voluntary religious society that gives greater place to individualism, thus reflecting a wider spectrum of styles and levels of aesthetic (musical) imagination.

6. In a curious writing, "Skyscrapers and Cathedrals" (in *The Gospel and the Modern World and Other Short Writings*), J. Gresham Machen reflects on Christian art and architecture as a religious and *cultural* symbol. Concerning the great cathedrals of the past, he speaks of them as "a living expression of the human soul," adding, "when every carving in every obscure corner, never, perhaps, to be seen by human eye, was an act of worship of Almighty God" (45). Unlike the "magnificently ugly" (yet impressive) city of New York, seen from the top of the Empire State Building, Machen yearned for an architectural feat in the modern world like that in the medieval age giving expression to the glory, grandeur, and worship of God. Somewhat uncharacteristically, Machen here confuses (religious) cult and (secular) culture. To be sure, there is a beauty to the City of Man in outward display, as a reflection of the glory of God. But the medieval age, like other ages of human civilization, confounded religious and cultural symbol in the building of the City of Man. Symbols and stylization change according to the times. Art and architecture acquire meaning from their place, role and functionality in society.

confessional statements of the church). The Presbyterian *Trinity Hymnal*, illustrative of confessional collections of Christian songs used in worship, reflects all of these styles. (Contemporary praise music is quite limited, largely due to the space requirements for this style of music on the printed page.) America, a melting pot of many peoples and races, has brought the global community to her doorsteps. Above all, the challenge for Christian congregations, wherever God has formed them, is to glorify the name and works of God in a manner pleasing to him—that is, in accordance to his Word. God's people are called to be a people united in Spirit and in truth, a spiritual edifice built upon the foundations of the apostles and prophets. The church of Christ holds a prophetic role in the world; unity in doctrine and practice remain the order of the day. Musical style is reflective of the cultural preferences that come to dominant the times in which the gathered saints worship.

Closing Thoughts

Needless to say, the writing of "psalms and hymns and spiritual songs" for the edification of believers in corporate worship is an ongoing enterprise and spiritual discipline. Musical settings of lyrics faithful to the teaching of the Bible is itself one of the fruits of the Spirit's work in the midst of his people. It is the Spirit of God who is the Author of artistic expression. True art in all of its forms is one of the distinguishing features of humankind made in God's image. Art that is good and true—including hymn/songwriting—requires aesthetic discrimination; it requires the selection of styles and idioms appropriate for Christian worship. Not all forms are conducive to the spirit of reverence and awe. Chiefly, music in the church is a ministry of the Word, one that impresses biblical truth upon the hearts and minds of the faithful, giving praise to God and offering thanksgiving and laments to him in song.

It must be remembered that music in the service of the church is not "performance music" or entertainment; it is spiritual worship. The Bible commands us to "worship God in the beauty of holiness" (1 Chr 16:29; Ps 29:2; 96:9): This means that our focus and our participation in worship must be directed exclusively to God, who as Creator/Redeemer of heaven and earth is altogether holy, righteous, and transcendent. Beauty and holiness are attributes (i.e., characteristics) of God. Earthly, artistic replicas of divine beauty serve to point us to God whom we alone worship. In the final analysis, the selection of appropriate music for corporate worship reflects the congregation's artistic and aesthetic discernment and sensibilities. This side of heaven, total agreement among Christians remains elusive. The employment of music in the church serves multiple purposes: the glorification of God, the edification of the saints (as catechetical instruction set to music), and witness to the nations. Music as one of God's great gifts has the power to arouse human emotion and thought.[7] In an oft-cited quotation John Calvin remarked that music "has great strength and power to move and to set our hearts on fire in order that we may call upon God and praise [God] with a more vehement and more ardent zeal." Likewise, Martin Luther concluded: "Music is a fair and glorious gift of God. I am strongly persuaded that after theology there is no art that can be placed on a level with music."

---

7. As Paul Westermeyer notes: "Music is also the means to *interpret a text*" (*Te Deum*, 28)—preferably, "a means" of interpreting the text of Scripture, one that is different in nature and function from the spoken word. Music is also an aid to memory. Recommended readings include: Dyrness, *Visual Faith* and *Reformed Theology and Visual Culture Protestant Imagination from Calvin to Edwards*; Routley, *Church Music and the Christian Faith*; Joby, *Calvinism and the Arts*; Farley, "What Is 'Biblical' Worship?"; Witvliet, "Church Music, Congregational Life, and Theological Education in Harmony; Wolterstorff, "Choir and Organ"; and Leaver, "Motive and Motif in the Church Music of Johann Sebastian Bach" (in this essay Leaver points out Bach's musical setting for the doctrine of the Trinity—e.g., three oboes, three-voice fugue, and the prominent Lutheran/Protestant Law/Gospel theme).

10

Theological Reflections on Church Music, Arts, and Architecture

THE YEAR 2009 MARKED the 500th anniversary of the birth of John Calvin, the most formative Reformed theologian from the time of the Protestant Reformation in the sixteenth century down to the present. No one since the close of the New Testament canon has had a greater impact upon Western civilization and culture than has Calvin. But that legacy in Western society has changed dramatically in the last fifty years or more. And change is rapidly coming to the Reformed churches as pressures continue to be exerted to conform to the spirit (culture) of this world. It is the duty of Christians, faithful to Christ and his teachings, to uphold the Word of truth and to live out the biblical life and ethic in the face of mounting opposition and ridicule. One of the many achievements of Calvin, alongside other Protestant reformers, was the return of Christian worship to its biblical principles. No longer would worship be based upon human traditions (good or bad), but solely upon the Word of God. This has been termed the "regulative principle" of worship.

What governs the shape and content of corporate worship is the revelation of God in Holy Scripture (specifically, in the New Testament canon which is regulative of the life and faith of the covenant community in the period between the advents of Christ). Under Calvin's oversight Christian worship once again became captive to God's Word. We gather together weekly to worship not in a way that suits our whims or desires (what "feels good," or what we think might be pleasing to God). God himself summons us to worship him as his people—by means of the Word and the Spirit. True worship is a manifestation of God's redemptive action in the world—calling sinners out of darkness into the light of the Gospel of Jesus Christ, gathering the elect from all corners of the earth. *Although certain cultural traits will be reflected among particular ethnic peoples, nevertheless, corporate worship will manifest an underlying similarity for all those called out of the world and adopted into God's family. This commonness is determined by Scripture.* According to the New Testament, the basic elements of worship include singing God's praises, offering up prayers and supplications, confession of sins personal and corporate (and the declaration of pardon), offering a portion of our financial resources into God's storehouse, the reading of Scripture, observance of the sacraments of baptism and the Lord's Supper, and the preaching of the Word by one ordained to the office of teaching elder.[1] It is the Spirit-filled saints who are inwardly renewed and empowered to declare God's praises, to worship him in Spirit and truth.

Reformation in doctrine led to one of the major alterations in worship, namely, the observance of the Lord's Supper. Architecturally speaking, the preaching pulpit became central, not the altar (the place of sacrifice). The "Mass," or "Eucharist" as it is also called, is neither an actual nor a symbolic (re)sacrifice of the body of Christ. Instead, it is *a memorial of Christ's once-for-all, unrepeatable sacrifice on Calvary.* As a genuine means of grace, God communes with his covenant people in the Supper by faith, as a ministration of the Spirit. Only those regenerated by the Spirit of God partake *spiritually* of the gracious benefits of the Supper.

The second major departure from Roman tradition came about as a result of Calvin's rethinking on the place of music and art in corporate

---

1. In the Anglican tradition the homily substitutes for expository preaching as practiced in the Presbyterian communion. What one finds in Anglican worship is the eclipse of the preached Word by the sacrament of the Mass, accompanied by choral music usually of a high caliber. Other (high church) accouterments include incense, liturgical-priestly vestments, and ritual acts. What was typological under the old covenant has been sacramentalized in the Anglo-Catholic tradition. A staple in the observance of Evensong are arrangements of the *Magnificat* and *Nunc dimittis*, focusing upon the birth narratives rather than the Easter narratives. Here again, we see an emphasis upon the old covenant ministration. In contrast the Eastern Orthodox tradition focuses upon the resurrection/glorification of Christ—God's glory is the theme. A classic choral text, named *Locus iste*, is the following: "This place is made by God, an inestimable sacrament without reproach. Amen" (commonly used in the Gradual at Mass for the dedication of a church).

In the Lutheran tradition the Masses of Johann Sebastian Bach, for example, function as prayers of confession, as a creedal statement of Christian faith, and as meditations in praise and supplication. The parts of the Mass include such as the following: the *kyrie*, *gloria*, Nicene Creed, *sanctus* and hosanna, ending with the *agnus dei*.

worship.[2] Calvin was, above all, a student of the Bible. He loved and cherished God's Word, and he set his mind and heart upon faithfulness to God's teachings in all facets of his pastoral ministry. To understand Calvin's view on the role of music and art in worship we must recall the practice of worship in the Roman Catholic Church at the time of the Protestant Reformation. Firstly, there were the magnificent buildings erected throughout Europe in the medieval period (notably between the eleventh and fifteenth centuries). The cathedrals were the focus of every town and city in which they were built.[3] (The steeple was the highest point in the physical landscape.) All life—social, cultural, religious, and political—revolved around the church, Roman or Orthodox. Upon entering the cathedral, one experienced a taste of heaven on earth by means of the visual and aural senses, light filtered through stained glass windows, the aroma of incense (symbolic of the prayers of the saints), and the ethereal sound of the choir singing highly complex forms of polyphonic music, notably the works of great Renaissance composers such as William Bryd and Giovanni Palestrina. Worship became more a spectacular display than a spiritual exercise of converted saints. Secondly, the tongue of the Roman Church was Latin, understood only by the learned few. All the "action" was performed by the clergy and the religious cast (including choristers and acolytes). Thirdly, there was the mandatory "taxation" for access to the church's sacraments, which were seven in number (baptism, Eucharist, penance, confirmation, marriage, holy orders, and extreme unction). It was Luther who decried the sale of indulgences as an abuse of church power and authority, as well as a corruption of God's way of salvation (by grace through faith alone—apart from all works of the law, the "doing of the law" viewed as an instrumental means of the sinner's justification).

Calvin and his fellow reformers gave worship back to the people. All that was spoken and sung was in the vernacular tongue; icons and statues

---

2. Anglicanism found a middle ground between the Roman and Genevan practice. Anglican liturgy offers a predictable structure and unity to corporate worship in its communion. In contrast, Presbyterians for the most part encourage free style, determined by the discretion of the local church. The Presbyterian communion is considered a voluntary religious society that gives greater place to individualism, thus reflecting in its corporate worship a much wider spectrum of musical styles and levels of aesthetic imagination. Over the course of Presbyterianism, those who moved away from exclusive, unaccompanied Psalm singing (on biblical grounds) joined others Protestants in expanding the repertoire of Christian songs and hymns.

3. See Machen, "Skycrapers and Cathedrals," in *Gospel and the Modern World and Other Short Writings*.

of Mary, Jesus, and venerated saints were removed from the site of worship. The worshipper was to gaze upon Christ through spiritual eyes of faith. Also forbidden were church choirs (at the same time, organs were destroyed); incense and other accessories of Roman worship were likewise abandoned. In its place, Calvin reintroduced (exclusive) unaccompanied Psalm singing, a very ancient practice in the Christian church, a practice that actually originated in Jewish synagogues during the time of the Babylonian exile several hundred years prior to Christ's birth. Where feasible in those cathedrals and churches taken over by Protestants, the pulpit became the visual center of the worship space. The table of the Lord's Supper was placed down (lower) in front of the pulpit. Once choirs were reintroduced within many Protestant communions, the choristers sang (preferably, but not always) from the rear gallery. In the later Puritan tradition, the English branch of Calvinism, worship was marked by simplicity—the worship place was a very plain, austere room. Happily, this strand of Calvinist thinking was not shared by the majority of Reformed Protestants, past or present.

We can credit Calvin with the reclamation of biblical worship in all its essentials, even though we may differ with him concerning some of the austere measures he implemented in his reform efforts (what we deem to be an overreaction to the abuses in Roman practice). There is a place for vocal groups and instruments in worship; art also has a contribution to make when employed with discernment (and proper education).[4] Christ has given us a *new song* to sing. For this very reason, the Psalms are no longer sufficient for Christian praise and worship (on this subject, Calvin and other proponents of exclusive Psalm singing erred in their interpretation of Scripture). More broadly, the regulative principle of worship is applied in accordance with what some reformers identified as the "light

---

4. Through the centuries music has served prominently as a means of religious expression (including Christian education). Since early times music had also became domesticated and commercialized for entertainment purposes. But music in the church has, above all, served to promote Christian faith and practice; from there Christian song moved into homes and into the marketplace (note especially the rise of commercialism in the Christian music beginning in the late twentieth century). The function of music in corporate worship is not to energize and arouse the passions, to usher worshippers into an ecstatic state, but rather to direct the praises of God's people to him, in exclusive homage to the triune God as revealed in Scripture. God's covenantal Word is central in all parts of corporate worship. Music in worship is also for the edification of the saints (Col 3:16). Where there is the use of drums and other rhythm instruments in worship, care must be exercised so that the rhythm is enhanced, but not controlling. For further study, see Jones, *Singing and Making Music*.

of nature," what pertains to the general ordering and government of the church as a local fellowship and communion of believers (and as a voluntary society). It should be noted in passing that Calvin himself greatly relished and promoted artistic expression as a gift of the God of all creation. As God's image-bearer, human beings engage in an array of creative arts, even though Calvin believed much of this was to be severely limited, or proscribed in the context of corporate worship. This brief overview serves to point out that down through the ages of church history there has been diversity of thinking with respect to the role of music and art in the context of Christian worship. What is absolutely vital, conducive to true spirituality, and healthy for the corporate worship and witness of the saints, is commitment to the Word of God as that which informs all we do in the exercise of our faith and obedience to our Redeemer and Lord.

Excursus

Presbyterian Versus Anglican Practice: Two Views on Church Music

A trip to London often includes attendance at Evensong in one or both of London's two most notable churches, Westminster Abbey (where the royal family marks special occasions in the life of the British Crown) and Saint Paul's Cathedral (a massive building designed by the famous architect Sir Christopher Wren). The visitor and worshipper alike are in awe of the beauty of the worship space and of the music sung by the equally famous men and boy choirs (the former called the "Gentlemen of the Choir," the latter the "trebles"). It is worthwhile and helpful to explain some of the differences between Anglican worship (in cathedral or church) and worship in the Presbyterian communion.

Presbyterian worship does not incorporate a "high" liturgy; that is to say, Presbyterians do not utilize set forms (notably fixed prayers, psalms and chants sung mostly by highly trained and highly skilled musicians). Nor in each and every service of Sunday morning worship do Presbyterians observe the Lord's Supper (called "Mass" in high churches). Rather, Presbyterians give focus to the Word preached and to music sung by the congregation (with assistance by choral leadership that has prepared the music in advance of the service). Additionally, most Presbyterian congregations prefer amateur vocalists in choir and praise teams drawn from the membership of the church, rather than paid professionals—this for the sake of fully involving the congregation in worship and witness to the Word. Music in the church, rightly understood, places the privilege and the responsibility for singing God's praises and for lifting up songs of lament/supplication upon the worshippers. Music that is pleasing to God is never "performance," although vocalists and instrumentalists who help lead the congregation in song need to prepare well, offering the best of their God-given musical talents for the glory of God. (Unless there is talent to be utilized in worship leadership, there would be no need for choirs or praise teams. Musical talent properly exercised in the church provides encouragement and support for strong, vibrant congregational singing.)

"Church cathedral music" is uniquely created for the acoustical space of the cathedral or large church. The Anglican view of choir and liturgical worship is drawn from the Old Testament—from the Levitical practice of ancient Israel in the time of the old Mosaic economy. Presbyterian doctrine, on the other hand, teaches that the Levitical practice is neither requisite nor commended for the worshipping saints under the new covenant established by Jesus Christ. Theologically speaking, form gives way to substance—or more accurately, shadow gives way to reality. The temple of Solomon (and its worship experience), grand and glorious as it was, and appropriate as it was for its time and place, has been superseded by the living temple of God, which is the Spirit of Christ himself dwelling in the very midst of the new covenant community. (The *Shekinah* glory in Old Testament times symbolized the greater glory of God to be revealed in the latter Day, the Day inaugurated at Pentecost.) Worship in the Solomonic temple was designed to create a distance between God and the worshipper entering the sanctuary in awe and fear. New covenant worship accentuates the intimacy of Father and his adopted family. Rather than turning the clock back to the day of symbolism and ritual in the Old Testament, Presbyterians take delight in the praises of God uttered from lips of Spirit-filled sons and daughters, those freely and graciously adopted into the family of God. By his grace new covenant worshippers have been freed from the terrors of the Law. In the words of the hymn "Let Us Love and Sing and Wonder":

> Let us love, and sing and wonder,
>   let us praise the Savior's name!
> He has hushed the law's loud thunder,
>   he has quenched Mount Sinai's flame:
> He has washed us with his blood,
>   he has brought us nigh to God.

Review—Section Three

John R. Muether, *Cornelius Van Til: Reformed Apologist and Churchman*
(Phillipsburg, NJ: P & R, 2008)

As part of the American Reformed Biographies series, John Muether's *Cornelius Van Til: Reformed Apologist and Churchman* offers a semi-popular historical biography, one that includes some theological analysis and critique. The author's prime objective is to lay out for his readers lessons drawn from the life and career of Van Til. Muether's overview is a window on developments in the seminary (Reformed church education more broadly) and in the church (viewed as a distinctively Reformed confessional body). Most important for Muether, as for Van Til, is the doctrine of the church; Muether highlights the role it played in shaping the life and teaching of the premier twentieth-century Reformed apologist, Westminster Seminary's greatest name to fame, or ill repute. Van Til was neither highly regarded nor respected in various quarters of the evangelical Reformed world. That is most unfortunate. Much of the misunderstanding of Van Til comes as the result of unfamiliarity with his writings, difficult and dense as they are to read. Van Til's work must be seen as an outgrowth, a blossoming, of historic Reformed theology—nothing more, and nothing less. Throughout Van Til's career, Westminster Seminary had close ties to the Orthodox Presbyterian Church, of which Van Til was a lifelong member (although his legacy was largely abandoned at the close of his life).

The four theological giants and pillars of the church whose work Van Til built upon were John Calvin, Geerhardus Vos, Abraham Kuyper, and J.

Gresham Machen. Muether remarks: "Calvin's theocentricity, Vos's biblical insights, Kuyper's antithesis, Machen's confessional consciousness—all of these influences came to bear upon Van Til's Reformed apologetics. Specifically, the Reformed faith produced in the pen of Van Til a Reformed militance that characterized Westminster Seminary and the OPC during his nearly half-century teaching career" (18). Equally influential was the work of Herman Bavinck. Muether's placement of Bavinck in the progressive "neo-Calvinist" camp requires qualification. The political and cultural aspirations of Kuperianism play a small role in Bavinck's *magnum opus* in Reformed dogmatics, and that is a significant point to note. Mention must also be made of the teaching of Louis Berkhof. (His one-volume systematics is the finest handbook of Reformed doctrine.)

The single most important feature of Van Til's work was his advancement of Reformed covenant theology. "Van Til argued that the theological basis for covenant theology is the doctrine of the self-contained ontological Trinity. Just as the relations among the divine persons of the Trinity are covenantal, so too is God's relation to every aspect of temporal existence" (54). This understanding played a decisive role in Van Til's theology and apologetic. "What Van Til learned from his teacher and what Machen admired in his student was an unrelenting insistence on the coherence of both Christian theology *and* apologetics. Christianity is a *system* of truth" (68). These two components lay of the heart of Van Tillian presuppositionalism. Van Til himself viewed his work as a refinement of the Reformed apologetic method, building on the Dutch Reformed tradition, notably that advanced by Vos and Bavinck. Muether draws attention to the fact that "Meredith G. Kline credited Van Til for his perception of the 'covenant-creature identification,' which John Murray 'strangely missed in spite of his specific role as theologian and his more directly exegetical method" (253 n. 40). This lacuna in Murray's theology would come to haunt Westminster's hallowed halls of learning, issuing in no small amount of debate and dispute. For this and other reasons, it is noted, Kline acknowledged that Van Til had "by far the most profound impact on my thinking of all my teachers" (cited 262 n. 3).

Van Til's name to fame appeared in connection with his scathing critique of Karl Barth, another theological giant—of a very different stripe—who was likewise difficult to read and comprehend. Some interpreters even accused Van Til of imbibing the Barthian dialectic between what is known by the creature and what is truly knowable. According to Barth, God is wholly other from his creation, and ultimately unknowable. Barth's doctrine of mystery bears no affinity with Reformed teaching. (Enter here the distinction between archetypal and ectypal knowledge: truth as it exists in the mind of God and truth imparted to the creature; the latter is analogical of the former.) Like his forebears identified in the above, Van Til developed a comprehensive grasp of the system of doctrine contained in the Bible and approximated in Reformed Protestant reformulation. Hence, "What alarmed Van Til about other American responses was their willingness to identify isolated elements of Barth's theology that seemed amenable to orthodoxy, as though it were possible to accept a selection of Barth's system and to discard others. Barth himself insisted that this dialectical principle was of a whole cloth and thus indivisible, and Van Til was eager to oblige him" (121).

Van Til's preoccupation with Barth is the explanation for "his relentless attack on Princeton" (74). Unbeknown to Van Til was the entry of Barthian teaching, chiefly Barth's law-grace construct, in the theology of Norman Shepherd, a professor of systematics at Westminster. No controversy was more destructive and more painful than the one addressing this doctrinal mutation at New Westminster. Muether cites only O. Palmer Robertson's history of the Shepherd controversy, published by the Trinity Foundation. (Some have had problems with Robertson's use of this publisher; John Robbins has had nothing but disdain for Van Til and Westminster for many decades. Yet, Robbins did have the discernment to publish other authors who otherwise differed with him on his critique of Old Westminster.) This part of Muether's biography, however, results in a minimalist reading of the history of Westminster Seminary. Muether concedes that a definitive history of Westminster is yet to be written. One correction to Muether's account: Edmund Clowney based his negative critique of Shepherd's teaching on decidedly theological grounds, not political expediency alone. Clowney had genuinely come to see the error of Shepherd's theology of justification, the covenants, and election. Muether's account of Van Til's unease with developments at Calvin College and Seminary in his early days of study bears repeating: "Student smugness, [Van Til] warned, results in trafficking in extremes, with the 'spirit of the mob.' Such arrogance would lead to 'intellectual and spiritual retardation' and should be awarded with 'Certificates of Incompetency.' Van Til even had a word for his instructors, urging them to mind the difference between discipling students and propagandizing them" (49). Later, Van Til would decry the shift in emphasis to practical theology at Princeton Seminary, which would contribute to her subsequent downfall. Old Westminster saw her mission as carrying on the work and witness of Old Princeton, the bastion of Reformed orthodoxy in America and beyond.

Regrettably, others disputes that left a bad taste for many evangelicals in their assessment of Westminster included those with (dispensational) premillennialism, the ongoing dispute with Arminianism, the Gordon Clark case, and theonomic reconstructionism. (Though not mentioned by Muether, one must also include in this list the present-day controversy with the Federal Visionists. Both the theonomists and the Federal Visionists mistakenly look to Van Til as their spiritual forefather.) Ultimately the seminary's militancy would give way to a new approach to discourse, one more suited to contemporary postfoundationalism (where theological diversity and tolerance, to one degree or another, prevails). Ironically, Van Til would come to view Clowney as the driving force behind the change of climate at Westminster. Van Til attributed his estrangement from seminary and church more immediately to Clowney's "ecumenical ambitions" (220). "No one was more symbolic of Westminster's less bellicose image than Edmund Clowney, about whose leadership of the seminary Van Til grew to develop deep suspicions" (224). The history of the seminary is more complicated than this, however.

Van Til's passion for Reformed theology and its apological defense is evident in the fact that he was not drawn to philosophy as a branch of Reformed theology, even though he had high regard for the "cosmonomic philosophy" of Herman Dooyeweerd, D. H. Th. Vollenhoven, and Hendrik Stoker. As handmaid to theology, philosophy begins and ends with the revelation of God in nature and Scripture. True philosophy thinks God's thoughts after him; at no point does philosophy proceed independently of the Word revealed. As it turns out, this is the sum and substance of Van Tillian presuppositionalism.

Muether's helpful study closes with the "Bibliographic Essay," providing ample additional readings. Interaction with these works would have enriched Muether's reading and critique of Van Til, a reading that is at odds with that furnished by John Frame in *Cornelius Van Til: An Analysis of His Thought*. Muether describes Frame's multiperspectival approach as "idiosyncratic, " and concludes that his analysis of Van Til produces "more of a creative expansion of Van Til's thought than a historical expression" (267).[1]

---

1. Compare my review of this work, "John Frame and the Recasting of Van Tilian

Looking back over the (at times) turbulent life and career of Van Til, Muether poignantly observes: "Church life was a struggle for Van Til as well" (116). Doubtless there were many great disappointments and periods of dismay—so much so that "The death of Van Til was the close of a remarkable story in twentieth-century American Calvinism" (228). One may even say that the Orthodox Presbyterian Church/Westminster Seminary experience in the twentieth century would turn out to be a short-lived experiment in American Presbyterianism. Perhaps the goal was set too high for life this side of heaven. Viewing the bigger picture, Muether concedes: "Here it is worth observing that recent assessments of American denominations are not encouraging. The identity crisis that is characterizing the decline in mainline Presbyterian identity is replaying itself in the conservative Reformed and Presbyterian churches, where aging memberships, geographic mobility, and the pursuit of individual forms of spirituality are combining to forge post-denominational sensibilities" (240). Though it is not easy to navigate amicably the turbulent waters stirred up by disputants who otherwise share much of the biblical faith in common, Van Til's militancy was balanced by his gentleness of spirit and demeanor. (The saying is *suaviter in modo, fortiter in re*; "gentle in persuasion, powerful in substance.") Van Til stands as a kindred spirit in a time when we are again shown that history has the uncanny ability of repeating itself over and over. There truly is nothing new under the sun.

Apologetics"; see also Karlberg, "On the Theological Correlation of Divine and Human Language."

Postlude

Theme and Recapitulation

REFORMED THEOLOGY IS, ABOVE all else, the theology of the covenants. From the opening decades of Protestantism on the continent and the isles, Reformed interpretation of the Scriptures was decisively shaped both by the history of redemption and the systematization of doctrine. Covenant theology, unlike any other theological tradition, brings together biblical theology and systematics into one, unified, coherent system of teaching. But the development of Reformed doctrine, i.e., the maturation of Reformed thought, takes place over the course of church history. The task is not yet completed. The church's efforts to set forth accurately the whole counsel of God will not reach conclusion until the return of Christ in Glory. The grace of God is manifested in history, in the redemption of the human race (as chosen in Christ). One of the challenges in articulating a theology of the Word is to discern the End from the Beginning. John Calvin never attempted a commentary on the Book of Revelation. In wisdom, he postponed that task for another time and place. Eschatology begins in the Book of Genesis. The doctrine of the covenants is thoroughly eschatological in nature and design.

The church's study of the doctrines of Scripture leads to confessional, dogmatic statement. Reformed hermeneutics, the "science" of theology, reaches its goal in the confessions of faith and in its apologetic defense. The Westminster tradition embodies some of Reformed hermeneutics at its very best. But it has shown to have its flaws, as is the case in all human enterprise, theological or otherwise. This simply underscores the need for vigilance and for the respect of competent theological voices in contemporary evangelicalism. The Westminster Seminary professors do not have all the answers (this may come as a surprise to them!). The Westminster Calvinism that has proven faithful to Scripture is but one manifestation of international Reformed catholicity, itself an expression of catholic orthodoxy over the course of church history. Whatever its strengths—and they are many—there are also weaknesses. We all do well to relearn and reconsider that truth.

New School Westminster has shown itself not only to be disruptive in the communion of Reformed churches, but also deviant in its distinctive teachings. The study of historical theology can best assess the nature and significance of its new doctrinal and exegetical meanderings. Perhaps a return to *theological prolegomina* (the study of theological foundations) will call Westminster back to Scripture as the formal principle of her theology, and in so doing recover the material principle of Protestant Reformed teaching: the doctrine of justification by grace through faith alone. What needs to be confessed *anew* is the sole instrumentality of saving faith in receiving the imputed righteousness of Christ, the sole ground of the believer's justification (hence a purely *passive* act on the part of the one united to Christ by the regenerating work of the Spirit of God). This reclamation of biblical truth requires the renunciation of false teaching that has prevailed at Westminster for more than four decades. Specifically, the conflating of (initial) justification with final judgment according to the good works of the justified must be renounced. In the second place, there is the need to acknowledge the role of the works-inheritance principle (enunciated in Lev 18:5), a principle antithetical to the faith-inheritance principle (the principle informing salvation by grace). This, in turn, will reopen the way to a biblical theology that is faithful to Scripture, not one distorted by a Barthian (i.e., Neo-orthodox) interpretation of the covenants.

With respect to the development of Reformed doctrine from the age of the Reformation to the present, the time has come for clarity, not confusion, regarding the peculiarity of the Mosaic Covenant in the economy of redemption leading up to Christ's first advent. It is the works principle of inheritance that informs temporal life in Canaan. It alone explains the loss of the land in the time of Babylonian exile. And recognition of this distinctive legal principle is requisite for a proper biblical understanding of Old Testament typology, all of which comes to fulfillment in the age of the Spirit. At this point in the history of doctrine there is need for consolidation and unity in the truths that have been advanced in faithfulness to Scripture (*sola scriptura*).

Appendix 1

Summary Statement of the Reformed Faith

As a Reformed evangelical congregation, we believe in the authority and supremacy of the Bible as the Word of God, free of all error by the inspiration of the biblical authors by the Spirit of God. Holy Scripture is unique among human writings (since it is the very Word of God), and is self-authenticating (not needing confirmation or proof by any standard external to Scripture itself). The Bible alone contains what Christians are to believe and practice for spiritual growth in grace and salvation (including the nurturing of fellowship and communion with the living, triune God).

God—Father, Son, and Holy Spirit—is both the Creator of all things and the Redeemer of fallen humanity (those numbered among God's elect). Both creation and recreation are the works of God's sovereign good pleasure, designed to bring glory to himself. Humans, originally created for fellowship with God, have suffered the consequences of the sin of our first parents in the initial state of probation in the Garden of Eden. Though now fallen and under God's displeasure, they remain the objects of God's love, made effective only by means of the sovereign, electing grace of God revealed in Jesus Christ. "Faith comes from hearing, and hearing by the Word of God" (Rom 10:17). Preaching is central to corporate worship, which is the dialogue between God and his people in prayer, praise, and exposition of the Word.

Salvation is found in Christ alone; there is no other name under heaven whereby sinners are reconciled and restored to life in covenant with God. Sinners are saved (justified, made right with God) by grace through faith. Obedience that is pleasing to God is possible only as a result of God's justifying grace. (Christ's perfect life of obedience is the sole basis of the

Appendix 1

salvation of sinners.) We believe the literal resurrection of Christ from the dead and his bodily return in glory.

The Spirit of God applies the saving benefits of Christ's death on the cross, without which no person is redeemed. What God begins in the spiritual life of the true believer he brings to completion on the day of Christ's second coming at the close of human history. Christ's return is both personal and visible, and marks the beginning of the eternal kingdom of God, which has no end.

The church as the body of Christ is the gathering of the saints for fellowship and upbuilding in the faith; it is ordained by God as that unique institution engaged in the extension of God's kingdom in the world by means of evangelism and global missions. Redemptive covenant is the sole means of the maintenance and spread of God's kingdom on earth, from the fall to the close of history.

As Presbyterians we stand in the historic Reformed tradition, whose confessional teaching is best summarized in the Westminster Confession of Faith and Catechisms.

Appendix 2

Statement on Baptism

BAPTISM AND CHRISTIAN DISCIPLESHIP are an integral part of the Great Commission. The sacrament of baptism is observed as a directive given by Christ to his church. Baptism by water points to the reality signified in the sacrament: regeneration and rebirth by the Spirit of God. As the outward sign of God's redemptive covenant, baptism identifies the recipient as belonging to Jesus Christ and a member of his Body, the visible church. Baptism is necessary for the governance and the growth of the church as it unfolds over the course of human history. By God's entering into covenant with his people, the spiritual kingdom is formed. The invitation to receive Christ's claim of ownership in baptism is extended to parent and child, even prior to the child's coming of age (personal accountability). The goal of the baptism of infants and adults alike is true, spiritual conversion (which can occur before or after the actual administration of baptism in the name of the triune God). Just as the bread and wine symbolize Christ's body and blood, so also the water of baptism symbolizes one's spiritual cleaning and renewal. In the Presbyterian tradition baptism is administered by the sprinkling of water, rather than by immersion.

Author Bibliography

Articles and Books

"Apostasy," "Backsliding," "Denial," and "Envy." In *Evangelical Dictionary of Biblical Theology*, edited by Walter A. Elwell. Grand Rapids: Baker, 1996.

The Changing of the Guard: Westminster Theological Seminary in Philadelphia. Unicoi, TN: Trinity Foundation, 2001. Also published as the March/April 2001 issue of *The Trinity Review*, available online at http://www.trinityfoundation.org.

"Covenant and Common Grace: A Review Article." *WTJ* 50 (1988) 323–37.

"Covenant Theology and the Westminster Tradition: A Review Article." *WTJ* 54 (1992) 135–52.

Covenant Theology in Reformed Perspective: Collected Essays and Book Reviews in Historical, Biblical, and Systematic Theology. Eugene, OR: Wipf and Stock, 2000.

"Doctrinal Development in Scripture and Tradition: A Reformed Assessment of the Church's Theological Task." *Calvin Theological Journal* 30 (1995) 401–18.

Engaging Westminster Calvinism: The Composition of Redemption's Song. Eugene, OR: Wipf and Stock, 2012.

Federalism and the Westminster Tradition: Reformed Orthodoxy at the Crossroads. Eugene, OR: Wipf and Stock, 2006.

"The Glory of God: Archetypal and Ectypal. Part One. The Theophanic Glory." *The Outlook* 60/3 (May/June 2010) 24–27.

"The Glory of God: Archetypal and Ectypal. Part Two: The Image of God." *The Outlook* (July/August 2010) 9–12.

Gospel Grace: The Modern-Day Controversy. Eugene, OR: Wipf and Stock, 2003.

"How Should Moses Be Read?: A Debate in Contemporary Reformed Theology." *The Outlook* 62/3 (May/June 2012) 24–26.

John Piper on the Christian Life: An Examination of His Controversial View of 'Faith Alone' in "Future Grace". Great Bromley: Christian Research Network, 1999.

"Justification in Redemptive History." *WTJ* 43 (1981) 213–46.

"Israel and the Eschaton: A Review Article." *WTJ* 52 (1990) 117–30.

"Israel as Light to the Nations: A Review Article." *JETS* 28 (1985) 205–11.

"Israel's History Personified: Romans 7:7–13 in Relation to Paul's Teaching on the 'Old Man.'" *Trinity Journal* 7, n.s. (1986) 65–74.

"John Frame and the Recasting of Van Tilian Apologetics: A Review Article." *Mid-America Journal of Theology* 9 (1993) 279–96.

Author Bibliography

"Judgment According to Works: The Crux of Today's Dispute [Part 2]." *The Outlook* 54/5 (May 2004) 6–8.
"Legitimate Discontinuities Between the Testaments." *Journal of the Evangelical Theological Society* 28 (1985) 9–20.
"Moses and Christ: The Place of Law in Seventeenth-Century Puritanism." *TrinJ* 10, n.s. (1989) 11–32.
"Music in Worship: A Historical Sketch and Theological Appraisal." *The Outlook* 49/9 (October 1999) 3–6.
"A (New) Systematic Theology for Our Times: A Review Article." *Foundations* 45 (2001) 23–41.
"On the Theological Correlation of Divine and Human Language: A Review Article." *JETS* 2 (1989) 99–105.
"The Original State of Adam: Tensions in Reformed Theology." *Evangelical Quarterly* 59 (1987) 291–309. Cited among collected essays in J. I. Packer, ed., *The Best in Theology*, vol. 3 (Carol Stream, IL: Christianity Today, 1989), 134.
"Patriotic Music in Worship." *The Outlook* 53 (July/August 2003) 4–5.
"Paul's Letter to the Romans in the *New International Commentary on the New Testament* and in Contemporary Reformed Thought." *EvQ* 71 (1999) 3–24.
"Paul, the Old Testament and Judaism: A Review Article." *Foundations: A Journal of Evangelical Theology* 43 (1999) 36–44.
"Recovering the Mosaic Covenant as Law and Gospel: J. Mark Beach, John H. Sailhamer, and Jason C. Meyer as Representative Expositors." *EvQ* 83/3 (2011) 233–50.
"Reformation Politics: The Relevance of Old Testament Ethics in Calvinist Political Theory." *JETS* 29 (1986) 179–91.
"Reformed Interpretation of the Mosaic Covenant." *Westminster Theological Journal* 43 (1980) 1–57.
"Reformed Theology as the Theology of the Covenants: The Contributions of Meredith G. Kline to Reformed Systematics." In *Creator, Redeemer, Consummator: A Festschrift for Meredith G. Kline*, edited by H. Griffith and J. R. Muether. Greenville, SC: Reformed Academic Press, 2000.
"The Search for an Evangelical Consensus on Paul and the Law." *JETS* 40 (1997) 563–79.
"The Significance of Israel in Biblical Typology." *JETS* 31 (1988) 257–69.
"Today's Church: Standing or Falling? [Part 1]." *The Outlook* 54/4 (April 2004) 5–8.
"Works and Grace," *New Horizons* 18 (1997), 23.

Book Reviews

Asselt, Willem J. van. *The Federal Theology of Johannes Cocceius (1603–1669)*. In *JETS* 45 (2002) 734–38.
Berkhof, Hendrikus. *Introduction to the Study of Dogmatics*. In *WTJ* 48 (1986) 385–88.
Coffey, John *Politics, Religion and the British Revolutions: The Mind of Samuel Rutherford*. In *JETS* 42 (1999) 543–44.
Engelsma, David J. *The Covenant of God and the Children of Believers: Sovereign Grace in the Covenant*. In *JETS* 49 (2006) 630–35.
Estelle, Bryan D., J. V. Fesko, and David VanDrunen, editors. *The Law Is Not of Faith: Essays on Works and Grace in the Mosaic Covenant*. In *JETS* 53 (2009) 407–11.

Author Bibliography

Farley, Benjamin Wirt. *The Providence of God*. In *JETS* 33 (1990) 265–66.
Ferguson, Sinclair B. *The Holy Spirit*. In *JETS* 42 (1999) 529–31.
Gamble, Richard C. *The Whole Counsel of God*, vol. 1, *God's Mighty Acts in the Old Testament*. In *TrinJ* 31 (2010) 141–43.
Garlington, Don B. *Faith, Obedience and Perseverance*. In *TrinJ* 18 n.s. (1997) 254–58.
Goppelt, Leonhard. *Typos: The Typological Interpretation of the Old Testament in the New*. In *JETS* 26 (1982) 490–93.
Hesselink, I. John. *Calvin's Concept of the Law*. In *WTJ* 55 (1993) 168–71.
Hoekema, Anthony A. *Created in God's Image*. In *WTJ* 49 (1987) 437–42.
Hoitenga, Dewey J., Jr. *John Calvin and the Will*. In *JETS* 42 (1999) 538–39.
Horton, Michael S. *Covenant and Eschatology*. In *TrinJ* 24 n.s. (2003) 125–29.
———. *God of Promise: Introducing Covenant Theology*. In *JETS* 49 (2006) 627–30.
Jewett, Paul K. *Election and Predestination*. In *WTJ* 48 (1986) 388–91.
Johnson, G. L. W., and G. P. Waters, editors. *By Faith Alone: Answering the Challenges to the Doctrine of Justification*. In *JETS* 50 (2007) 640–43.
Lidgett, J. S. *The Fatherhood of God*. In *JETS* 32 (1989) 373.
Mathison, Keith A. *Given for You: Reclaiming Calvin's Doctrine of the Lord's Supper*. *JETS* 48 (2005) 174–78.
McCoy, Charles S., and J. Wayne Baker, *Fountainhead of Federalism: Heinrich Bullinger and the Covenantal Tradition*. In *WTJ* 54 (1992) 396–400.
McGowen, Andrew T. B. *The Federal Theology of Thomas Boston*. In *JETS* 42 (1999) 544–46.
Moore, Russell D. *The Kingdom of Christ: The New Evangelical Perspective*. In *JETS* 48 (2005) 410–15.
Muether, John R. *Cornelius Van Til: Reformed Apologist and Churchman*. In *TrinJ* 30 (2009) 305–8.
Muller, Richard A. *Christ and the Decree: Christology and Predestination in Reformed Theology from Calvin to Perkins*. In *WTJ* 49 (1987) 442–46.
———. *Post-Reformation Reformed Dogmatics*, vol. 1. In *WTJ* 50 (1988) 364–70.
Piper, John. *Future Grace*. In *New Horizons* 17/5 (May 1996) 23–24.
Rainbow, Paul A. *The Way of Salvation: The Role of Christian Obedience in Justification*; and Richard B. Gaffin. In *"By Faith, Not by Sight": Paul and the Order of Salvation*. *JETS* 50 (2007) 423–28.
Rohr, John von. *The Covenant of Grace in Puritan Thought*. In *TrinJ* 8, n.s. (1987) 84–87.
Sandlin, P. Andrew, editor. *Backbone of the Bible: Covenant in Contemporary Perspective*. In *TrinJ* 26 n.s. (2005) 149–50.
Shepherd, Norman. *The Call of Grace: How the Covenant Illuminates Salvation and Evangelism*. In *TrinJ* 22 n.s. (2001) 131–36.
Strickland, Wayne G. editor. *The Law, the Gospel, and the Modern Christian: Five Views*. In *JETS* 37 (1994) 447–50.
Thomas, G. Michael. *The Extent of the Atonement: A Dilemma for Reformed Theology from Calvin to the Consensus*. In *TrinJ* 20 n.s. (1999) 116–19.
VanDrunen, David, editor. *The Pattern of Sound Doctrine: Systematic Theology at the Westminster Seminaries*. In Karlberg, *Federalism and the Westminster Tradition*, 131–35.
Vickers, Brian. *Jesus' Blood* and *Righteousness: Paul's Theology of Imputation*. In *JETS* 50 (2007) 419–23.

Author Bibliography

Doctoral Dissertation

"The Mosaic Covenant and the Concept of Works in Reformed Hermeneutics: A Historical-Critical Analysis with Special Attention to Early Covenant Eschatology." ThD diss., Westminster Theological Seminary, 1980. Available at University Microfilms International (Ann Arbor, MI; London, England), #8024938.

Master's Thesis

"Law in Pauline Eschatology: The Historical Qualification of Justification by Faith." ThM thesis, Westminster Theological Seminary, 1977.

General Bibliography

Asselt, Willem J. van. *The Federal Theology of Johannes Cocceius (1603–1669)*. Translated by Raymond A. Blacketer. Studies in the History of Christian Thought 100. Leiden: Brill, 2001.

Beach, Mark. *Christ and the Covenant: Francis Turretin's Federal Theology as a Defense of the Doctrine of Grace*. Göttingen: Vandenhoeck & Ruprecht, 2007.

Beale, G. K. *A New Testament Biblical Theology: The Unfolding of the Old Testament in the New*. Grand Rapids: Baker Academic, 2011.

———. *The Temple and the Church's Mission: A Biblical Theology of the Dwelling Place of God*. New Studies in Biblical Theology 17. Downers Grove, IL: InterVarsity, 2004.

Beale, Gregory K. *A New Testament Biblical Theology*. Grand Rapids: Baker Academic, 2011.

Bovell, Carlos R. *Inerrancy and the Spiritual Formation of Younger Evangelicals*. Eugene, OR: Wipf and Stock, 2006.

Casselli, Stephen J. "'Anthony Burgess' *Vindiciae Legis* and the 'Fable of Unprofitable Scholasticism': A Case Study in the Reappraisal of Seventeenth Century Reformed Scholasticism." PhD diss., Westminster Theological Seminary, 2007.

Clark, R. Scott, editor. *Covenant, Justification, and Pastoral Ministry: Essays by the Faculty of Westminster Seminary California*. Phillipsburg: P & R, 2007.

Clark, R. Scott, and Joel E. Kim, editors. *Always Reformed: Essays in Honor of W. Robert Godfrey*. Escondido, CA: Westminster Seminary California, 2010.

Coxhead, Steven. "John Calvin's Subordinate Doctrine of Justification by Works." *WTJ* 71 (2009) 1–19.

Dennison, J. T., S. F. Sanborn, and B. W. Swinburnson. "Merit or 'Entitlement' in Reformed Covenant Theology: A Review." *Journal of Northwest Theological Seminary* 24/3 (2009) 3–152.

Dyrness, William A. *The Reformed Theology and Visual Culture Protestant Imagination from Calvin to Edwards*. New York: Cambridge University Press, 2004.

———. *Visual Faith: Art, Theology, and Worship in Dialogue*. Grand Rapids: Baker, 2001.

Edwards, William R. "John Flavel on the Priority of Union with Christ: Further Historical Perspective on the Structure of Reformed Soteriology." *WTJ* 74 (2012) 33–58.

Edwards Wilaim R., and William B. Evans. "*Sic et Non.* Views in Review: Westminster Seminary California Distinctives?" *Confessional Presbyterian* 8 (2012) n.p.

Engelsma, David J. *Federal Vision: Heresy at the Root*. Jenison, MI: Reformed Free Publishing Association, 2012.

Estelle, Bryan D., J. V. Fesko, and David VanDrunen, editors. *The Law Is Not of Faith: Essays on Works and Grace in the Mosaic Covenant*. Phillipsburg: P & R, 2009.

General Bibliography

Evans, William B. "Déjà vu All Over Again?: The Contemporary Reformed Soteriological Controversy in Historical Perspective." *WTJ* 72 (2010) 135–51.

———. "*Sic et Non*. Views in Review: Westminster Seminary California Distinctive?" *The Confessional Presbyterian* 8 (2012).

Farley, Michael A. "What Is 'Biblical' Worship? Biblical Hermeneutics and Evangelical Theologies of Worship." *JETS* 51 (2008) 591–613.

Fesko, John. *Beyond Calvin: Union with Christ and Justification in Early Modern Reformed Theology (1517–1700)*. Göttingen: Vandenhoeck & Ruprecht, 2012.

Frame, John M. *The Escondido Theology: A Reformed Response to Two Kingdom Theology*. Lakeland, FL: Whitefield Media, 2011.

Gaffin, Richard B. *"By Faith, Not by Sight": Paul and the Order of Salvation*. Bletchley, UK: Paternoster, 2006.

———. "Response to John Fesko's Review." *Ordained Servant Online*, n.d. Online: http://opc.org/os.html?article_id=140.

Gamble, Richard C. *The Whole Counsel of God*. Vol. 1, *God's Mighty Acts in the Old Testament*. Phillipsburg: P & R, 2009.

Genderen, J. van. and W. H. Velema. *Concise Reformed Dogmatics* Phillipsburg: P & R, 2008.

Godfrey, W. Robert and D. G. Hart. *Westminster Seminary California: A New Old School*. Escondido: Westminster Seminary California, 2012.

Hahn, Scott W. *Covenant and Communion: The Biblical Theology Pope Benedict XVI*. Grand Rapids: Brazos, 2009.

———. *Kingship by Covenant: A Canonical Approach to the Fulfillment of God's Saving Promises*. New Haven, CT: Yale University Press, 2009.

Hart, D. G. *Between the Times: The Orthodox Presbyterian Church in Transition, 1945–1990*. Willow Grove, PA: Committee for the Historian of the Orthodox Presbyterian Church, 2011.

Hewitson, Ian A. *Trust and Obey: Norman Shepherd and the Justification Controversy at Westminster Theological Seminary*. Minneapolis: NextStep Resources, 2011.

Howard L. Rice. and Mames C. Huffstutler. *Reformed Worship*. Louisville: Geneva, 2001.

Hughes, J. J., editor. *Speaking the Truth in Love: The Theology of John Frame*. Phillipsburg: P & R, 2009.

Joby, Christopher Richard. *Calvinism and the Arts: A Re-Assessment*. Dudley, MA: Peeters, 2007.

Jones, Paul S. *Singing and Making Music: Issues in Church Music Today*. Phillipsburg: P & R, 2006.

Kline, Meredith G. *God, Heaven, and Har Magedon: A Covenantal Tale of Cosmos and Telos*. Eugene, OR: Wipf and Stock, 2006.

Leaver, Robin A. "Motive and Motif in the Church Music of Johann Sebastian Bach." *Theology Today* 63 (2006), 38–47.

Lillback, Peter A. *The Binding of God: Calvin's Role in the Development of Covenant Theology*. Grand Rapids: Baker, Academic, 2001.

———. "The Rev. Dr. Richard B. Gaffin, Jr.: *Sancti Libri Theologicus Magnus Westmonasteriensis*." *WTJ* 74 (2012)1–31.

Machen, J. Gresham. "Skyscrapers and Cathedrals." In *J. Gresham Machen's The Gospel and the Modern World and Other Short Writings*, edited by Stephen J. Nichols. Phillipsburg: P & R, 2005.

General Bibliography

Melton, Julius. *Presbyterian Worship in America: Changing Patterns Since 1787.* Richmond: John Knox, 1967.

Meyer, Jason C. *The End of the Law: Mosaic Covenant in Pauline Theology.* NAC Studies in Bible and Theology. Nashville: B&H, 2009.

Muether, John R. *Cornelius Van Til: Reformed Apologist and Churchman.* Phillipsburg: P & R, 2008.

———. "Who Narrates the Orthodox Presbyterian Church?: The Church and Its Historians." *Ordained Servant Online*, August/September 2011. Online: http://www.opc.org/os.html.

Muether, John R., and Danny E. Olinger, editors. *Confident of Better Things: Essays Commemorating Seventy-Five Years of the Orthodox Presbyterian Church.* Willow Grove, PA: Committee for the Historian of the Orthodox Presbyterian Church, 2011.

Murray, John. *The Call of Grace: How the Covenant Illuminates Salvation and Evangelism.* Phillipsburg: P & R, 2000.

Ogasapian, John. *Church Music in America, 1620–2000.* Macon, GA: Mercer University, Press, 2007.

Oliphint, K. Scott., editor. *Justified in Christ: God's Plan for Us in Justification.* Fearn, Scotland: Mentor, 2007.

Piper, John. *Counted Righteous in Christ: Should We Abandon the Imputation of Christ's Righteousness?* Wheaton: Crossway, 2002.

———. *Future Grace: The Purifying Power of the Promises of God.* Colorado Springs: Multnomah Books, 2005.

———. *The Future of Justification: A Response to N. T. Wright.* Wheaton, IL: Crossway, 2007.

Rainbow, Paul. *The Way of Salvation: The Role of Christian Obedience in Justification.* Bletchley, UK: Paternoster, 2005.

Rice, Howard L. and Mames C. Huffstutler, *Reformed Worship.* Louisville: Geneva, 2001.

Robertson, O. Palmer. *The Current Justification Controversy.* Unicoi, TN: Trinity Foundation, 2003.

Routley, Erik. *Church Music and the Christian Faith.* Carol Stream, IL: Agape, 1978.

Sailhamer, John. *The Meaning of the Pentateuch: Revelation, Composition and Interpretation.* Downers Grove, IL: IVP Academic, 2009.

Schreiner, Thomas R. *The Law and its Fulfillment: A Pauline Theology of Law.* Grand Rapids: Baker, 1993.

Shepherd, Norman. *The Call of Grace: How the Covenant Illuminates Salvation and Evangelism.* Phillipsburg: P & R, 2000.

———. *The Way of Righteousness: Justification Beginning with James.* La Grange, CA: Kerygma, 2009.

Silva, Moisés. *Explorations in Exegetical Method: Galatians as a Test Case.* Grand Rapids: Baker, 1996.

Tipton, Lane. "Biblical Theology and the Westminster Standards Revisited: Union with Christ and Justification *Sola Fide*." Inaugural lecture, Westminster Theological Seminary, November 13, 2012.

———. "Union with Christ and Justification." In *Justified In Christ: God's Plan for us in Justification*, edited by K. Scott Oliphint, 23–49. Fearn, Scotland: Mentor, 2007.

Trueman, Carl R. *John Owen: Reformed Catholic, Renaissance Man.* Great Theologians Series. Hampshire, UK/Burlington, VT: Ashgate, 2007.

Van Til, Cornelius. *Christianity and Barthianism.* Grand Rapids: Baker, 1965.

General Bibliography

Venema, Cornelis P. "The Mosaic Covenant: A 'Republication' of the Covenant of Works? A Review Article." *Mid-America Journal of Theology* 21 (2010), 35–101.

Vickers, Brian. *Jesus' Blood and Righteousness: Paul's Theology of Imputation*. Wheaton, IL: Crossway, 2006.

Westermeyer, Paul. *Te Deum: The Church and Music*. Minneapolis: Fortress, 1998.

Williams, Michael D. "Adam and Merit." *Presbyterion* 35 (2009) 87–94.

Wilson-Dickson, Andrew. *The Story of Christian Music*. Oxford: Lion, 1992.

Witvliet, John D. "Church Music, Congregational Life, and Theological Education in Harmony: Toward a New Approach for Musical Advocacy." *The American Organist* (December 2006) 76–81.

Wolterstorff, Nicholas. "Choir and Organ: Their Place in Reformed Liturgy." Calvin Institute of Christian Worship. Online: http://www.calvin.edu/worship/presentations/wolterstorff.php.

Yeo, John J. *Plundering the Egyptians: The Old Testament and Historical Criticism at Westminster Theological Seminary (1928–1998)*. Lanham, MD: University Press of America, 2010.

Name Index

Asselt, Willem J. van, 74 n.30
Allison, C. FitzSimons, 55
Aquinas, Thomas, 63
Bach, Johann Sebastian, 128, 143, 147 n.7, 150 n.1
Bahnsen, Greg, 55
Barth, Karl, 1, 12–13, 25 n.8, 57, 80 n.49, 88, 156–157
Baugh, Stephen M., 92
Bavinck, Herman, 156
Baxter, Richard, 37
Beach, J. Mark, 61–69
Beale, Gregory K., 26–29, 95
Beisner, Calvin, 54
Belcher, Richard, 92
Berkhof, Louis, 72
Bolt, John, 56
Bovell, Carlos R., 22 n.3
Bruckner, Anton, 144 n.4
Bryd, William, 151
Bucer, Martin, 17, 37
Calvin, John, 13, 37, 72–73, 128, 149–152, 155
Casselli, Stephen, J., 63 n.2
Clark, Gordon, 158
Clark, R. Scott, 25 n.8, 50
Clowney, Edmund P., 7 n.7, 157–158
Cocceius, Johannus, 72, 74
Conn, Harvie, 94
Coxhead, Steven, 32 n.28
Curtis, Bryan G., 92
DeLong, Richard, 144 n.4
Dennison, William, 80 n. 48
Dillard, Raymond B., 94
Dooyeweerd, Herman, 158
Dryness, William A., 147 n.7
Duguid, Iain, 50.
Edwards, Jonathan, 37

Edwards, William R., 3 n.3, 23–26
Elmore, Robert, *xi*
Engelsma, David J., 23 n.3, 25 n.8, 26 n.11, 30–34
Enns, Peter, 22 n.3, 94
Estelle, Bryan D., 29 n.19, 80 n.48, 89–90
Evans, William B., 23 n.4
Farley, Michael A., 147 n.7
Ferguson, Sinclair, 93
Flavel, John, 3 n.3, 23, 25
Ferry, Brenton, 91
Fesko, John V., 22 n.3, 25 n.9, 89
Frame, John M., 3 n.1, 31, 70 n.17, 94, 158
Gaffin, Richard B., Jr., 3, 22, 23, 25 n.8, 26 n.10, 27 n.12, 28, 35–44, 45, 50, 59, 89
Gamble, Richard C., 60, 80 n.48, 94–96
Genderen, J. van, 96
Godfrey, W. Robert, 7 n.7, 25 n.8
Gordon, T. David, 54–55, 92
Graham, Billy, 145
Gundry, Robert, 55
Hafemann, Scott, 76
Hahn, Scott W., 26 n.12, 80 n.49
Hancock, Gerre, *xi*
Handel, George Frederick, 128, 143
Hart, D. G., 7 n.7, 25 n.8 and 9, 91
Hewitson, Ian A., 22 n.3
Hodge, Charles, 88
Hooker, Richard, 37
Horton, Michael S., 27 n.12, 90, 93–94
Hugenberger, Gordon P., 27 n.12
Huffstutler, Mames C., 122 n.6
Hustad, Donald, 130
Joby, Christopher Richard, 147
Johnson, Gary. L. W., 52
Jones, Mark, 29 n.19

175

Name Index

Jones, Paul S., 152 n.4
Kaiser, Walter C., Jr., 75
Keven, Ernest R., 79 n.46
Kim, Joel E., 25 n.8
Kline, Meredith G., *xii*, 6, 27 n.12, 31 n.24, 50, 57, 80, 89, 91, 95, 100, 119 n.4, 156
Küng, Hans, 80 n.49
Kuyper, Abraham, 155
Leaver, Robin A., 147 n.7
Lee, Brian, 29 n.19
Leithart, Peter, 92
Lillback, Peter A., 3 n.3, 22 n.3, 32 n.28, 50–51, 93
Longman, Tremper, II, 94
Luther, Martin, 6, 12, 37, 53
Machen, J. Gresham, 6, 145 n.6, 151 n.3, 156
Melancthon, Philip, 37
Melton, Julius, 122 n.7
Mendelssohn, Felix, 128
Meyer, Jason C., 75–79
Mohler, Albert, 52
Moo, Douglas, 76 n.33
Muether, John R., 3 n.1, 22 n.3, 25 n.9, 70 n.17, 97, 155–159
Muller, Richard A., 62
Murray, John, 7, 15, 18, 47, 55–56, 59, 62, 79 n.46, 85, 88, 92–93, 156
Ogasapian, John, 122 n.6
Olinger, Danny E., 22 n.3, 25 n.9
Palestrina, Giovanni, 151
Phillips, Richard, 55
Piper, John, 27, 39, 57
Rainbow, Paul A., 35–44, 50, 55
Rice, Howard L., 122 n.6
Robertson, O. Palmer, 22 n.3, 26 n.11, 157
Robbins, John, 157
Routley, Eric, 147 n.7
Sailhamer, John H., 69–75
Sanders, E. P., 48.
Schreiner, Thomas, 45, 76 n.33
Shepherd, Norman, 3, 7, 22, 25 n.8, 26 n.10, 27–28, 30–32, 41, 50, 55, 57, 59, 79 n.46, 85, 87, 157
Silva, Moisés, 57, 78 n.46

Sproul, R.C. (Sr.), *xi*
Snodgrass, Klyne R., 28
Spencer, Stephen, 66
Stoker, Hendrik, 158
Strimple, Robert B., 7 n.7, 25 n.8
Tipton, Lane, 22 n.3
Trueman, Carl R., 63 n.2
Turretin, Francis, 62–68, 72, 80
Van Til, Cornelius, 3 n.1, 69 n.17, 97, 155–159
VanDrunen, David, 56, 90–91, 94
Velema, W. H., 96
Venema, Cornelis P., 50, 54, 80 n.48
Vickers, Brian, 45–51, 77 n.43
Vollenhoven, D. H. Th., 158
Vos, Geerhardus, 45, 50, 100, 155–156
Ward, James, 137
Waters, Guy P., 25 n.8, 52, 92
Watts, Isaac, 128
Wells, David F., 27 n.12, 52–53
Wesley, Charles, 37, 128
Westermeyer, Paul, 122 n.6, 147 n.7
White, R. Fowler, 54
Williams, Michael D, 63 n.2
Wilson-Dickson, Andrew, 137 n.1
Witvliet, John D., 147 n.7
Wolterstorff, Nicholas, 147 n.7
Wren, Christopher, 153
Wright, N. T., 37, 48, 52, 54–55
Yeo, John J., 22 n.3

www.ingramcontent.com/pod-product-compliance
Lightning Source LLC
Chambersburg PA
CBHW071515150426
43191CB00009B/1536